Saving Spaces

Saving Spaces offers an historical overview of the struggle to conserve both individual parcels of land and entire landscapes from destruction in the United States. John H. Sprinkle, Jr. identifies the ways in which the identification, evaluation, and stewardship of selected buildings and landscapes reflect contemporary American cultural values. Detailed case studies bring the text to life, highlighting various conservation strategies and suggesting the opportunities, challenges, and consequences of each. Balancing close analyses with a broader introduction to some of the key issues of the field, *Saving Spaces* is ideal for students and instructors of historic preservation.

John H. Sprinkle, Jr. is an historian with the National Park Service and an Adjunct Associate Professor, School of Architecture, Planning, and Preservation, University of Maryland, College Park.

Saving Spaces

Historic Land Conservation
in the United States

John H. Sprinkle, Jr.

Routledge
Taylor & Francis Group

NEW YORK AND LONDON

First published 2019
by Routledge
711 Third Avenue, New York, NY 10017

and by Routledge
2 Park Square, Milton Park, Abingdon, Oxon, OX14 4RN

Routledge is an imprint of the Taylor & Francis Group, an informa business

Library of Congress Cataloging-in-Publication Data
A catalog record for this book has been requested

ISBN: 978-1-138-88866-1 (hbk)
ISBN: 978-1-138-88867-8 (pbk)
ISBN: 978-1-315-71324-3 (ebk)

Typeset in Bembo
by Apex CoVantage, LLC

For my parents, who entrusted me with a legacy of open space and agricultural heritage:

Jane Vickers Brooks (Librarian and Farmer)

John Harold Sprinkle (Architect and Archaeologist)

Contents

Acknowledgments

This study began at the Lloyd House, 220 North Washington Street, in Alexandria, Virginia. For several years it was my privilege to serve on the Alexandria Historical Restoration and Preservation Commission. Chartered in 1962, this nine-member group of local citizens oversees, at the behest of the local city council, a collection of historic preservation easements in Alexandria. In the late 1960s, far-sighted citizens secured an open space acquisition grant from the Department of Housing and Urban Development to purchase Lloyd House. The preservation story of Lloyd House, and the ongoing work of the so-called Long Name Commission, sparked my interest in the interaction of the historic preservation and land conservation movements.

Over the years, many friends and colleagues within the historic preservation community have helped in the creation of this book, including Brenda Barrett, Eric Benson, Nancy Boone, Warren Brown, John Burns, Ethan Carr, Priya Chhaya, David Clarke, Rebecca Conard, Dennis Connors, Al Cox, Grant Dehart, Andrew Dolkart, Bruce Donovan, Jodey Elsner, Chris Floyd, Ehren Foley, John Fowler, Denis Galvin, James Glass, Tom Greene, Lisa Hayes, Destry Jarvis, Ian Johnson, Aimee Jorjani, Robert Kapsch, Tom King, Laura Kolar, Jane Loeffler, Eleanor Mahoney, Lance Mallamo, Maria McCollester, Janet McDonnell, Catherine Miliaras, Hugh Miller, Marla Miller, Robert Montague, Donald Murphy, Elizabeth Novara, Mark Peckham, Jess Phelps, Constance Ramirez, Jerry Rogers, William Rudy, Stephanie Sample, Michele Scalise, Richard Sellars, Earle Shettleworth, Carol Shull, Wayne Strum, Charles Trozzo, Richard Weingroff, David Weir, and Robert Utley. I am indebted to each of these individuals, many of whom have endured my often unbridled fascination with conservation easements, surplus property, open space, and urban renewal. I would be remiss in not acknowledging the exemplary work of the professional staff at the Department of the Interior Library in Washington, DC; the Hornbake Library at the University of Maryland, and the National Archives and Records Administration, Archives II, both in College Park, Maryland; the manuscripts division of the Library of Congress; the National Park Service's Harpers Ferry Center, the Wilson Library at the University of North Carolina, Chapel Hill; and the Wyoming History Center. While the views and conclusions in this book are mine alone and should not be interpreted as representing the opinions or policies of the National Park Service of the U.S. government, over the years my understanding of the historic preservation and land conservation movements has grown from numerous conversation with colleagues at the National Park Service, including Christine Arato, Michael Commisso, Jeffrey Durbin, Emily Ferguson, James Gabbert, Anna Holloway, Lu Ann Jones, Turkiya Lowe, Paul Lusignan, Joel Lynch, Mary McPartland, John Renaud, Travis Senter, Angie Sirna, and Kelly Spradley-Kurowski.

For more than three decades, my wife Esther has been a continuous source of inspiration, comfort, and copious amounts of laughter. Our two sons, Harry and Jack, have grown to become engaging, talented, and delightful young men during the time that I worked on this book. Together we share in the stewardship of our own cultural landscape—a family legacy that has, over the last decade, shaped my understanding of saving spaces.

A Note on the Sources

This work rests upon research conducted at the following collections and archives. Abbreviations used in the notes are given in parentheses.

Advisory Council on Historic Preservation (ACHP)

- Advisory Council on Historic Preservation, Executive Director's Administrative Files (ACHP ED AF)

College of Southern Maryland (CSM), Southern Maryland Studies Center

- Moyaone Collection (MC)

Library of Congress (LOC), Manuscript Division

- Papers of David E. Finley (DEF)
- Papers of Nathaniel A. Owings (NAO)

Mount Vernon Ladies' Association of the Union (MVLA); Fred W. Smith National Library for the Study of George Washington

- Minutes of the Council of the Mount Vernon Ladies' Association held at Mount Vernon, Virginia (Minutes)
- Superintendent's Monthly Report (SMR)
- Operation Overview Collection (Overview)
- Papers of Charles Cecil Wall, Resident Director (CCW)
- Papers of the Regent or various Vice Regents (VR), e.g. Frances Bolton (VR Bolton)

National Archives and Records Administration

- RG 79: National Park Service

- RG 207: Department of Housing and Urban Development (HUD). This record group includes records produced by its predecessor, the Urban Renewal Administration (URA).
- RG 368: Heritage, Conservation, and Recreation Service (HCRS). This record group contains the records of the Bureau of Outdoor Recreation (BOR) and the Land and Water Conservation Fund (LWCF).
- RG 421: National Trust for Historic Preservation (NTHP). Certain records of the NTHP are housed at NARA, including some associated with the Advisory Council on Historic Preservation (ACHP).
- RG 429: Council on Environmental Quality (CEQ)
- RG 515: Records of the Historic American Buildings Survey (HABS)

National Park Service (NPS)

- Harpers Ferry Center (HFC)

  - Papers of Ronald F. Lee (RFL) include files on individual properties such as the Old San Francisco Mint (OSFM).

- National Historic Landmark (NHL) Program files related to individual properties, both designated National Historic Landmarks and "other sites considered" (OSC) for possible designation, theme studies and records and meeting minutes associated with the National Park System Advisory Board (NPSAB) and its National Historic Landmark Consulting Committee (CC) and the History Areas Committee (HAC).
- Park History Program (PHP) collection includes the working files of the agency's Chief Historian and Bureau Historian. Files are generally arranged by subject, individual, or location, e.g., Old San Francisco Mint (OSFM).
- Park-specific files are arranged by a four-letter code, e.g., Appomattox Courthouse National Historical Site (APCO).

University of North Carolina, Chapel Hill, Wilson Library (UNC)

- Papers of Gordon Gray (GG)

University of Maryland, College Park (UMCP)

- UMCP hosts the National Trust for Historic Preservation (NTHP) library and the papers of Charles Hosmer (CBH) which include a collection of oral history interviews, particularly Ernest Connally (EAC). The library also hosts the papers of Charles E. Peterson (CEP) and William A. Murtagh (WAM)

University of Mary Washington (UMW)

• Remembering the Future (RTF) was a 1986 conference celebrating the 20th anniversary of the National Historic Preservation Act. Papers presented at this meeting are in manuscript.

Wyoming History collection

• Papers of Frederick A. Gutheim (FAG)

Introduction

How Will They Know It Was Us?

Oscar never called. Produced by the Modern Talking Picture Service in 1968 as a work of cinematic art, the 28-minute film *How Will They Know It's Us?* never received much recognition. Focusing on a collection of historic preservation success stories from across the country, the film highlighted creative transportation design in Monterey, California; the adaptive use of a former chocolate factory at Ghirardelli Square in San Francisco; residential rehabilitations and the introduction of a new school and community center in Wooster Square, New Haven, Connecticut; and small-town business sustainability in Galena, Illinois. A collaboration between the National Trust for Historic Preservation (NTHP) and the Department of Housing and Urban Development (HUD), the film's title is adapted from a scene in *The Grapes of Wrath*, where a group of women are deciding what possessions they can take with them as they abandoned Oklahoma during the Great Depression: "How can we live without our lives? How will we know it's us without our past?"[1]

While use of the Steinbeck quote invited comparisons between the economic and social turmoil of the 1930s with the racial, social, economic, and demographic upheavals of the 1960s, it was not meant to cast aspersions on the operation of the newly established agency. The department was proud of its accomplishments in urban renewal:

> In cities across the country, at an ever increasing rate, buildings and even whole areas are being rehabilitated and restored. Older houses and commercial structures which are given useful new lives help us relate to our past and assist in finding answers to the question: How will they know it's us?[2]

Like the women in *The Grapes of Wrath*, each generation has decided, either through action or inaction, what parts of the past to preserve for the future. The material presence of the past remains a finite resource linked with the land and landscape upon which it was seated. Thus the historic preservation and land conservation movements are inherently linked because of the underlying factor of land, and with it the fundamental role of private property within the American system. As the long-standing Maryland politician

Louis L. Goldstein was fond of saying, investing in land was a good idea "because the Good Lord isn't making any more of it."[3]

Saving Spaces

This book approaches the wide-ranging subject of "saving spaces" from an admittedly federal perspective—a result of the readily available primary sources and an acknowledgement of the increasingly important role that the national government had on landscape and historic conservation efforts from the 1950s through the 1970s. Each chapter presents a case study, as it were, of one particular aspect of the interaction of the conservation and preservation movements. Taken together, they examine the collaboration between these two social movements, which have at their core, the premise that the identification, evaluation, and long-term stewardship of land and landscapes provides important values to communities across the country. In many ways it was a story of how a maturing preservation movement operated at the fringes of other, more-well-funded, governmental endeavors, especially those designed to renew urban environments, provide access to open space in cities and towns, dispose of surplus federal infrastructure, and ensure the development of recreational resources.

Chapter 1 presents a broad-brush review of the historic preservation movement from the mid-1920s through the mid-1970s. Since its birth during the mid-19th century, American historic preservation has been most interested in the stewardship of individual historic buildings and sites, those associated with notable persons or dramatic events. During this period it was not uncommon for museum curators and other collectors acquired architectural elements from historic properties threatened with demolition in order to provide a background for collections of furniture or works of art. This practice illustrates the educational and inspirational branch of the social movement prior to World War II. That particularistic view was expanded during Cold War to include a concern for the setting and environs of historic properties; the recognition of ensembles of buildings within historic districts; and eventually, an engagement with cultural landscapes on a large scale. It was the recognition of beauty—whether in art, architecture, scenic views, or natural settings (and shared threats to its continuity)—that linked preservationists, advocates within the National Park Service (NPS), and land conservationists during the third quarter of the 20th century.

Early preservation successes, such as the preservation of George Washington's Mount Vernon estate saw new challenges at mid-century. Flying into Washington's National Airport in the early 1950s, Ohio Congressperson Frances Bolton may have observed tendrils of suburban development creeping out into Prince George's County, Maryland, across the Potomac River from Mount Vernon. Serving as the vice regent from Ohio for the Mount Vernon Ladies' Association, Bolton established Operation Overview: a multi-year effort to ensure the stabilization of the historic views from Washington's home. Chapter 2 describes the creation of Piscataway Park, an experiment in creating protected areas through a mosaic of public and private steward-ship, and the only NPS unit designed to protect the viewshed from a historic property.[4]

Much of the conservation movement was experimental, as the country sought to deal with post–World War II conditions of growth that confronted valued natural and cultural resources. In 1970, Ernest Connally, the head of the NPS's Office of Archaeology and Historic Preservation (OAHP) learned that the Smithsonian Institution was about to acquire fireplace mantles and other interior woodwork salvaged prior to the proposed demolition of the old U.S. Mint in San Francisco. The fate of the Old Mint was the subject of an long and intense debate and, as described in Chapter 3, its story illustrated the post–World War II concern for the future of surplus federal buildings and the administrative conflicts that often imperiled their long-term stewardship or survival.

Metropolitan challenges were at the core of many conservation planning debates facing the Baby Boom generation. Chapter 4 describes the Depart-ment of Housing and Urban Development's open space grant program, which helped localities set aside more than 380,000 acres of urban land in communi-ties across the country from 1961 to the mid-1970s. In 1962, for example, the city of Alexandria, Virginia, took advantage of this program to purchase parts of Fort Ward, a remnant of one of the Civil War defenses of Washington, DC. Acknowledging the role of historic properties in the revitalization of urban communities, this program fostered the acquisition and protection of historic sites while also pushing for the liberalization of federal criteria to recognize historic districts as a category of official memory.

Urban open space grants provided an important precedent for operation of the Land and Water Conservation Fund (LWCF) described in Chapter 5. In 1962, NPS Director Conrad Wirth detailed a creative funding source to help states acquire additional lands for recreational purposes. Established in 1964, the LWCF has since provided more than $11.7 billion in funding, preserving 2.6 million acres in perpetuity. Creation of the LWCF was the result of a decade-long campaign to expand the recreation estate within the United States in order to provide increased access to outdoor activities for a growing urban and suburban population. The LWCF presented a signifi-cant opportunity for collaboration between advocates for the preservation of scenic beauty, open space, and historic resources where the "conservation clock" was "ticking too fast to be turned back."[5]

As described in Chapter 6, conservation easements were viewed as one of the most important tools available to the land-use protection communities during the 1960s and 1970s. In 1974, Secretary of the Interior Cecil Andrus accepted a bundle of conservation easements on Green Springs, a 7,000-acre cultural landscape in central Virginia that was threatened by mining and insti-tutional development. At that time it was the largest historic district in the United States. This protection established the principle that federal conser-vation assistance must come with some form of perpetual protection. The acquisition and administration of conservation easements was a double-edged sword for many bureaucrats: on the one hand it appeared to reduce the initial costs of ownership, while on the other hand it presented a cluster of managerial headaches that soured their utility in many government applications. Despite this administrative hesitancy, conservation easements remain an important legal pathway for saving spaces.

The final chapter describes how the New Conservation of the 1960s, a bureaucratic component of the wider environmental movement, transformed the land conservation and historic preservation movements within the United States and suggests that the integrated concept expressed in the phrase the "preservation and enhancement" of the natural and cultural environment established a foundation for saving spaces in the future. As described by Hal Rothman, this book addresses the period from the "democratization of conservation" through the "rise of aesthetic environmentalism."[6] During the third quarter of the 20th century, despite advancing seemingly similar goals for the identification and protection of special places, the land conservation and historic preservation movements were often poorly integrated, existing in a relationship that limited the success of nationwide efforts to save valued spaces for future generations.

Notes

1. John Steinbeck, *The Grapes of Wrath, 75th Anniversary Edition* (New York: Viking, 2014), p. 92. The paragraph concludes: "No. Leave it. Burn it."
2. HUD, "How Will They Know It's Us? A Film Featuring HUD Programs used for Preservation Purposes." Tri-Fold Brochure, 1968. HFC EAC Box 5.
3. "Louis L. Goldstein," *The Washington Post*, July 7, 1998.
4. See: John H. Sprinkle, Jr, "Operation Overview and the Creation of Piscataway Park," *The Public Historian*, Vol. 38, No. 4 (November 2016), pp. 79–100.
5. Department of the Interior, *A Special Report to the Nation on: The Race for Inner Space* (Washington, DC: Government Printing Office, 1964), p. 69.
6. Hal Rothman, *Saving the Planet: The American Response to the Environment in the Twentieth Century* (Chicago: Ivan R. Dee, 2000), pp. 85–107, 108–130.

1   From Period Rooms to Large Landscapes

George Washington danced here—in 1797. Each February since 1932, Gadsby's Tavern in Alexandria, Virginia, has hosted a celebration of George Washington's birthday. Known as the "Birth Night Ball," the event is held in the 22-by-38-foot rectangular ballroom of the 1792 hotel, a room that includes a raised balcony (or "orchestra") from which the musicians would provide entertainment. Since 1924, however, the original ballroom woodwork has resided at the Metropolitan Museum of Art in New York City, as part of the exhibition of American interior design portrayed in an assemblage of "period rooms." In 1929, American Legion Post No. 24 acquired Gadsby's Tavern as a memorial to Washington and to honor the veterans of World War I. In order to foster the building's continued use as a house museum, the distinguished and distinctive ballroom woodwork was authentically reproduced in 1941 to reflect its historic appearance.[1] The removal of the Gadsby's Tavern ballroom woodwork and its reinstallation in a museum setting illustrated what was a common practice within American museum culture prior to World War II. Curators considered the creation of period rooms an ideal way to display growing exhibits of American and European decorative arts, and museums were encouraged to expand their collections to include entire buildings.[2] This piecemeal approach to the preservation of architectural fragments was part of a maturing historic preservation movement during the middle of the 20th century.

Traditionally defined by the preservation and presentation of places associated with heroic events or individuals, the historic preservation movement expanded after World War II to include an increasing appreciation for beauty. The concept of scenic beauty, and the inspirational public values embodied by distinctive landscapes, in the western United States took shape in the east and in urban settings as a concern for the protection of authentic historic scenes. With this background, the conservation of American heritage grew from the interpretation of the individual building, usually maintained as a house museum, to the recognition of the historic community. This was first described as area preservation, but is more commonly known as historic districts. By the 1970s the scale and scope of the movement had grown to include "cultural landscapes:" large areas inhabited by a mosaic of historic

Figure 1.1 Gadsby's Tavern Interior, Alexandria, Virginia. This image shows the ballroom that hosted a Birth Night Ball for George Washington in 1797. The woodwork was removed and reinstalled at the Metropolitan Museum in New York City to serve as a backdrop for the display of furniture and other 18th-century decorative arts. The woodwork was reproduced and installed at Gadsby's Tavern in 1941.

Source: LOC Prints and Photographs Division, HABS VA,7-ALEX, 19–14.

resources valued by diverse communities. Parallel to this expanding vision for heritage conservation was the creation of an administrative structure, seated within the federal government, which implemented the often-bifurcated mandates to both use and protect valued landscapes across the county.

Period Rooms

During the first half of the 20th builders, antique dealers, collectors, and museum curators sometimes treated woodwork and other architectural materials purchased from the often-impoverished owners of historic buildings in both urban and rural communities as portable culture. Room by room, the architectural heritage of individual buildings was removed and transported, often miles away from the original locations, or even across the Atlantic from European settings. Curators and collectors reinstalled the decorative elements to serve as stages upon which to display and interpret other types of material culture. The practice was often justified and legitimized because an individual building was in danger of neglect or demolition.[3]

Confessing in 2006 that there was "no cohesive body of writing" on the subject, Trevor Keeble introduced a collection of essays on the modern period room with the conclusion that the practice was a "key representational device of social history" within the museum field, as it humanized collections of decorative arts.[4] In Europe, museum acquisition of rooms as backdrops appears to have begun in the late 1860s. In the United States the Metropolitan Museum of Art in New York City opened its American Wing of period rooms in 1924.[5] Other museums soon followed suit, perhaps most notably, the Philadelphia Museum of Art (as orchestrated by the architect and curator Fiske Kimball) and the Winterthur Museum in Delaware, which was the creation of Henry Frances Du Pont. By the late 1920s the success of this widespread practice led the American Institute of Architects (AIA) to urge the museum community to abstain from the trade in old houses and their furnishings, calling it a "rather shoddy and uncultured act":[6]

> The house thus mutilated becomes a loss to their community with a very doubtful benefit to another. Such old work, placed in a new setting with new materials, bears with it the element of deception and inconsistency, and the historical value of these unrelated fragments is destroyed.[7]

The room-by-room vandalism that fed the antiquarian's desire for period rooms was fostered by twin concerns: first, that saving the craftsmanship demonstrated by quality interior and exterior woodwork was one means of ensuring the survival of beauty, as reflected in the quality of design; and second, that such architectural elements could provide the appropriate setting and context for other forms of decorative arts.

Private residences were not the only targets of the vandals. Soon after establishing the Society for the Preservation of New England Antiquities in 1910, William Sumner Appleton reported a rumor that the Metropolitan Museum was "after" the interior woodwork at the Touro Synagogue (1759–1763) in Newport, Rhode Island. Unfamiliar with the building or its architect, Peter Harrison, Appleton was surprised by the museum's apparent interest until he saw a picture post card of the synagogue's interior, after which he declared that it would be a "terrible calamity" for the woodwork to leave Newport. Fortunately, the building had an active congregation and an endowment overseen by prominent individuals, including Arthur Sulzberger, the publisher of *The New York Times*. The Touro Synagogue would be among the first properties recognized as a National Historic Site under the auspices of the Historic Sites Act of 1935, not only for its historical associations but also its architectural achievement.[8]

During the 1930s the recycling of older buildings extended beyond the reuse of woodwork to other architectural materials. The owners of Eltham, a 17th-century planation located near West Point, Virginia, remarked: "those Williamsburg people had carried off everything that remained above ground."[9] Hard times during the Great Depression meant that families throughout the original 13 states looked favorably upon an offer to purchase woodwork, windows, or other pieces of their architectural heritage. Eventually though, as recalled by National Park Service (NPS) architect Charles Peterson, it became easier for architects to design and fabricate architectural reproductions "rather than hustle old mantle pieces around from one place to another."[10]

Figure 1.2 The Lindens, or King–Hooper House, was built in Danvers, Connecticut, in 1754. This building was disassembled and transported to Washington, DC, where it was reconstructed in the Kalorama neighborhood. The relocated home served as the setting for a distinctive private collection of American furniture and decorative arts.

Source: LOC Prints and Photographs Division, HABS, MASS, 5-DAV, 2–4.

This concern for beauty in the form of a unique architectural assemblage was the prompt for one of the most ambitious relocations of a historic home during the 20th century. The Lindens (also known as the King–Hooper House) was seated in Danvers, Connecticut, from 1754 until the early 1930s, when the building was deconstructed, inventoried, moved to the Kalorama neighborhood of Washington, DC, and reconstructed. During the late 1920s, the owner, antiques dealer Israel Sack, had used the building as a showroom—and not only were the furniture, ceramics, and paintings for sale, but also the woodwork itself. After selling the parlor features for installation in the Nelson–Adkins Museum in Kansas City, Missouri, Sack sold the rest of the house to George and Miriam Morris, who were well-regarded collectors of American decorative arts.[11]

Removing the Lindens from its original site was quite controversial. The supervising architect, Walter Macomber, was widely criticized within the emerging field of historic preservation. Rarely an advocate for moving historic properties, Charles Hosmer, the chronicler of the preservation movement, eventually became convinced that moving the home almost intact was far preferable to having its individual components extracted and reinstalled at diverse new locations. Relocating the building to Washington, DC, the Morrises felt, allowed its architectural qualities to be appreciated much more than if it had remained in Connecticut.[12]

As the historic preservation movement matured, dismantling and reinstalling old woodwork increasingly fell out of favor—yet moving buildings for conservation purposes still remains a viable practice. Relocating historic properties was defined as an automatic adverse effect by the regulations that implemented Section 106 of the National Historic Preservation Act. However, recognizing the tradition of house moving, the National Register of Historic Places has accommodated horizontal relocation with Criterion Consideration B. Challenges delivered by sea-level rise and increased flooding have prompted renewed consideration of both the elevation and relocation of historic properties as a preservation tool.[13]

House Museums to Historic Districts

Prior to World War II, the American historic preservation movement was primarily driven by a particularistic concern for individual buildings, often associated with political, cultural, or economic elite figures, or momentous events such as famous battles. This period was characterized by a focus on the educational and inspirational benefits that historic properties deliver to the visiting public, which reinforced dominant social and political values of the period. In addition to the practice of preserving authentic woodwork and hardware by installation in museum-curated period rooms, this period embraced the house museum as the most appropriate use for historic properties, after their original function was superseded by change—or once they were recognized as being historic. By the 1930s, period rooms and house museums were well known to the American public. Laurence Coleman estimated that there were more than 400 house museums in the country,[14] which could be classified into three categories:

> There is the house which, due to a combination of circumstances and architectural inspiration, merits the public's attention from the date of building. There is the house which, because of the birth, death or visit of a distinguished individual; by being the scene of an important event, or by housing the arts and sciences, reflects glory upon itself and is therefore of interest to the public. And there is the old house, whose claim to fame rests only on its persistence in surviving when all about it falls away. Much as the oldest inhabitant is a character, no matter how inferior he may have seemed to his contemporaries, so the oldest house in a locality, or of a type, is essentially historic and important.[15]

House museums saw their ultimate expression with the living history museum, most famously illustrated by Colonial Williamsburg in Virginia, a product of seemingly unending patronage. The restoration provided four-dimensional exhibits where history came alive through reenactment within a community that was—like the musical village of Brigadoon—purported to be frozen in time so that the future could learn from the past. The success of the Williamsburg restoration encouraged communities across the United States to look beyond the individual property to include ensembles of historic properties that gave character and beauty to urban settings.[16]

Before World War II, a few local communities began using local zoning laws to manage urban change brought primarily by the new automobile-centered landscape—most commonly illustrated by the gasoline station. In 1929, for example, Alexandria, Virginia, agreed to preserve the memorial character of Washington Street as it carried the George Washington Memorial Parkway through the city; and in 1946 (following Charleston, South Carolina's 1931 model), the city established an Old and Historic District where development was regulated by a Board of Architectural Review. Local zoning districts designed to protect *le tout ensemble* of historic neighborhoods expanded in the Cold War era of urban renewal, eventually prompting the federal recognition of area conservation in 1965 (see Chapter 4).[17]

Large Landscapes

The overall trend in American historic preservation since World War II was the expansion of the number, type, and size of cultural resources valued as part of the patrimony of American heritage. At the end of the 1960s, the residents of Green Springs, a rural community in central Virginia, faced a dilemma: Their commonwealth government had recently proposed the construction of a new prison that, from the local perspective, would degrade, denude, and destroy many aspects of the unique qualities of the cultural landscape they called home. The struggle to obtain official recognition of this Louisa County community and its resources (see Chapter 6) echoed the long-running campaign to preserve a large landscape that comprised the viewshed from Mount Vernon across the Potomac River into Maryland (see Chapter 2). Prior to World War II, the historic preservation movement might begrudgingly accept the need to disassemble significant works of art (in the form of architectural woodwork) for installation as a stage setting for the display of decorative arts in period rooms or accommodate the necessity to move entire historic structures. Due to the wide swaths of demolition left by urban renewal and interstate highway construction activities during the mid-1950s through the mid-1960s, individuals and organizations began to appreciate the impact of inappropriate features within larger settings that contained historic properties. Historic preservation's progress marched quickly from the consideration of individual components, to the care of whole buildings and their original settings (expanding to recognition of neighborhoods and districts), and finally to entire landscapes that reflected a community's ongoing cultural impact within a natural world. One theme that flows through this progression, and one that was a significant component of the wider land conservation movement during the same period, was the concern for beauty and authenticity.

Beauty worth Preserving

Beautiful buildings came to be as valued as beautiful scenery after World War II.[18] In 1948 the landscape of preservation was expanded by the federal recognition of Hampton Mansion, located outside of Baltimore, Maryland, as a National Historic Site. This property met neither of the two traditional elements of historic places in that it was not associated with any nationally significant persons or events in the past. It was, however, a dramatic example of architectural design and craftsmanship that was thought worthy of long-term stewardship by the federal government. At Hampton, the idea was that beauty, expressed in architecture, was equal to the nationally significant scenic beauty presented by the wonders of nature within the national park system.

Scenic values and views lay at the core of the conservation agenda during the 20th century. The intellectual foundation for perpetual protection of natural and scenic values laid by John Muir was articulated through the Antiquities Act of 1906, which gave the President Theodore Roosevelt (and his successors) significant power to shape the American landscape, especially vast areas of ineffable natural beauty in the western states, through the process of declaring national monuments. This preservation approach contrasted with the conservation model promoted by Gifford Pinchot at the U.S. Forest Service (established in 1905 within the Department of Agriculture), which saw these public lands as primarily economic resources.[19]

According to historian Donald Swain, during the 1920s the concept of "aesthetic conservation" was institutionalized within the leadership of the NPS. This set the stage for the transformation of the agency during the 1930s, growing from 31 units in 1933 to more than 140 in 1940, with a similar expansion in its workforce (from 2,000 to more than 7,000 employees). Secretary of the Interior Harold Ickes even went so far as to propose rebranding his agencies within a new Department of Conservation, with an eye toward ending the long-standing competition between the NPS and the Forest Service. Fundamentally opposed to the more utilitarian approach to land-use management favored by the Forest Service, the NPS, with its unique mandate among federal agencies, "considered itself the citadel of aesthetic values" as it embraced heritage and scenic tourism to bolster public and congressional support for its expanding system. As civic activist Harleen James noted, the general public did not really care which federal agency managed a particular parcel of public land: they were simply confused by the diversity of policies and practices.[20]

This bureaucratic conflict over values—utilitarian versus aesthetic—was reflected in the use of frontier metaphors. For Westerners, the pragmatic challenges of a frontier landscape were ongoing and federal assistance was warranted to enhance economic activities within the region. Following Frederick Jackson Turner's "end of the frontier" thesis espoused in the 1890s, Easterners saw growing congestion and competition for parks and open space in a predominately urban and suburban landscape. For those who saw the parks as "temples for the worship of nature," the expansion of the NPS during the 1930s was troublesome: the additional responsibilities within historic preservation and recreational planning somewhat lessened the central place of natural beauty within the system of protected areas. Easterners feared that western public lands would be managed based on local practices and need rather than from a national perspective. This sectional division would shape the land conservation movement during the second half of the 20th century.[21]

Americans have always had an uneasy relationship with beauty. Alexis De Tocqueville thought our democracy would "habitually prefer the useful to the beautiful and . . . want the beautiful to be useful."[22] Nineteenth-century poets and pundits, from Ralph Waldo Emerson to Andrew Jackson Downing and John Muir, espoused the diverse values of natural beauty within a rapidly changing American society. With the creation of the NPS in 1916, visionaries like Stephen Mather became bureaucrats with a mandate to preserve and present the natural and scenic beauty embodied by the original national parks. During the post–World War II era of urban renewal, some developers saw "beauty as costing too much and yielding too little."[23] During the 1960s, however, there was significant federal focus on the concept of natural beauty that in many ways coincided with an emphasis on the value of good design within the built environment as the Kennedy administration took steps to improve the quality of federally sponsored architecture.[24] At a 1964 conference held in Venice, Italy, the architect Carl Feiss lamented current contradictions within the historic preservation movement:

So we find in the United States a combination of active preservation in the big cities, a scattering of preservation activities in certain well known smaller historic areas, and in the rest a general reduction to banality and sameness which is characterized by the least common denominator of the automobile, the filling station, supermarket and the false colonial house.[25]

Despite this appraisal, Feiss was hopeful for the future: The conservation movement was "sufficiently deep-seated and of sufficient validity to promise the permanent protection" of areas of great beauty, architectural importance, and historic significance.[26]

In many ways, the historic preservation movement bridged the gap between a concern for the conservation and enhancement of natural beauty and the retention and revitalization of quality designs from the past. The revitalization of federal conservation activities embraced by the Johnson administration resulted from ideas about the values of scenic beauty, open space, wilderness, and trails; and the cooperative and competitive roles of government and the private sector as advocates for landscape protection—all seated within the historical context for landscape conservation during the middle of the 20th century.[27] At the center of this new conservation was an expanding role for the NPS within the land conservation and historic preservation movements.

Enjoyment versus Impairment

Since 1916, the American people have entrusted the NPS with the care of their national parks; and since the 1930s, with the incorporation of more than 50 historic properties into its stewardship portfolio, the agency has played a significant role in the conservation of both natural and historic landscapes. The agency's mandate is to preserve, unimpaired, the natural, cultural, and recreational resources and values of a system of national parks for the enjoyment, education, and inspiration of current and future generations. In general, parklands are areas set aside by a federal, tribal, state, or local government that illustrate some distinctive natural or historical element, characteristic, or theme that is best manifested in the unique qualities of an individual place. Through their identification, selection, and protection, parks convey, in a very pragmatic way, the resources and stories that a community thinks are worthy of sharing with the future. The administrative dilemmas faced by the NPS illustrated the transformation of the land conservation and historic preservation movements during the third quarter of the 20th century.[28]

In 1955 at the invitation of Harlean James, NPS Director Conrad Wirth spoke at a conference entitled "Parks and Open Spaces for the American People." That year the equivalent of about one-third of the 165 million people in the United States visited one of the NPS units, and planners forecasted that an even higher percentage would take advantage of the available cultural, natural and recreational resources by the end of the 20th century. Ever mindful of the mandate to preserve parklands for future generations, NPS planners, and those at the state and local level, considered rationing access because the carrying capacity of the resources had been, or were about to be, overwhelmed by increasing visitation. Looking toward 50th anniversary of the agency in 1966, Wirth recounted that:

> Our first goal is to solve, by that time, the difficult problem of protecting the scenic and historic areas of the National Park System from over use and, at the same time, of providing optimum opportunity for public enjoyment of the parks.[29]

Complicating Wirth's vision was the fact that states and local governments were often unable to "carry their share" of the steadily increasing need for outdoor recreational facilities and continued to rely on federal support. Park traditionalists—those who considered natural and scenic values to be transcendent—begrudgingly accepted the presence of nationally significant historic properties within the system, but they were reticent in their tolerance of units designated primarily for active outdoor recreation. The expansion of the nation's outdoor recreation estate during the Cold War era would prove a

Figure 1.3 NPS directors (left to right) Newton Drury, Horace Albright, George Hartzog, and Conrad Wirth at the 1963 National Historic Landmark dedication of the Darien, Connecticut home of the first NPS director, Stephen Mather.

Source: Box 409, Charles E. Peterson papers, Special Collections, University of Maryland Libraries.

challenge to the NPS as well as to other federal, state, and local land management agencies.

"Encroachment" became the watchword as cities and towns came to recognize that not enough open spaces, historic sites, and parklands had been previously acquired to accommodate an expanding population. Because of their concentration within and near existing metropolitan areas, American historic places faced a grave crisis caused by the rapid urban and suburban expansion that accompanied the Baby Boom generation (1945–1964). One consequence was that numerous historic properties (and the values they represented) were significantly endangered by the construction of new housing, highways, and airports, as well as other commercial, residential, and industrial infrastructure. Severing linkages to the past was troubling to many, and appalling to some. These historic properties, like places of natural beauty, presented the "only possible authentic environment." Since the mid-1930s, their identification, evaluation, preservation, and presentation had become a tremendous undertaking that increasingly required administrative cooperation among all levels and branches of government as well as collaboration with private organizations, like the National Trust for Historic Preservation. During the Cold War this mission took on a distinctly patriotic and nationalistic tone and the expansion of broad-based historical conservation programs was justified as an effective means of preserving the American way of life in the face of rapid change and challenges from abroad.[30]

As the NPS approached its 50th anniversary, in 1966, there were 231 units in the system, which encompassed nearly 27 million acres across the United States. Despite the just-completed billion-dollar infrastructure investment program known as Mission 66, in the early 1960s the NPS retained the same fundamental mission and character as in 1916: it was a (mostly western) land management agency dedicated to the stewardship of nationally significant historical, natural, and recreational resources. All this was about to change. Federal conservation activities that stated as part of President John F. Kennedy's "New Frontier," were expanded in President Lyndon B. Johnson's "Great Society" to transform the mandate of the NPS, adding major roles and responsibilities that focused attention beyond the boundaries of its traditional activities. Adjustments to the mandates and missions of the NPS during the third quarter of the 20th century highlighted the constellation of administrative dilemmas that continued to challenge the agency, its leadership, and its employees as the institution embraced its centennial.[31]

The dual goals expressed in the agency's 1916 legislative mandate established a Janus-like binary conflict (enjoyment of the people versus impairment of the resources) that has perplexed its leadership over the last century. This enjoyment-versus-impairment dilemma is the basis of an interconnected series of challenges—ones shared by both institutions and individuals who seek to ensure the conservation of parcels small and large.[32]

Gaps in the System

One perennial debate swirls around the question of government's manifest destiny toward an ever-expanding system of protected areas. It encompasses not only the idea of the kinds and distribution of conserved lands, but also these questions: How many of any particular type of resources are warranted? How many battlefields are necessary to tell the comprehensive story of the American Civil War? How much open space do urban, suburban, and exurban communities need to ensure a healthy and happy population? What is the cost of preserving natural beauty and setting aside wilderness for future generations? Traditionalists within each generation have decried the addition of what were seen as less-than-nationally significant units—sometimes called "park-barrel" projects (a sly reference to the pejorative "pork-barrel" projects that is applied to federal undertakings that agencies have conducted for no other reason than to cater to political support), where agency guidelines, standards, and analysis were swept away by a deliberate application of political pressure. On the occasion of the agency's 65th anniversary in 1981 at the start of the Reagan administration, NPS Director Russell Dickenson exclaimed that the growth of the system "must now be curtailed." The NPS, it was frequently argued, could not adequately fulfill its role as steward to an ever-increasing portfolio without substantial reinvestment in stewardship and interpretation, as well as maintenance and operations. This pattern of management issues was repeated at the state, local and tribal levels of government. Others were more pragmatic in recognizing the reality that Congress and the executive branch rarely tire of creating new units. They viewed the park ecosystem as organic and mutable, and embraced the episodic ability to fill gaps in the system so that it reflects a representative panorama of the United States.[33]

The story of how the national park system has grown over the last century, *Shaping the System*, illustrates the assemblage of forces that have influenced the creation of protected areas within the United States. Every collection of parklands requires a strong set of criteria that define what should (and should not) be included within the system, with clearly defined goals that shape how political forces decide what properties are selected. This is vital, because once properties are acquired it is rare for them to be de-accessioned. Traditionally, the choice of what to include has ultimately been a political decision, somewhat influenced by systems of evaluation to defer, deflect, and delay the acquisition of new properties. The fact remains that some themes in American history are difficult to recognize through park designations.[34]

The national park system was designed to be the apex of the pyramid of recognition and stewardship, with state, tribal, and local government taking care of places of less-than-national significance. In the aftermath of World War II, park planners and historians recognized that there were many more nationally significant sites than could be maintained by the federal government; thus the goal was to develop overlapping systems that identified layers or levels of significance. Reflecting the widely held belief that federal conservation responsibilities should be limited to nationally significant properties and resources, in 1966 Congressman Craig Hosmer, comically proclaimed that "If Jubilation T. Cornpone's birthplace is to be preserved, let Dogpatch do it!"[35]

The NPS has long recognized that the philosophical and pragmatic quandaries regarding the shape and content of the system are influenced by a wide variety of forces. In 1972, an immediately controversial national park system plan called for the addition of nearly 200 new units in order to acquire sites that presented a comprehensive panorama of American history. From the mid-1930s until the mid-1990s the agency's approach to gaps in the system was shaped by a thematic framework that presented a consensus view of American history. This chronological and geographic structure was replaced, via a congressional mandate, with a collection of themes and concepts presented in a complex Venn diagram. By the late 1990s the agency formally acknowledged that a national system of protected areas could never be completed, especially with regard to the recognition of historic properties.[36]

Great Society Conservation

Prior to the mid-1960s, the mission of the NPS was focused almost entirely on the internal management of the units in the system. During the agency's first half century, most administrative forays into looking at the broader context of land conservation, historic preservation, or recreation were limited and designed to ensure that the system acquired or retained only a limited number of nationally significant properties. Over the last 50 years the agency's mandated portfolio has expanded to encompass a diversity of external programs that extended American park philosophy and influence beyond federal parkland boundaries. Several of the Great Society conservation programs, such as the Land and Water Conservation Fund (LCWF 1964), the National Historic Preservation Act (NHPA 1966), and the National Scenic Trails Act (NSTA 1968), gave the NPS a substantially enhanced roles in conserving areas that would never be national parks. Prior to 1966, for example, the NPS was legislatively hindered in its ability to assist states, local communities, or other federal agencies in addressing historic preservation issues at sites that were not deemed nationally significant. Efforts to assist federal urban renewal agencies in accommodating historic preservation concerns within redevelopment projects were thwarted during the early 1960s because of this limitation. Expansion of the National Register of Historic Places, the execution of the Section 106 process on federal undertakings, the rehabilitation tax credit program, and the creation of a diverse array of departmental standards and guidelines, each represented another layer of administrative responsibility that was external to what some saw as the agency's core mandate.[37]

Another factor was the transformation of the agency's conservation message into an environmental focus. In the 1950s the interpretive program had a significant obligation and opportunity to advance the preservation and enjoyment aspects of the agency's mission. By the early 1970s it had become imperative that the system serve as more than a showplace of natural, historical, or recreational assets; it had become a tool by which to "fashion a deep and permanent public awareness and concern for fundamental environmental issues." In addition, at several points in its history the agency has embraced job training and other social programs that sought to use outdoor experiences to foster the development of engaged and productive citizens.[38]

In 1962 the magazine *Changing Times* called attention to a rising trend in the transformation of the American landscape caused by the growth of automobile culture. This "infestation of tourist blight" across the country resonated with large sections of the public who wondered would "America the Beautiful" still exist in the modern world. Taking a phrase from the song "It's Only a Paper Moon," where a "honky-tonk parade" was set in a "Barnum and Bailey world, just as phony as it can be," of principal concern was the authenticity of American historic places. Carl Feiss decried the "false and imitation historic buildings" which had dominated domestic architecture and "demeaned the historic by repetition and cheap copy." Officials at Colonial Williamsburg, trading on its tradition of historical research and accurate restoration, worried that its environs were infected with "honky-tonkitis," where poorly planned and executed amusements, and recreational and commercial businesses, might overwhelm the historic triangle created by Williamsburg, Yorktown, and Jamestown. But in a Cold War world of international competition on so many fronts, where pragmatism and patriotism went hand in hand, the question remained: "Does beauty really pay?"[39]

In 1946 Bill Goodwin, the announcer on the popular radio program, *Maxwell House Coffee Time With George Burns and Gracie Allen*, described a beautiful melody picture created by the recently deceased composer Jerome Kern, "which naturally brings to mind a lot of wonderful scenes; the redwoods, orange groves, beautiful old missions, contrasted with deserts, mountains, and the sea; all a dramatic part of our American scene." It was the contrast between what was seen as natural beauty and the distinctiveness of manmade cultural manifestations that separated the land conservation and historic preservation movements during the third quarter of the 20th century. At the dawn of the Cold War, the challenges of implementing urban renewal, disposing of surplus property, and creating recreational facilities would shape how these social causes developed. But it was a return to the site of the 19th century origins of American historic preservation, George Washington's Mount Vernon estate on the Potomac River in Virginia, that would illustrate the complexities of integrating the values inherent in land conservation and historic preservation.

Notes

1. Gretchen Bulova, *Images of American: Gadsby's Tavern* (Charleston, SC: Arcadia Publishing, 2015). Dorthy Kabler, *The Story of Gadsby's Tavern* (Alexandria: Newell-Cole

Printers, 1952). Alexandria Historical Restoration and Preservation Commission, "Celebrating our Past: Highlights of Preservation Efforts in Alexandria," May 1982. Thomas Waterman, "Written Historical and Descriptive Data: Gadsby's Tavern," Historic American Buildings Survey, 1941. A noted architectural historian, Waterman may have executed the replication of the ballroom woodwork. See also: Nicolas Vincent, "The Alexandria Ballroom in the American Wing of the Metropolitan Museum of Art," in *Our Town Revisited: Historic Alexandria Foundation Antiques Show* (Alexandria: Historic Alexandria Foundation, 2009), pp. 39–41.

2. See a series of essays in *Winterthur Portfolio*, Vol. 46, No. 2/3, Period Room Architecture in American Art Museums (Summer/Autumn 2012), including: David Barquist, "'The Interior Will Be as Interesting as the Exterior Is Magnificent': American Period Rooms in the Philadelphia Museum of Art" (pp. 139–160); Neil Harris, "Period Rooms and the American Art Museum" (pp. 117–138); Morrison Heckscher, "The American Wing Rooms in the Metropolitan Museum of Art" (pp. 161–178). Horace Jayne, "The Georgian Room," *Bulletin of the Pennsylvania Museum*, Vol. 17, No. 71 (May 1922), pp. 9–11. "Farewell to the Past on Mount Vernon Place," *Baltimore Sun*, December 10, 1940. Commenting on a crowd of visitors to a prominent residence prior to an estate sale, the unidentified author noted: "the era of the recapitulation of history in period rooms" is over. Laurence Coleman, "Collecting Old Houses," *The Scientific Monthly*, Vol. 41, No. 5 (November 1935), pp. 461–463.

3. Charles Hosmer, *Presence of the Past: A History of the Preservation Movement in the United States before Williamsburg* (New York: G. P. Putnam's Sons, 1965), pp. 193–236.

4. Trevor Keeble, "Introduction," in Penny Sparke, Brenda Martin, and Trevor Keeble, eds., *The Modern Period Room: The Construction of the Exhibited Interior, 1870 to 1950* (New York: Routledge, 2006), pp. 1–7.

5. Jeremy Aynsley, "The Modern Period Room: A Contradiction in Terms?" in Penny Sparke, Brenda Martin, and Trevor Keeble, eds., *The Modern Period Room: The Construction of the Exhibited Interior, 1870 to 1950* (New York: Routledge, 2006), pp. 8–30.

6. See: Kathleen Curran, *The Invention of the American Art Museum: From Craft to Kulturgeschichte, 1870–1930* (Los Angeles: The Getty Institute, 2006). Leicester Holland, "Colonial Interiors as Museum Trophies," *The Octagon: A Journal of the American Institute of Architects* (November 1932). Holland, who chaired the AIA committee on the preservation of historic buildings, cited Frank Mather's, "Atmosphere vs. Art," in the August 1930 edition of *The Atlantic Monthly*.

7. Lawrence Kocher, "Annual Report to Executive Committee, American Institute of Architects, Sixty-Third Annual Convention, Committee on Preservation of Historic Monuments and Natural Resources," April 24, 1928.

8. Charles Hosmer, *Presence of the Past: A History of the Preservation Movement in the United States before Williamsburg* (New York: G. P. Putnam's Sons, 1965), p. 218. William Sumner Appleton to Edith May Tilly (Newport), October 27, 1913. Tilley to Appleton, October 29, 1913. UMCP CBH, Series II: Research Notes, Box 4.

9. Charles Wall to Rutherford Goodwin, March 9, 1939. MVLA CCW Papers.

10. Constance Greiff, "Interview with Charles Peterson, January 8, 1981," p. 5. UMCP CEP Box 136.

11. "The Lindens, Site of National Significance," NPS, 1968. The NPSAB did not recommend that the property be designated as a National Historic Landmark. Ernest Connally to John Warner November 20, 1968. NPS NHL OSC Files. Jeanne Schinto, "Israel Sack and the Lost Traders of Lowell Street," *Maine Antique Digest*, April 2007.

12. Charles Hosmer to Mrs. George Morris, June 9, 1974. Mrs. George Morris to Charles Hosmer, June 16, 1974. UMCP CBH.

13. The Col. Paul Wentworth house provided an unusual case study. Seated in Rollinsford, New Hampshire from ca. 1701–1936, the house was carefully removed by the family and reconstructed in Dover, Massachusetts, where it remained until 2002, when it was returned to New Hampshire, and re-erected near its original site. Paul Edwards to Charles Peterson, October 16, 1936, UMCP CEP Box 11. See: John H.

Sprinkle, Jr., *Crafting Preservation Criteria: The National Register of Historic Places and American Historic Preservation* (New York: Routledge, 2014), pp. 173–195.

14. Laurence Vail Coleman, *Historic House Museums* (Washington, DC: The American Association of Museums, 1933), pp. 99–109.

15. Milby Burton, "Historic House Restoration," 1941 Yearbook: Park and Recreation Progress, NPS, 1941, pp. 60–65.

16. Albert Good, "Historical Preservations and Reconstructions," Park and Recreation Structures: Part II, Recreational and Cultural Facilities, NPS, 1938. Chapter 13, pp. 185–196.

17. Lewis Mumford, *The Highway and the City* (New York: Harcourt Brace Jovanovich, Inc., 1963). John H. Sprinkle, Jr., *Crafting Preservation Criteria: The National Register of Historic Places and American Historic Preservation* (New York: Routledge, 2014), pp. 149–172.

18. John H. Sprinkle, Jr., *Crafting Preservation Criteria: The National Register of Historic Places and American Historic Preservation* (New York: Routledge, 2014), pp. 68–86.

19. Maria McCollester, *Executive Power in Unlikely Places: The Presidency and America's Public Lands*, Ph.D. Dissertation, Boston College, September 2016. Daniel Nelson, *Nature's Burdens: Conservation and American Politics, the Reagan Era to the Present* (Boulder: University Press of Colorado, 2017).

20. James was the executive secretary of the American Planning and Civic Association, an organization that combined the American Civic Association and the National Conference on City Planning and that was headed by former NPS Director Horace Albright and Ulysses S. Grant III, who also played a prominent role in the leadership of the National Trust for Historic Preservation. Donald Swain, "The National Park Service and the New Deal, 1933–1940," *Pacific Historical Review*, Vol. 41, No. 3 (August 1972), pp. 312–332. Donald Swain, *Wilderness Defender: Horace M. Albright and Conservation* (Chicago: University of Chicago Press, 1970), pp. 277–278. NPS managed more than $218 million in conservation projects during this period. James' testimony appears in "Consolidation of Federal Conservation Activities," Hearings before the Special Committee on Conservation of Wild Life Resources, United States Senate, January 12–13, 1933, pp. 72–80.

21. Donald Swain, "The National Park Service and the New Deal, 1933–1940," *Pacific Historical Review*, Vol. 41, No. 3 (August 1972), p. 327.

22. Alexis de Tocqueville, *Democracy in America*, Book II: The Influence of Democracy on Progress of Opinion in the United States, Translated and edited by Harvey Mansfield and Delba Winthrop (Chicago: University of Chicago Press, 2000), p. 439.

23. Charles Abrams, "The City Is the Frontier," in Jewel Bellush and Murray Hausknecht, eds., *Urban Renewal: People, Politics, and Planning* (New York: Anchor Books, 1967), p. 401.

24. Daniel Patrick Moynihan, "Guiding Principles for Federal Architecture," 1962. Karen Patricia Heath, "Daniel Patrick Moynihan and His 'Guiding Principles for Federal Architecture' (1962)," *Political Science*, Vol. 50, No. 2 (April 2017), pp. 384–387.

25. Carl Feiss, "An Introduction to the Preservation of Historic Areas in the United States of America," International Federation for Housing and Planning Standing Committee on Historic Urban Areas, Venice, Italy, May 22–24, 1964. RG 421 NTHP Feiss.

26. Carl Feiss, "An Introduction to the Preservation of Historic Areas in the United States of America," International Federation for Housing and Planning Standing Committee on Historic Urban Areas, Venice, Italy, May 22–24, 1964. RG 421 NTHP Feiss.

27. Some of the literature on landscape conservation includes: John Ise, *Our National Park Policy: A Critical History* (Baltimore: The Johns Hopkins University Press, 1961); Donald Swain, *Federal Conservation Policy, 1921–1933* (Berkeley: University of California Press, 1963); Donald Swain, *Wilderness Defender: Horace M. Albright and Conservation* (Chicago: University of Chicago Press, 1970); Roderick Nash, *Wilderness*

and the American Mind (New Haven: Yale University Press, 1967); Edgar Nixon, ed., *Franklin D. Roosevelt and Conservation, 1911–1945* (2 vols., Hyde Park: Franklin D. Roosevelt Library, 1957); Sarah Phillips, *This Land, This Nation: Conservation, Rural America, and the New Deal* (New York: Cambridge University Press, 2007); Henry Clepper, ed., *Origins of American Conservation* (New York: The Roland Press, Co., 1966). Martin V. Melosi, "Lyndon Johnson and Environmental Policy," in The Johnson Years, Volume Two: Vietnam, the Environment, and Science, ed. Robert A. Divine (Lawrence: University Press of Kansas, 1987).

28. On the history of the national park system see: Denise Meringolo, *Museums, Monuments, and National Parks: Toward a New Genealogy of Public History* (Amhurst: University of Massachusetts, Amhurst, 2012) and Richard West Sellars, *Preserving Nature in the National Parks: A History* (New Haven: Yale University Press, 1997).
29. Conrad Wirth, "An Adequate National Park System for 300 Million People," National Citizens Planning Conference on Parks and Open Spaces for the American People, Washington, DC, May 24, 1955. RG 368 HCRS Subject Box 2.
30. George Dickie to Tom Wallace, "Suggestions for Statement of Principles of Park Protection," May 19, 1955. Wallace was second vice president of the American Planning and Civic Association. RG 368 HCRS Subject Box 2. John Hurst, "That the Past Shall Live: the History Program of the National Park Service," NPS, 1959, p. 32. This publication was funded by the Old Dominion Foundation as part of the agency's publicity program supporting Mission 66.
31. At the end of the centennial year the national park system contained 417 units, comprising 84 million acres, which supported nearly 300 million visits annually, as managed by about 20,000 employees with an annual appropriation of $3 billion. The "new preservation," "new archaeology," and "new social history" were also launched during the 1960s.
32. See: Lary Dilsaver, ed., *America's National Park System: The Critical Documents* (New York: Rowman & Littlefield, 1994). The mandate is "to conserve the scenery and the natural and historic objects and the wild life therein and to provide for the enjoyment of the same in such manner and by such means as will leave them unimpaired for the enjoyment of future generations." Newton Drury, "The Dilemma of Our Parks," *American Forests*, Vol. 55, No. 6 (June 1949), pp. 6–11, 38–39. His recognition of a postwar crisis in the management and use of the parks was echoed in a variety of publications, most notably Bernard de Voto, "Let's Close the National Parks," *Harper's Magazine*, Vol. 207, No. 1241 (October 1953), pp. 49–52. The binary mission (visitor use versus resource protection) is a component of the feasibility criteria for adding new park. Carol Hardy Vincent, *National Park System: Establishing New Units* (Washington, DC: Congressional Research Service, March 26, 2014).
33. Reflecting on his 30-year career with the National Park Service, Ronald Lee thought that the agency's disparate management of natural, historical, and recreation areas had "grown like Topsy" Ronald Lee to Roy Appleman, July 11, 1969. Russell Dickenson, "Our Challenge Today," in *National Park Service: 65th Anniversary* (Washington, DC: NPS, 1981). John H. Sprinkle, Jr., "'An Orderly, Balanced and Comprehensive Panorama . . . of American History': Filling Thematic Gaps within the National Park System," *The George Wright Forum*, Vol. 27, No. 3 (2010), pp. 269–279.
34. Barry Mackintosh and Janet McDonnell, *The National Parks: Shaping the System* (Washington, DC: NPS, 2005). Barry Mackintosh, *Former National Park System Units: An Analysis* (Washington, DC: NPS, 1995). Between 1930 and 1994, 23 units were transferred out of NPS ownership. "The System is indeed imbalanced, but this is not necessarily bad. The problem lies less with the imbalance than with those who either deny it—pretending the Service is telling the whole story—or deplore it and urge expansion into subject areas better communicated by other media." Barry Mackintosh, *Interpretation in the National Park Service: A Historical Perspective* (Washington, DC: NPS, 1986).

35. Cornpone was a fictional Confederate general from Dogpatch, Kentucky, in Al Capp's long-running comic strip, *Li'l Abner.* Congressional Record, September 19, 1966, p. 22957.

36. NPS, *Part One of the National Park System Plan: History* (Washington, DC: NPS, 1972). Some 120 units were added between 1973 and 2000. *History in the National Park Service: Themes and Concepts* (Washington, DC: NPS, 1994; revised 2000). NPSAB, Committee on Standards and Criteria, Final Report, June 10, 1997. NPS PHP Files. The recent work of the NPSAB under the leadership of historian John Hope Franklin and the National Parks Second Century Commission illustrated the ongoing debate about the future of the agency and its mission. NPSAB, "Rethinking the National Parks for the 21st Century," NPS, 2001; National Parks Conservation Association, *Advancing the National Park Idea,* 2009. The Second Century Commission specifically called for updated criteria for the designation of new park units, developed in consultation with the National Academy of Sciences.

37. Part of this pattern harkens back to the 1930s when regional offices were developed to oversee Depression-era work on state and local parks. Helping state park systems was an effective means of reducing pressure on additions to the already overburdened natural and historical units of the national park system. See: Advisory Board on National Parks, Historic Sites, Buildings and Monuments, "Papers," 60th Meeting, April 21–24, 1969. NPS PHP.

38. Director, NPS to All Field Offices, "Securing Protection and Conservation Objectives through Interpretation," April 23, 1953. Robert T. Dennis, *National Parks for the Future* (Washington, DC: The Conservation Foundation, 1972), p. 9. Angela Sirna, *Recreating Appalachia: Cumberland Gap National Historical Park, 1922–1972.* Ph.D. Dissertation, Middle Tennessee State University, 2015.

39. Harold Arlen, Yip Harburg, and Billy Rose, "It's Only a Paper Moon," 1933. This jazz standard was revived after World War II with covers by Ella Fitzgerald and Nat King Cole and by the 1973 Paramount Pictures production of the Peter Bogdanovich film, *Paper Moon.* Carl Feiss, "An Introduction to the Preservation of Historic Areas in the United States of America," International Federation for Housing and Planning Standing Committee on Historic Urban Areas, Venice, Italy, May 22–24, 1964. (p. 15) RG 421 NTHP Feiss. Michael Frome, "America the Beautiful: Let's Not Lose It," *Changing Times,* September 1963, pp. 25–29 and "America the Beautiful: Heritage or Honky Tonk?" *Changing Times,* November 1962, pp. 7–10.

2 Valuing Vision

During the first months of 1966, rather than anticipation for the soon-to-be proposed National Historic Preservation Act, the principal headline in American historic preservation was the enhancement of scenic easements as important tools in the preservation of historic properties. Officials in Prince George's County, Maryland, took advantage of recent changes in state law to reduce, by half, property taxes on parcels (five acres or greater) that were permanently protected from development through the application of conservation easements. The first local law in the United States granting tax credits for historic preservation was executed on the piazza of George Washington's Mount Vernon plantation, a ceremonial event recognizing that the inspirational view across the Potomac River into Maryland was worthy of investment and protection. This was an important moment in the history of conservation as it recognized the tangible contribution of individual landowners in the protection of open space associated with historic properties. Just as the purchase of Mount Vernon was a watershed during the mid-19th century, so too was the mid-20th century success of the campaign known as Operation Overview.[1]

Operation Overview

Soon after the Mount Vernon Ladies' Association (MVLA) celebrated its centenary in 1953, the organization that had purchased, preserved, and presented George Washington's Virginia plantation was faced with a serious challenge to the physical integrity of its mission. The almost pristine view from the piazza of Washington's iconic home, which overlooked more than 5,000 acres of fields and forests across the Potomac River into Maryland, became threatened by the encroachment of potential suburban, commercial, and industrial development that would have substantially impaired the experience of the estate's many visitors. Recognizing the significance of this challenge, the MVLA's leadership launched a campaign in partnership with a number of like-minded Maryland-based organizations, called Operation Overview, to preserve the viewshed and protect the scenic values that so enhanced the site's historic setting. This goal necessitated a creative vision for land conservation

Figure 2.1 View across the Potomac River into Maryland from the Piazza at Mount Vernon, ca. 1961. The interpretive signage described threats to the viewshed from proposed industrial and residential developments within the area that would become Piscataway Park.

Source: Mount Vernon Ladies Association, Operation Overview

that led to the establishment of Piscataway Park, the only unit of the national park system with the mandate to protect the vista from a historic property.[2]

The MVLA entered its second century of operation just as the United States was enveloped by the post–World War II transformation of society, culture, and landscape. Growing federal support for highway construction and suburbanization began to send tendrils of development into areas that surrounded metropolitan centers across the country. Opened in 1932 and built by the federal government as a lasting reminder of the celebration of the bicentennial of George Washington's birth, the George Washington Memorial Parkway provided not only a stately approach to the historic shrine, but had ironically also spurred the spread of suburban and commercial development south from Alexandria, Virginia, toward its terminus at Mount Vernon. As more and more visitors came to the estate via automobiles (as opposed to traveling by riverboat as was most common before World War II), the MVLA remained protective of the memorial highway and worked closely with its steward, the National Park Service (NPS), to enhance its design qualities and scenic values. For example, at a congressional hearing in 1949 on allowing additional automobile access to the parkway from a residential development just south of Alexandria, Representative Frances Bolton (and Mount Vernon vice regent from Ohio) testified that it would be a "national tragedy" if the parkway were to be "turned into a commercial road."[3]

The stewards of Mount Vernon were well aware of the threats proposed by suburbanization of the Virginia side of the Potomac River during the post–World War II period. Beginning in the early 1940s residential developments such as Tauxemont, Hollin Hills, and Waynewood began the spread of suburbia southward along the George Washington Memorial Parkway. MVLA Resident Director Charles Wall quipped: "We have a friendly interest in the growing community about Mount Vernon."[4] Concern for the estate's larger environment grew as the MVLA approached its centennial in 1953:

> With the rapid postwar growth of the Mount Vernon community, the possibility of residential development immediately adjacent to the old West Gate has been a matter of growing concern to us. It would be unfortunate if the original atmosphere there were to be impaired by the intrusion of modern housing. Such a development could intrude, also, upon the vista which extends from the Mansion courtyard to the West Gate.[5]

Increasing suburban development during the late 1950s stimulated (ultimately unsuccessful) interest to extend the memorial parkway from Mount Vernon to Woodlawn, a Washington family estate that was the first property acquired by the National Trust for Historic Preservation (NTHP). At some level the MVLA's experience with the expansion of suburbia on the Virginia side of the Potomac during the early 1950s must have served as an alarm for the Mount Vernon leadership. The Woodrow Wilson Memorial Bridge—authorized in 1954 and proposed as part of the Interstate Highway System and the beltway (or ring road) around nearby Washington, DC—was certain to increase automobile access and development pressure to both sides of the Potomac River. Limited by its state charter, its fiscal resources, and its administrative traditions, Mount Vernon looked toward an expanded vision to secure the conservation of the Maryland shoreline, one that involved a package of partnerships, philanthropy, and political machinations.[6]

The View across the River

The NPS was an important partner in Operation Overview. During the 1950s the agency crafted an administrative justification that legitimized consideration of a federal role in the preservation of the Mount Vernon viewshed. In July 1953, Murray Nelligan, a NPS historian, prepared a memorandum on Mockley Point that described the archaeological significance of the area across Piscataway Creek from Fort Washington, a defensive fortification that had itself been added to the national park system only 20 years before. Highlighting

Alice Ferguson's archaeological excavations at a purported Susquehannock fort, Nelligan recommended investigating the national park "potentialities" of the property before urban expansion into Prince George's County overwhelmed the area. From an NPS perspective, the site had three principal qualities: First, it was relatively accessible to the Washington, DC, metropolitan area. Second, it could open up an entirely new field for archaeological and historical interpretation in the region, rounding out coverage of all significant periods in history. Since the mid-1930s the NPS had been charged with creating a system of units that together could illustrate a comprehensive panorama of American history. Third, the site offered a spectacular view up the river to Washington, DC, and down the river and across to Mount Vernon.[7]

While some in the NPS discounted the historical qualities of the Piscataway area, Ronald Lee, the agency's Chief of Interpretation, disagreed. In early 1954, Lee wondered whether there was any legal authority for the NPS to accept "this kind of property"? The obvious administrative path was to have the area designated as a National Historic Site under the auspices of the Historic Sites Act of 1935.[8] During this period, National Historic Sites could be either under private or government stewardship—such as at Jamestown Island. "Much would depend," concluded NPS historian Charles Porter, "on the weight to be given to the logical balance in the overall program of acquiring archaeological sites for addition to the National Park System."[9] During the 1950s, "logical balance" was often a bureaucratic code phrase for the application of "Criterion P," meaning the availability of political power to ensure congressional approval of a recommended site. As the national survey of historic sites was reinvigorated after World War II during the NPS's Mission 66 program, it had become increasingly apparent that there were far too many nationally significant historic sites for the NPS to steward them all. In 1954 the idea was to incorporate the Mockley Point archaeological site into a proposed parkway to Fort Washington, similar to the one on the Virginia shore. NPS historians remained concerned that the currently isolated area would be open to encroachment and that it would be difficult to justify the cost of securing the site when the restoration and maintenance of Fort Washington was so underfunded. "It is a rugged dilemma that we face," reflected Charles Porter, "Unhappily, it looks like the times are not favorable to the acquisition" of this important historical and archaeological site.[10]

If its archaeological resources brought Mockley Point to the attention of the NPS, its scenic qualities quickly became the focus of federal interest. During the summer of 1954, NPS developed a preliminary justification for a proposed Accokeek Park that focused on the area's outstanding scenic values as well as its significant archaeological components.

> Though relatively undeveloped at present, the area cannot be expected to remain so much longer in view of the accelerating expansion of the urban areas out into this part of Prince George's County. Therefore if the park values . . . are to be conserved, the land needed should be

acquired with the least possible delay. . . . Because of its location . . . the park site offers spectacular views of the river and the surrounding countryside. Mount Vernon, the most important historic home in the United States, lies directly across the river, and the proposed park would permanently preserve this important vista from this hallowed spot.[11]

Spurred into action by Ronald Lee's directive to find a mechanism by which the NPS could acquire property along the Maryland shoreline to protect the vista, this memorandum was clearly crafted in response to the possible sale of Vaughan Connelly's farm, a 485-acre property seated across the river from Mount Vernon. Acquisition of this tract was "key to the conservation and interpretation of an area of outstanding scenic and historic importance."[12]

Acquiring the Key

In the conclusion to his 1954 essay, "The Big Change in Suburbia," the editor of *Harper's Magazine*, Frederick Lewis Allen, enumerated the values of open space in the postwar world and called for communities to take immediate action to develop a "ways and means for preserving open land for the benefit of succeeding generations."[13] In light of this challenge, the MVLA, in close cooperation with NPS officials, began preparations for a national campaign to stabilize the view across the Potomac River. Considering the rising prices of suburban land in Virginia, Charles Wall correctly predicted that "our hopeful project across the river" would require significant fiscal resources.[14] Believing funds might come from a visionary and patriotic benefactor, the MVLA unsuccessfully approached several philanthropists who had previously sponsored historic preservation projects in Virginia.[15] Discouraged, Wall reflected on the dim prospect of securing a timely congressional appropriation to purchase Connelly's farm despite the NPS's strong support for its acquisition. "Time is of the essence," he concluded. "Land values there are bound to be pushed upward by the prevalent local speculative fever and a housing development is one of the lesser evils to be feared." He reported that across the Potomac, Connelly, "who first crystalized our interest in the preservation of the status quo," had been approached by some Texas investors with a proposal for a residential development that would have included a clubhouse replica of Mount Vernon.[16]

Fortunately, a new ally had appeared on the horizon. Representing a group of landowners with property within the viewshed called the Moyaone Association, Charles Wagner contacted Wall to discuss their mutual interest in preserving the Maryland shoreline. It was Wagner who suggested that the MVLA partner with a charitable organization to acquire and hold property while waiting for Congress to fund its acquisition by the NPS.[17] By August 1955, while planning an extensive congressional trip to Africa, Representative Frances Bolton purchased the Connelly farm using her own financial resources. Despite her best efforts, Bolton's acquisition became public knowledge while she was abroad.[18] Positive reaction to her substantial generosity launched an unintended career in land conservation and historic preservation. Through Charles Wagner, Bolton and Wall came to know like-minded conservationists across the Potomac in Maryland, including Robert Ware Straus from the Moyaone Association and Henry Ferguson, who in 1952 had created the Alice Ferguson Foundation in honor of his wife's archaeological exploration of Mockley Point.[19] As the overall complexity of Operation Overview became clearer, Bolton established the Accokeek Foundation in 1957 to oversee efforts to protect the view across the Potomac, inviting David Finley, one of the founders of the NTHP, to serve on its Board of Trustees. Initially the foundation avoided any recognition for its land acquisition program, fearing that publicity would increase land values. Determining that property values had risen by 30 percent in the first two years of its operation, the Accokeek Foundation abandoned this stealth approach when another significant threat appeared on the horizon.[20]

Let One Spot Be Saved From Change[21]

News in summer of 1960 that the MVLA was to be honored as the first recipient of the Louise du Pont Crowninshield Award from the NTHP was tempered by the shocking discovery that the Washington Suburban Sanitary Commission (WSSC) had plans for the construction of a sewage treatment plant along Piscataway Creek near Mockley Point.[22] The proposed introduction of a modern industrial structure motivated and mobilized the consortium of individuals and institutions participating in Operation Overview. Stabilizing the viewshed was "infinitely more important" than any other undertaking at Mount Vernon, as noted by one of MVLA vice regents:

> It was useless to pay thousands of dollars for memorabilia and documents, which are never seen by the public, while neglecting the one aspect of Mount Vernon which is probably best remembered by the majority of our visitors—the view.[23]

Convinced of the impending threat of the proposed sewage treatment facility, the MVLA took the unprecedented step of providing substantial funding to the Accokeek Foundation in support of their common goal. The newly elected MVLA regent, Rosamund Beirne, took it upon herself to write each member of the NTHP in Maryland decrying this "first encroachment on the scenic environment of Mount Vernon."[24] In mid-January 1961 Operation Overview marshalled its combined forces in opposition to the proposed sewage treatment plant at a public meeting in Prince George's County. As a result the WSSC deferred consideration of a site along Piscataway Creek— but this episode, augmented by President Kennedy's conservation message to

Congress in February 1961, convinced the MVLA and the Accokeek Foundation to publically join forces in Operation Overview.[25]

Soon after the initial purchase of the Connelly farm in 1955, Charles Wall and Ronald Lee worked together to develop a legislative formula to authorize federal land acquisition in the area. Discussions regarding the preservation of the Potomac shoreline also included the Maryland National Capital Park and Planning Commission, a state agency with oversight on regional park proposals. While a congressional bill was finally introduced in June 1961, proponents continued to seek possible donations from major philanthropic organizations, with the goal of avoiding the need for federal ownership. Because of extensive private landholdings within the viewshed, the park was envisioned as a hybrid, with a core of publically owned parcels surrounded by private property that was protected by a patchwork of scenic easements.[26]

Public visibility was a key component of Operation Overview. On July 11, 1961, the President and Mrs. Kennedy hosted a diplomatic dinner commemorating the visit of the President of Pakistan on the east lawn at Mount Vernon overlooking the Potomac. In preparation for the event, Mount Vernon temporarily removed a four-by-seven-foot interpretive panel that had been recently installed on the riverfront describing potential threats to the vista and plans for its protection (see Figure 2.1). Although the event, planned by the First Lady, was not without some controversy, it had the "providential effect of bringing public and official attention to our scenic environment."[27]

In the fall, as the congressional session drew to a close, MVLA Regent Rosamund Beirne presented an elaborate analogy as to how Mount Vernon's viewshed was America's front yard:

> What strangers see here may affect their whole conception of this country because first things make the greatest impression. The far horizon and peacefulness of our view from the portico have given more foreigners food for thought than you can possibly imagine.[28]

Focusing on the need for sanitary treatment infrastructure to support suburban growth in the region, representatives from the WSSC questioned whether a sewage treatment facility located at a new site located further up Piscataway Creek from Mockley Point would be visible from Mount Vernon. NPS officials argued that any site along the lower Piscataway would impair the setting of Fort Washington and the memorial highway to Mount Vernon. WSSC representatives had the unenviable task of arguing that it was "not inconsistent" to have a sewage treatment plant seated within a scenic park area.[29]

Much of the congressional debate centered on the complex mosaic of areas proposed for federal fee-simple acquisition, donated parcels, and those slated for the purchase of scenic easements. One local farmer and landowner,

Manning Clagett, charged that the NPS's cost estimates for land acquisition, set at $1,600 per acre, did not represent the true fair market value for land in this area.[30] Cost considerations forced Congress to remove Marshall Hall, the downriver site of an existing amusement park, from the initial area set aside for acquisition. As the Accokeek Foundation had seen during the late 1950s, land values in the Piscataway area continued to increase rapidly during the 1960s. The average price per acre for fee-simple acquisition was about $5,000 per acre, while scenic easements were purchased for just over $2,000 per acre. Across the country during the 1960s, local park proponents, like those at Piscataway, encountered escalating land prices that quickly outpaced the appropriation ceilings established by Congress.[31]

Accepting the necessity of federal involvement in Operation Overview was troublesome to many of the local conservationists, who had hoped to avoid federal intervention. To some, the Piscataway area was considered a "quiet back-water to the great city of Washington, lived in modestly by people who like country life and who have no political influence or power to enforce some sort of planning or zoning."[32] Yet, as Denise Meringolo demonstrated in a 2008 article on Piscataway Park, the membership of the Moyaone Association had independently established a cooperative venture of residential covenants designed to preserve of the open and wooded cultural landscape visible from Mount Vernon. Moyaone, concluded Maryland Senator John Butler, was an "almost unique or pilot project in cooperative individual activity for the development and use of the countryside without destroying its natural attraction."[33] By necessity, the Accokeek Foundation, the Moyaone Association, and their local partners were also in the real estate development business, acquiring additional land within the viewshed, subdividing parcels, attaching restrictive covenants, and then re-selling new residential lots seated in the periphery of the park. Incorporating federal assistance would backstop private efforts to control land use in the area by removing the threat of condemnation by regional authorities such as the WSSC.

President Kennedy signed the bill authorizing establishment of Piscataway Park on October 4, 1961, completing the initial stage of Operation Overview.[34] It took another seven years to secure the appropriations necessary to acquire additional lands within the viewshed (those not previously protected by the Accokeek Foundation) as well as more than 100 easements from local property owners. This debate centered on the cost associated with acquiring parcels and easements and whether this conservation effort was truly a federal responsibility. Proponents of Operation Overview were hopeful that the establishment of the Land and Water Conservation Fund (see Chapter 5) might provide an immediate solution to the problems of land acquisition. Representative Bolton and her allies had to maintain pressure to secure the necessary funds to even after the public opening of Piscataway Park in 1968.[35]

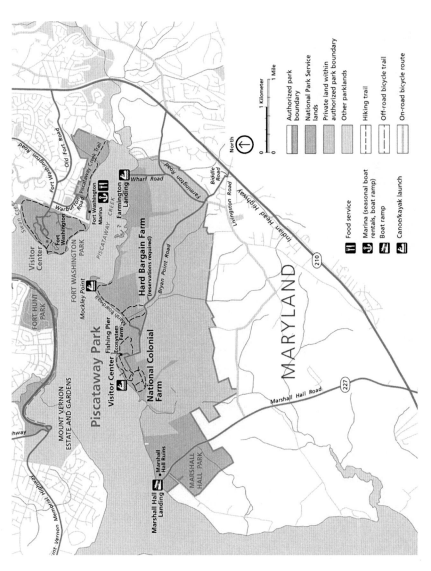

Figure 2.2 Piscataway Park. This map shows the relationship between the George Washington Memorial Parkway and Mount Vernon on the Virginia side of the Potomac with Fort Washington, Piscataway Creek, and the National Colonial Farm on the Maryland shoreline. It also shows distribution of federally owned properties and those protected via conservation easements.

Source: Courtesy of the NPS

Park Planning Challenges

The Piscataway authorization presented a variety of challenges for the NPS planners. In 1956 the national park system comprised 181 units and contained a total of 25 million acres. Seventy new areas were added to the national park system during the decade-long Mission 66 program, and more than 100 proposed parks were studied for their significance, feasibility, and suitability for inclusion in the system. Trained as a landscape architect, NPS Director Conrad Wirth had an expanded vision for the area that included rebranding the various publicly and privately held historic resources along the Potomac as components of a larger George Washington Memorial Park to be integrated by a water transportation network. The undeveloped character of Piscataway Park was atypical of national park system units created near urban centers during the Mission 66 expansion. And yet this quality, of undisturbed fields and forest that matched George Washington's view from the piazza, was exactly what the park's proponents—on both sides of the Potomac—had in mind as Representative Bolton acquired the Connelly farm in 1955.[36]

Understandably, the residents living within the area proposed for the new park were concerned, not only by the potential encroachment of additional suburban, industrial, or commercial developments, but also the "undesired expansion" of the park itself.[37] Initial proposals called for the creation of extensive riverine swimming facilities at Fort Washington, building a visitor's center along Piscataway Creek (near the location of the proposed sanitary plant), and establishing a network of trails connecting camp sites for more than 600 overnight visitors. Some local landowners thought that Operation Overview was fundamentally misguided, arguing that the greatest impact to the Mount Vernon viewshed was the presence of the honky-tonk atmosphere found downriver at the Marshall Hall Amusement Park.[38] Across the river from Mount Vernon, local land-use planning was not well developed, so neighborhood groups such as the Moyaone Association creatively attempted "zoning on a do-it-yourself basis," by voluntarily restricting development to one modest house per five-acre parcel.[39] Although Robert Straus had previously complained that the Accokeek area was "deficient in everything—riverfront parks, transportation, communication, water, housing—all factors of modern metropolitan life," his community remained hesitant about NPS plans for the area.[40]

Discussions with the local residents became "somewhat more cordial" when NPS gave assurances that only the minimum amount of land would be acquired by the federal government and that easements on the remaining potions of the viewshed would not impact existing buildings or land uses.[41] The Accokeek Foundation retained the services of a prominent regional planner, Frederick Gutheim (see Sidebar 2.1), to assist in planning for the development of a "diversified program of open space uses along the waterfront, involving a variety of conservation, recreational and cultural uses" that included primitive camping areas for scouts, a wildlife sanctuary, and a living history museum called the National Colonial Farm. Any expectation that local conservation groups and other landowners would quickly convey their landholdings to the federal government and drop out of the picture proved incorrect. Illustrating its vision for the future of the property, the Acco-keek Foundation developed its own plans for the limited development of the park's resources.[42]

Sidebar 2.1   The Sage of the Potomac

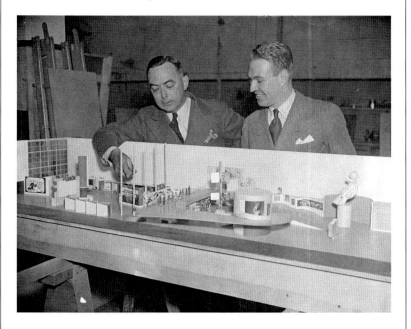

Figure 2.3 Frederick Guthiem. This late 1930s photo Harry Stubman shows Fritz Gutheim an exhibit model.

Source: LOC Prints and Photographs Division. Harris & Ewing, Photographer. LC-H22-D-2935.

In 1987 after a presentation to an assembly at George Washington's Mount Vernon, Jim Rees, the estate's resident director, called Frederick (Fritz) Gutheim (1903–1993) the "sage of the Potomac" for his lifelong devotion to the river valley and its cultural and natural resources.[43] Edu-cated at the University of Wisconsin's Experimental School, Gutheim considered himself an "instigator" who collaborated with a broad range of partners to study social and cultural problems from a land-use planning and public policy perspective. Among a variety of public service posi-tions, he served as the staff director for the Joint Congressional Commit-tee on Washington Metropolitan Problems (1958–1960), after which he established an urban think tank, the Washington Center for Metropolitan Studies (1960–1965).[44] His publications included a regional history, *The Potomac* (1949); *The Federal City: Plans and Realities* (1976), written with the historian Wilcomb Washburn; and *Worthy of a Nation* (1977), a history of Washington, DC. A passionate advocate for historic preservation and open space conservation, Gutheim was often critical of federal, state, and local government programs, taking on federal architecture programs, highway programs, and a variety of urban renewal issues.[45]

Gutheim made significant contributions to Operation Overview and the preservation of the Mount Vernon vista. From his perspective, few people recognized how long and complex an endeavor saving the viewshed would become. From the start, Gutheim concluded that Piscataway Park could never be developed like a traditional recreational facility, with extensive bathing beaches, fishing piers, camp grounds, and other infrastructure. Protecting the overview from Mount Vernon was too important, leading him to propose development of the National Colonial Farm, a living history museum that mimicked an idealized 18th century agricultural landscape, as an appropriate compromise. After the establishment of Piscataway Park in 1961, Gutheim also helped the Accokeek Foundation secure funding from the Bureau of Outdoor Recreation to study the use of conservation easements as a new tool for landscape preservation.[46]

In retrospect, Gutheim recalled the overall "background of inexperience" among the conservation proponents; their "congenial political relationship," and their tenacious ability to drag the Department of the Interior "along kicking and screaming" to achieve Operation Overview's goals.[47] Always the partisan, the Accokeek Foundation's Robert Straus could never comprehend any opposition to Piscataway Park, and yet Gutheim understood the NPS's reluctance. The unit was relatively small and relatively undeveloped, yet, because of the scenic easements, seemingly difficult to administer. Its fundamental purpose—to preserve a historic landscape (for the most part) sealed in amber—was too new and too untried a conservation technique during the 1960s. Long-range plans for the conservation of open space in the Washington, DC, metropolitan region, as described by Gutheim in 1964, called for the protection of nearly 250,000 additional acres of land, an approach that illustrated his constant emphasis on regionalism as the only way to secure sufficient fiscal resources and to overcome narrowly concentrated special interests.[48] Gutheim's pragmatic vision enhanced the long-term stewardship of Piscataway Park and the Potomac River that he loved.

A site's scenic values and setting had always been considerations in the NPS's evaluations of potential new units, but embracing a new area designed primarily for the protection of Mount Vernon's Potomac River overview was a significant step, not only for the agency but also for the MVLA. The proposed park generated a unique and creative land conservation plan with the core of the viewshed to be wholly acquired by the federal government and the outlying areas subject to protection through conservation easements. During this period the NPS was distrustful of inholdings, or privately held parcels located within one-third of park units. "As long as such lands are not under the exclusive control" of the NPS, they posed a "continuing threat to the integrity" of the park, which in the past had resulted in conflicts between the agency and local landowners.[49] Moreover, at this time the growing trend in park planning was to create substantially developed recreational areas adjacent to metropolitan areas to provide access to the out-of-doors for urban and suburban residents (see Chapter 5).

Scenic Easements

Creation of a system of easements that allowed private owners to receive income tax deductions for the donation of a conservation interest in their lands was one of the prime accomplishments of Operation Overview (see Appendix 2.1). Reflecting a general characteristic of historic preservation policy makers during the period, this vision of a system of conservation easements had tangible aspects to its financial value. Operation Overview started during a vanguard period (see Chapter 6) for the use of easements as part of conservation efforts—a time in which questions raised during the late 1950s regarding legislative mandate, methods of assessing value, and enforcement led to what was called a "welter of confusion."[50]

Operation Overview did not represent the first use of easements to protect scenic values: The NPS had had such authority since at least the early 1940s, and several state highway departments had used such legal mechanisms to protect scenic views along various rights of way. In 1940, as the NPS began the interpretive development and reconstruction of several important buildings located at the mid-19th century crossroads village of Appomattox Court House, Virginia, it relied upon scenic easements to protect the views of the "surrender grounds," where General Robert E. Lee had capitulated to General Ulysses S. Grant to end the Civil War (see Sidebar 6.4). During the first half of the 1960s, the Potomac River Valley became the focus of several efforts to preserve its natural beauty and to improve its water quality. Scenic easements were considered valuable conservation tools and were used to restrict development at several parcels upriver of the capitol, including at Merrywood, a 47-acre estate associated with Jacqueline Kennedy's youth (see Sidebar 6.2). However, these easements were not designed to protect the vistas associated with historic properties.[51]

The Old Line state was at the forefront of efforts to encourage the preservation of open space, a strongly endorsed land-use planning goal supported by more than a dozen federal programs in the 1960s. State and local governments in Maryland were concerned with the rapid disappearance of urban open space and rural farmland.[52] "When it is not always possible to make a park," noted Mount Vernon Regent Rosamund Beirne, "voluntary offers of scenic easements and preservation of open space constitute real conservation."[53] In 1960 the Lee-Robinson Act authorized the state's Department of Forests and Parks to acquire easements for conservation purposes—however, few communities sought such protections. As a newly devised method of land protection, the impact of scenic easements on overall land values was uncertain and landowners within the proposed Piscataway Park who had established easements anxiously awaited a decision from the Department of the Treasury as to the value of such donations. After more than a year of debate, on May 5, 1965, Maryland Governor Millard Tawes executed a bill that would allow certain counties seated along the Potomac River to provide tax relief for individuals who encumbered their properties with scenic easements.[54] NPS Director George Hartzog was on hand to endorse the action as an important contribution to the Johnson administration's plans to conserve and enhance the natural beauty of the Potomac River Valley.[55] Now with a clear mandate from the state, Prince George's County officials moved quickly to propose tax abatement for landowners that placed scenic easements on their property. This effort was let by two Mayonne activists: Belva Jensen and Dixie Otis.[56] In January 1966, the local law was enacted at a ceremony held within the large dining room at Mount Vernon, a clear indication of the ongoing involvement of the MVLA in fostering the program.[57] Secretary of the Interior Stewart Udall called the example set by Operation Overview's creative use of easements "a conservation tool of national significance."[58]

Values and Vision

Operation Overview took place during a transformational period of American historic preservation. What had been an elite-led movement generally centered on house museums and battlefields prior to World War II was changing—within the context of urban renewal, suburbanization, and social upheaval—into a more democratic and increasingly bureaucratic system that focused grassroots recognition efforts and the adaptive use of historic properties.[59] In some ways the movement was a relatively young endeavor in 1955 when Representative Bolton purchased the Connelly farm: The phrase "preservation movement" had been first used in 1941; nationally significant achievements in architecture had only been federally recognized in 1948; and the NTHP had just two years before merged its operations with the National Council for Historic Sites and Buildings.[60]

The creation of Piscataway Park illustrated many of the conflicts inherent in the intersection of the historic preservation and land conservation movements of the mid-20th century. In 1962, announcing the first White House conference on conservation in more than 50 years, President Kennedy said that the ultimate goal was to "harmonize conflicting objectives" through "comprehensive and integrated planning."[61] But, according to the NPS, there were

> Certain areas . . . that simply cannot afford to wait. Nature and historical accident have combined thus far to protect these irreplaceable remnants of our American heritage. . . . Unnecessary delay in acquiring these park and recreation areas so vital to an adequate public recreation system results in tremendously increased costs.[62]

Piscataway's problem was that the values it possessed as the overview from Mount Vernon were in contrast to the recreational needs of the metropolitan area. As noted by Ethan Carr in his analysis of the Mission 66 program, there was frequent conflict between the goal of providing increased public access to recreation and the potential impairment of those values (preservation of a historic vista) that the park was designed to preserve. The struggle to protect the Mount Vernon vista continued even after the Piscataway Park dedication in 1968. While the beauty of the vista could be recognized and appreciated, its value lay in its seemingly undeveloped condition, and while the scenic qualities of nature could be considered of national significance and worthy of federal stewardship, that concept had never before been applied to historic sites. Whatever recreational or other interpretive developments might occur at Piscataway had to be invisible from across the Potomac.[63]

While the establishment of each national park is unique, Piscataway's path to creation "showed no direct precedent" nor has its pattern of acquisition been widely duplicated.[64] The constellation of partners involved in the park's development and the administrative creativity regarding the fiscal value of easements when donated for preservation purposes are important precedents for the conservation and preservation movements. At the Urban Renewal Administration, Arthur Davis pointed to the success of scenic easements and Maryland's support of reduced taxation for conservation easements in protecting the view from Mount Vernon. Others were not so enamored of the utility presented by the scenic easement tool. Philip Stewart, the chief of NPS land acquisition, viewed the acquisition and maintenance of scenic easements resulting from Operation Overview as comprising an expensive path to landscape conservation.[65] The Accokeek Foundation model, wherein a nonprofit organization acquires and holds tracts under consideration for permanent protection as parklands in anticipation of subsequent government acquisition and as a hedge against increasing property values, was adopted as the justification for the creation of the National Park Foundation in 1968. The land conservation and historic preservation success of the Operation Overview experiment was thus legitimized and nationalized by congressional legislation.[66]

Although it began as an effort by private citizens and organizations to preserve the Mount Vernon viewshed, Operation Overview was transformed by fiscal and political necessity into a public campaign that embraced the necessity of public funding and public ownership while still holding onto the vision that "broadened the narrow horizons" of current conservation practice to recognize the ineffable value of the view from George Washington's piazza.[67] For half a century Piscataway Park has continued as a unique enterprise within the constellation of American land conservation and historic preservation.

Notes

1. "The Nation's First Local Law Granting Tax Credits for Preservation," *Preservation News*, February 1, 1966.
2. Since the mid-19th century the MVLA has been the stewards of George Washington's Potomac River plantation. Thirty-five women serve as vice regents (one per state), under the leadership of a regent and a resident director (formerly called a superintendent). Barry Mackintosh and Janet McDonnell, *The National Parks: Shaping the System* (Washington, DC: NPS, 2005).
3. Although he appreciated it as a "magnificent conception," Charles Wall thought that the George Washington Memorial Parkway had been "virtually destroyed" by the establishment of Washington's National Airport and commercial development along Washington Street in Alexandria. From experience on the Fairfax County Planning Commission he was convinced that "as long as undeveloped land . . . is privately owned, there is always a possibility" that local authorities "will be persuaded to impair the residential character of the community" along the parkway. Wall to Mrs. Warner Snider, February 12, 1955, MVLA Overview. House Resolution No. 1936, "A Bill to Authorized the Secretary of the Interior to Grant a Right of Way," House Committee on Public Lands, May 24, 1949. Frances Payne Bingham Bolton (1885–1977) served as a member of the U.S. House of Representatives (1940–1969) and as vice regent for Ohio with the Mount Vernon Ladies' Association from 1938 to the late-1970s. As the leader of Operation Overview, she was later described by Charles Wall as "second only to Ann Pamela Cunningham" for her contribution to the preservation of Mount Vernon. David Loth, *A Long Way Forward, a Biography of a Congresswoman: Frances P. Bolton* (New York: Longmans, 1957).
4. Although completed by another federal agency in 1932, the George Washington Memorial Parkway was transferred to the NPS on August 10, 1933 under Executive Order 6166. It is also called the Mount Vernon Memorial Highway. Wall to W. G. Rawlings, August 5, 1954. MVLA CCW.
5. Wall to August Buch (one of the landowners outside the West Gate), August 27, 1954, MVLA CCW.
6. In 1951 Wall reported that the estate's Virginia setting was protected "with the exception of two corners opposite the West Gate." MVLA Minutes, 1951, p. 100. The Regent was given authority to negotiate for the purchase of the "minimum acreage" that would protect the view toward the West Gate. At that time Wall estimated that four or five acres costing $1,200 to $1,500 per acre should be acquired. In late 1952 Wall first met with Vaughan Connelly, who owned land immediately across Little Hunting Creek from Mount Vernon, as well as two miles of shoreline across the Potomac opposite the estate. Wall reported that Connelly manifested a "friendly interest in avoiding any development of either tract which would be objectionable to the Association." SMR December 19, 1952. In 1957, with 90 employees (mostly guards and gardeners), Mount Vernon had only a $12,000 operating surplus in its annual budget. MVLA Minutes, 1957, pp. 33–34.

7. Murray Nelligan to Superintendent, through Chief, National Memorials and Historic Sites Division, "Mockley Point, Prince George's' County, Maryland," July 30, 1953. NPS PHP.
8. Charles Porter to Herb Kahler, September 17, 1953. Charles Porter to Ronald Lee, "Mockley Point, Near Fort Washington, Maryland," March 11, 1954. NPS PHP.
9. In fact, during the late 1930s representatives of the NPS had sought to declare Mount Vernon as the first National Historic Site, a new level of federal designation created with the Historic Sites Act of 1935. The MVLA appreciated the honor, but declined, citing its charter issued by the Commonwealth of Virginia. Charles Porter to Ronald Lee, "Mockley Point, Near Fort Washington, Maryland," March 11, 1954. NPS PHP.
10. John H. Sprinkle, Jr., *Crafting Preservation Criteria: The National Register of Historic Places and American Historic Preservation* (New York: Routledge, 2014), pp. 26–44. The Capper-Crampton Act of 1930 authorized construction of an interconnected system of parks and parkways in and around Washington, DC. On the Virginia shore, the "memorial highway" ended at Mount Vernon, while Fort Washington was the proposed southern end of the parkway in Maryland. Charles Porter to Ronald Lee, "Mockley Point, Near Fort Washington, Maryland," March 11, 1954. NPS PHP.
11. Superintendent (Edward Kelly) to Director, NPS, "Preliminary Justification for the Proposed Accokeek Park, Prince George's County, Maryland," July 2, 1954. MVLA Overview.
12. Edward Kelly to Director, NPS, "Preliminary Justification for the Proposed Accokeek Park, Prince George's County, Maryland," July 2, 1954. MVLA Overview.
13. Frederick Lewis Allen, "The Big Change in Suburbia," *Harpers*, June and July 1954.
14. Wall thought so highly of Frederick Lewis Allen's article that he sent a copy to Ronald Lee at the NPS. CCW to RFL, July 26, 1954, MVLA CCW.
15. Kenneth Chorley to Armistead Boothe, May 26, 1954; Armistead Boothe to Kenneth Chorley, June 2, 1954. MVLA Overview. Frances Bolton, Charles Wall, and Ronald Lee met with representatives from the Rockefeller Brothers Fund in New York City on June 6, 1955; by mid-July they learned that support was not forthcoming. See also: Robin Winks, *Laurance S. Rockefeller: Catalyst for Conservation* (Washington, DC: Island Press, 1997).
16. Conrad Wirth to Frances Bolton, June 10, 1955, MVLA Overview. Wirth had met with Representative Bolton earlier in June to discuss the "mutual interest" between NPS and MVLA regarding the Maryland shoreline. Wall to Bolton, May 4, 1955, MVLA Overview.
17. In January 1955 Wall reported to Ronald Lee that Charles Wagner had relayed concerns about proposed sewage disposal into the Potomac River. Wall to Lee, January 12, 1955, MVLA CCW. Wall to Bolton, May 4, 1955, MVLA Overview.
18. CCW Notes for July and August 1955, MVLA Overview. Connelly offered to sell the property to Frances Bolton at below market value if he could secure some tax benefit. For her part, Bolton wanted assurances that NPS had the authority to accept the property when offered. Bolton to Wall, August 18, 1955, MVLA Overview. "From the Office of Mrs. Frances P. Bolton," September 15, 1955, MVLA Overview. Bolton preferred to contribute to worthy causes "without announcement," but the land transaction was a matter of public record.
19. Robert Ware Straus, *The Possible Dream: Saving George Washington's View* (Accokeek, MD: The Accokeek Foundation, 1988); Denise Meringolo, "The Accokeek Foundation and Piscataway Park," *CRM: The Journal of Heritage Stewardship*, Vol. 5, No. 1 (Winter 2008).
20. Bolton to David Finley, April 11, 1967, LOC DEF Box 1. The Accokeek Foundation, "Minutes of Meeting of Board of Trustees of August 7, 1957." LOC DEF Box 2. Straus to Accokeek Foundation (AF) Board of Trustees, June 30, 1959, LOC DEF Box 2. By 1960, Bolton had purchased land valued at $770,000 within the viewshed. Straus, "Report to the Mount Vernon Ladies' Association of the Union, Committee on Lands," October 20, 1960, CSM MC Box 5.

21. Charles Wall, *Let One Spot Be Saved from Change* (Mount Vernon, VA: MVLA, February 1961). MVLA published this essay as part of the Operation Overview campaign.

22. As a public utility, the WSSC had powers of eminent domain that gave it the ability to locate its infrastructure without regard to private property or other factors. Local conservationists Robert Straus and Charles Wagner testified in 1958 in support of increased efforts to clean up the Potomac River south of Washington, DC, but were concerned that Piscataway Bay had been indicated as a possible location for a proposed treatment facility. "Washington Metropolitan Area Water Problems," Hearing before the Joint Committee on Washington Metropolitan Problems, Government Printing Office, Washington, April 22, 23, and 25, 1958, pp. 338–341.

23. MVLA Minutes, 1960, pp. 40–41.

24. MVLA Regent, "To the Maryland Members of the National Trust," MVLA Overview. Wilbur Hubbard, a preservationist from Chestertown and a WSSC bond holder, opined that Maryland was "becoming so cluttered with buildings and unsightly structures that the scenic beauty of the state is being rapidly destroyed." Hubbard to Governor Millard Tawes, December 29, 1960, MVLA Overview.

25. Wall to Wirth, February 24, 1961; Wall to Wilmarth Lewis, February 27, 1961, MVLA Overview; SMR March 1961.

26. Laurence Stern, "Mt. Vernon Fears Unsightly Homes," The Washington Post, August 18, 1956. Wall said that legislation was being drafted to allow NPS to acquire scenic easements to "create federal curbs against undesirable riverside development." Some local officials were against fee-simple acquisition by the federal government because it further reduced the local tax base. Wall to Vice Regent (VR) Beirne, November 9, 1955, MVLA Overview. Wall to Beirne, November 17, 1955. "Plans for 4 Nearby Md. Parks Discussed," The Washington Post, April 6, 1956. In early 1961 one of the vice regents reported on conversations with officials at the Old Dominion Foundation. VR Elinor Lamont to Wall, March 23, 1961. MVLA Overview. These overtures were unsuccessful, as were other private fund-raising attempts among the Vice Regents.

27. SMR July 1961. The panel was installed on July 4, 1961. MVLA Regent to all VRs, July 19, 1961, MVLA Overview. Some newspaper editorials questioned the legitimacy of using a historic shrine as a backdrop for a state dinner.

28. MVLA Minutes, 1961, pp. 4–9.

29. Senate Report 1082, September 18, 1961, pp. 77 and 108. WSSC asked Congress for additional funds needed to move the proposed Piscataway facility south to a location in Charles County, Maryland.

30. Senate Report 1082, September 18, 1961, p. 122. Allen Bible (1909–1988) was a NPS advocate, helping to establish more than 80 new units during his tenure (1954–1974). Regarding the creation of new parks, he declared: "I have dealt with these NPS people long enough to know that quite often miss boundaries and prices both."

31. Department of the Interior Figures on Piscataway Park as Received November 20, 1973. NPS PHP.

32. House of Representatives Report No. 1045, August 28, 1961, pp. 24 and 31. Rosamund Beirne, Senate Report 1082, September 18, 1961, p. 9.

33. Denise Meringolo, "The Accokeek Foundation and Piscataway Park," *CRM: The Journal of Heritage Stewardship*, Vol. 5, No. 1 (Winter 2008). Moyaone residents limited development to modest single-family homes on five-acre parcels. John Butler, Senate Report No. 1082, September 18, 1961, p. 6.

34. Public Law 87–362. See: House of Representatives Report No. 1045, August 28, 1961 and Senate Report 1082, September 18, 1961.

35. Piscataway Park was formally established on February 22, 1968, the anniversary of George Washington's Birthday. The MVLA and its partners were frustrated by opposition from a powerful congressman, Michael Kirwan, who was a substantial supporter of the NPS Mission 66 program and who believed that protection of the

overview was not nationally significant. CCW to Mrs. Thomas F. Bayard, September 4, 1964. MVLA Overview 3. Efforts to enhance the protection of the viewshed are ongoing: "Cardin, Hoyer Announce Addition of 73 Acres to Piscataway National Park," Senator Benjamin Cardin Press Release, April 28, 2008.

36. NPS, "Mission 66 Progress Report," March 1966, p. 20. Less than 3 percent of the area contained within park unit boundaries were privately held. NPS, "Mission 66 Progress Report," March 1966, pp. 7, 17. Wirth to Bolton, June 10, 1955, MVLA Overview. Ethan Carr, *Mission 66: Modernism and the National Park Dilemma* (Amherst: University of Massachusetts Press, 2007).

37. Straus to Moyaone Company Members, January 9, 1956, MVLA Overview.

38. NPS, "Proposed Piscataway Park: Possible Development," 1962; NPS, "General Development Plan, Fort Washington, Md," n.d. NPS PHP. Roger Faw to VR Katharine Isham, February 27, 1962, MVLA VR Katharine Isham. Marshall Hall was owned by the operators of the passenger ferry service that docked at Mount Vernon.

39. Robert Straus, House of Representatives Report No. 1045, August 28, 1961, p. 2.

40. "Washington Metropolitan Area Water Problems," Hearing before the Joint Committee on Washington Metropolitan Problems, Government Printing Office, Washington, April 22, 23, and 25, 1958, pp. 338–341.

41. Elizabeth Kenah to Alice Ferguson Foundation Membership, January 10, 1956, MVLA Overview.

42. Frederick Gutheim, "Relation of the Accokeek Foundation to the Area Development Program," May 1, 1957, CSM MC Box 4. Wall to Mrs. Douglas Gibson (VR-Iowa), December 19, 1961. MVLA Overview.

43. Jim Rees to Frederick Gutheim, May 16, 1987. FAG Papers, Box G 58.

44. For a complete description of Gutheim's career see: Jane Loeffler, "Frederick Gutheim, Capital Catalyst," *Washington History*, Vol. 10, No. 1 (Spring/Summer 1998), pp. 25–45. "Area Officials and Gutheim Meet Tonight," *The Washington Post*, January 28, 1958; "Gutheim Proposes District Area Budget," *The Washington Post*, January 30, 1958; "Conservation Societies' Record of Open Spaces Support Cited," *The Washington Post*, April 26, 1964; Frederick Gutheim, "Open Spaces Project," *Letter to the Editor, Washington Post*, May 4, 1964; "Ford Foundation Grants $250,000 to Center for Metropolitan Studies," January 6, 1960; "Metropolitan Studies," *The Washington Post*, January 3, 1962.

45. "Expert Tells of Problems in Rebuilding," *The Washington Post*, January 24, 1958; Frederick Gutheim, "This Is the Past Now Menaced at Lafayette Sq," *The Washington Post*, June 24, 1960; "Gutheim Declares Revised Design Puts District Forward 10 Years," *The Washington Post*, May 19, 1960; Frederick Gutheim, "Low Estate of Public Building," *The Washington Post*, January 5, 1961; Frederick Gutheim, "Looking at Architecture: Is Renewal Needed for Georgetown?" *The Washington Post*, January 7, 1962; Frederick Gutheim, "Need Highways be Ugly Scars?" *The Washington Post*, January 11, 1962; Jean White, "Preserving a City by Renewal is Item of Parley," *The Washington Post*, May 5, 1962.

46. Robert Straus, "Oral History Interview with Frederick Gutheim," October 13, 1983, Accokeek Foundation. FAG Papers Box G 102. Frederick Gutheim, "An Introduction to Scenic Easements," A Portion of a Longer Survey Prepared for the Department of the Interior by the Accokeek Foundation, February 1967. FAG Papers Box G 104.

47. Robert Straus, "Oral History Interview with Frederick Gutheim," October 13, 1983, Accokeek Foundation. FAG Papers Box G 102.

48. Ira Gabrielson, a member of the Accokeek Foundation board, reportedly quipped that the group had spent the first decade saving Piscataway Park for the NPS and the next century saving it from the agency. Robert Straus, "Oral History Interview with Frederick Gutheim," October 13, 1983, Accokeek Foundation. FAG Papers Box G

102. Frederick Gutheim, "Open Spaces Project," *Letter to the Editor, Washington Post,* May 4, 1964.

49. NPS, "Mission 66 Report," September 1955, pp. 19–20. Mission 66 envisioned accelerating the acquisition of inholdings through an increased federal appropriation ($500,000) that would match an annual donation by a private individual, raising the acquisition budget from $250,000 to $2 million per year.

50. "Remarks of the Honorable Frances P. Bolton at the White House Conference on Natural Beauty, Water and Waterfronts Panel," May 24, 1965, MVLA Overview. NPS Director George Hartzog was on hand at the May 4, 1965 ceremony in Annapolis, Maryland where Governor Millard Tawes signed the bill allowing certain counties to permit tax credits for lands protected by scenic easements. "Tawes Signs Scenic Shoreline Bill," *The Washington Post,* May 5, 1965. Straus to Frederick Gutheim, "Public Use of Private Land," July 22, 1959, CSM MC 4.

51. Walter Douglas, "Battle to Save Potomac Beauty Persists," *The Washington Post,* September 26, 1964.

52. Andrew Scheeffey, "Open Space: A Metropolitan Resource Problem," *Trends in Parks & Recreation: A Publication of the Park Practice Program, National Park Service,* Vol. 2, No. 3 (July 1965), pp. 7–9. *Baltimore Sun,* "Scenic Easements Cut Property Values," June 9, 1968. This story was based on a study published in the *Appraisal Journal* that compared values of parcels with and without easements along the Blue Ridge Parkway in North Carolina. RWS to Assistant Secretary of the Interior John Carver, March 3, 1964. Straus tried to establish a formula for the value of scenic easements in time for the 1963 federal tax return filing deadline on April 15. Lowdon Wingo, ed., *Cities and Space: The Future Use of Urban Land* (Baltimore: The Johns Hopkins Press, 1963), published for Resources for the Future. See also Lowdon Wingo, "The Uses of Open Space," Planning Conference on Open Spaces, Maryland-National Park and Planning Commission, Riverdale, MD, 1961.

53. Rosamund Beirne to Maryland Delegate Roy Staten, March 10, 1964, MVLA Overview.

54. Proposals to allow local jurisdictions to offer tax relief to property owners who have placed open space or scenic easements on their property had been working their way through the Maryland legislature for several years. Despite favorable testimony from members of the Moyaone Association, the *Maryland Legislative Council, Committee on Taxation and Fiscal Matters, 1963 Report* delayed recommending new open space legislation until after completion of a federal open space study, probably a reference to the ongoing work of the Accokeek Foundation on the encouragement of open space acquisition through easements and tax concessions. According to press reports, the Maryland bill was patterned after similar legislation enacted in California in 1959. Charles Whiteford, "House O.K.'s Bill Designed to Preserve Open Country," *The Baltimore Sun,* February 16, 1960.

55. "Bill Signed to Protect Scenic Maryland Shore," *Washington Post,* May 5, 1965.

56. John Eddinger, "Scenic Easement Plan Wins Support," *The Evening Star,* October 27, 1965. Owners who placed scenic easements on their lands would be taxed at 50 percent of the regular rate. "Prince George's Plan Would Use Tax Rebate to Save Scenic Spots," *Washington Post,* October 27, 1965. Strauss, *The Possible Dream: Saving George Washington's View* (Accokeek, MD: The Accokeek Foundation, 1988), pp. 45–52. "Prince George's Passes First Law to Exchange Tax Credit for Open Space," *The Washington Post,* January 15, 1966.

57. The event received extensive press coverage: Jerry Lipson, "Prince George's Enacts 1st Law to Save Scenery," *The Washington Star,* January 11, 1966; "Nation's First 'Scenic Space' Law Enacted Here," *Upper Marlboro, MD Paper,* January 20, 1966; "Scenic Easements," *The Washington Post,* January 16, 1966; Richard Homan, "Prince George's Passes First Law in U.S. to Exchange Tax Credit for Open Space," *The Washington Post,* January 12, 1966; "Incentive for Easements," *The Washington Sunday Star,* January 16,

1966; "Accokeek Foundation Lauds Tax Reform Ordinance," *The Washington Star*, January 19, 1966.

58. "Remarks of the Honorable Frances P. Bolton at the White House Conference on Natural Beauty, Water and Waterfronts Panel," May 24, 1965, MVLA Overview. Jerry Lipson, "Udall to Push Piscataway Park Action," *The Washington Star*, January 14, 1966.

59. For example, consider the American Scenic and Historic Preservation Association. Established in 1895, this group championed the preservation of historic properties and scenic views within New York. Most active prior to World War II, it brought together consideration of both scenic and historical values at individual parks and buildings. Randall Mason, "Historic Preservation, Public Memory, and the Making of Modern New York City," pp. 131–162; Max Page and Randall Mason, eds., *Giving Preservation a History: Histories of Historic Preservation in the United States* (New York: Routledge, 2004).

60. Fiske Kimball, "The Preservation Movement in America," *The Journal of the American Society of Architectural Historians*, Vol. 1, No. 3–4 (July–October 1941), p. 16; David Doheny, *David Finley: Quiet Force for America's Arts* (Washington, DC: National Trust for Historic Preservation, 2006), pp. 257–291.

61. President John F. Kennedy, "Special Message to the Congress on Conservation," March 1, 1962.

62. NPS, "New Parks for the Nation," White House Conference on Conservation, Washington, DC, May 24–25, 1962.

63. Ethan Carr, *Mission 66: Modernism and the National Park Dilemma* (Amherst: University of Massachusetts Press, 2007), p. 280. "The Mount Vernon Overview: What Can We Do?" *Preservation News*, June 1, 1970.

64. The Accokeek Foundation, June 12, 1959, "Accokeek Foundation Annual Report: The First Two Years," June 12, 1959, MVLA Overview. Bolton remarked: "To protect and preserve the natural beauty of that historic stretch of Tidewater country called for something more than ordinary determination and organization."

65. Arthur Davis, "Reserving Open Space so Cities May Breathe," *Outdoors USA: The Yearbook of Agriculture, 1967.* 90th Congress, First Session, House Document No. 29, pp. 308–311. Philip Steward to Assistant Chief, Administration, Division of Land Acquisition, "Restrictive (Development) easements over National Historic Landmarks," October 9, 1974. NPS PHP Green Springs File.

66. Rep. Hervey Machen, Congressional Record, H-11982 to H-11983, September 18, 1967.

67. MVLA Minutes, 1959, p. 13.

3   San Francisco Surplus

In June 1970 while at a cocktail party in Washington, DC, Ernest Connally, the chief historic preservation official at the National Park Service (NPS), accidently found out that the Smithsonian Institution intended to acquire selected fireplace mantles, decorative lighting, and ornately carved wood-work salvaged prior to the proposed demolition of the former U.S. Mint in San Francisco, California. Connally knew that the fate of the Old Mint (one of the few buildings that had survived the city's disastrous 1906 earthquake) had been the subject of an intense historic preservation debate since the end of World War II. Decades later, the Old Mint remains an ongoing preserva-tion project that continues to illustrate the choice between the adaptive use and surplus disposal of federal sites, structures, and, buildings. Developing a case for conventions that would allow for the continued productive use of historic buildings—while not substantially compromising their character— was a significant goal as American historic preservation matured during the mid-20th century. The story of surplus federal buildings like the Old San Francisco Mint included some unique attributes, including:

• an opinion from the Attorney General that property disposal law trumped historic preservation mandates;
• the federal codification of historic preservation's so-called 50-year rule;
• an early Section 106 consultation case that helped establish the concept of alternatives analysis in project reviews; and,
• a controversial restoration project that helped lay the groundwork for creation of the Secretary of the Interior's Standards for Rehabilitation.

In major urban centers across the United States, the location of a federal custom house or courthouse had traditionally been an outward and visible sign of the national government's economic and political role, while in many more communities, large and small, the local post office was symbolic of the federal presence.[1] After the Civil War the construction of federal buildings within the former Confederate states also demonstrated the administrative reunification of the country. Generally, federal buildings reflected current building styles and technologies. Their design was overseen by the Treasury Department's Office

Figure 3.1 Old San Francisco Mint. This photograph, showing Mission and Fifth streets in San Francisco's Tenderloin district, was taken by the Historic American Buildings Survey in 1958 as part of an NPS effort to generate public support for the conversion of the property into the agency's western regional headquarters.

Source: LOC Prints and Photographs Division, HABS CAL, 38-SANFRA,5 –10.

of the Supervising Architect, where from 1866 to 1874 the prolific Alfred Mullett designed 40 buildings, most in the Second Empire style. Federal buildings during the 19th century were aspirational:

> The evolution of American public architecture paralleled and reflected the development of the country itself and the cities and towns contained within it. From a collection of single building projects, a unified program of federal building construction emerged by the mid-nineteenth century. The design of federal buildings represented democratic ideas, reflecting a growing sense of national identity. Because such federal buildings such as custom houses and federal courthouses were usually located in expanding urban centers, their construction signaled the arrival of that particular city into the community of major U.S. cities. The placement of federal buildings also portended excellent prospects for continued growth and prosperity.[2]

As part of its mission—mandated in the Historic Sites Act of 1935—to identify, document, and interpret the history of the United States, the NPS saw federal buildings constructed during the 19th century as important symbols of the expansion and continuity of the American system.

> Embodying the highest levels of achievement in contemporary building arts, they set the standard of civil architecture for their times. They were the best built and most permanently conceived of structures in the United States. They expressed the national confidence, public aspirations, and governmental stability of 19th century America.[3]

This respect for how the qualities of federal buildings illustrated the advance of American architectural practice was visible in the operation of the Historic American Buildings Survey and the work of the Society for Architectural History and the American Institute of Architect's historic preservation committee.[4]

The architecture that housed federal offices within communities across the United States was transformed during the first half of the 20th century. During the course of the Great Depression, the national government constructed approximately 1,300 new buildings. At the same time, many federal office buildings dating from the last third of the 19th century were classified as old and obsolete. However, within the parameters newly adopted by the growing historic preservation movement, some of these properties retained inherent value as historic properties within their communities.[5]

In 1939 the management of federal buildings nationwide was delegated to the Public Buildings Administration, the predecessor to the General Services Administration (GSA). Management of federal government buildings focused on economic efficiency, which was usually expressed in a cost per square foot. Conventional wisdom at that time was that older buildings were always more costly to maintain than was new construction. For example,, in Washington, DC, upkeep on the Old Patent Building (1837), which contained a large interior courtyard (that was capped by a floating glass canopy in 2006), was nearly twice as expensive as upkeep on the newer Internal Revenue Building (1930). Early in its tenure, the Old Post Office building (1899) on Pennsylvania Avenue was considered one of the most uneconomical buildings within the federal portfolio because its vast interior courtyard was considered wasted space. Despite this pejorative analysis, Congress has never been willing to fund its demolition and replacement.[6]

When Congress furnished the NPS with the responsibility to identify, evaluate, and recognize nationally significant historic properties across the nation, it also gave the Treasury Department—the agency that since the 1850s had housed the Office of the Supervising Architect and managed the portfolio of non-military federal buildings—the ability to suitably dispose of certain federal buildings and sites that had been supplanted by new structures.[7]

One of the first applications of this surplus property mandate was in 1938 when the agency offered the Second Bank of the United States in Philadelphia for sale. A prominent architect and museum curator, Fiske Kimball, insisted that Secretary of the Interior Harold Ickes use his Historic Sites Act authority to designate the property as a National Historic Site because of its historical and architectural significance. Kimball then helped to identify the Carl Schurz Memorial Foundation, a German/American cultural exchange group (named after a former Secretary of the Interior) to serve as an appropriate steward for the property. NPS saw this project as a successful example of adaptive use for surplus federal buildings.[8]

In certain ways, federal efforts to manage surplus property was similar to efforts to locate and evaluate historic buildings across the country. Both endeavors required substantial efforts to survey the landscape of structures that might be designated as being eligible for consideration. The process of designating a property involved an evolving concept of what was either historic or surplus and was influenced by a fair amount of political considerations.

The federal footprint expanded greatly as part of the industrial, institutional, and agricultural mobilization associated with World War II. Existing factories were converted to war production, and new factories, roads, airports, hospitals, and housing were built with funding from the Reconstruction Finance Corporation, a federal agency created to manage the war effort. The federal bureaucracy expanded to oversee this work, which increased the need for office space. In addition, industrial mobilization fostered migration throughout the country as people left home for war-related jobs. For example, more than 18,000 housing units were constructed in the Hampton Roads area of Virginia between 1940 and 1941.[9] During World War II the real estate community estimated that there were potentially 12 million acres of surplus federal property, including several hundred thousand residences "too good to be demolished," that might flood the market at the end of the conflict. Because of these surplus properties, certain aspects of World War II demobilization were just as complex as preparing for global war (see Sidebar 3.1).[10]

Sidebar 3.1   A Four-Story White Elephant

Described as a "four-story white elephant" attached to a 28-story hotel, the building located at 100 McAllister Street in San Francisco, California, provides an illustration of the intersection of federal surplus property, church–state relations, and historic preservation in the middle third of the 20th century.[11]

In 1928 several Methodist churches in San Francisco sold their disparate real estate interests and pooled resources to construct a combination church and hotel at the corner of McAllister and Leavenworth Streets in the Tenderloin neighborhood. Located near the civic center and city hall, the Temple Methodist Episcopal Church's spiritual works were augmented by the operation of a 28-story secular hotel with more than 600 rooms and a 400-seat auditorium adjacent to a separate religious sanctuary. Hotel rooms were located on the sixth through 14th floors, with apartments for permanent residents found from the 15th through 26th floors. Designed by Lewis Hobart and based on a design by Timothy Pflueger, the then-contemporary Gothic-revival style skyscraper included, after 1938, an Art Deco–styled "sky room" located on the 24th floor that provided panoramic views of the city and avoided city zoning regulations regarding the location of cocktail bars near houses of worship.[12]

Launching such a cooperative venture was poorly timed as the church/hotel opened in 1930 and was adversely impacted by the widespread economic and social dislocation of the Great Depression. The property was renamed the Empire Hotel in 1936 and acquired by the federal government at the onset of World War II to supply needed administrative office space for the war effort. During the war the interior of the gothic-styled hall was substantially altered for conversion to a garage, and a floor and drop ceiling were inserted into the sanctuary.

As prosperity returned due to the economic revitalization associated with the war, the church leadership tried to reacquire the religious portion of the building, which triggered consideration of the building as potentially surplus federal property. "Certainly," argued the Chaplain of the U.S. Senate, "a nation which is pouring out billions [in defense spending] to preserve its heritage cannot afford to allow consideration of such a paltry amount [potentially generated by the sale of the site to secular developers] to rob a great city the powerhouse of spiritual energy."[13] Following standard procedure, in 1945 the NPS assessed the possible historical significance of the former Empire Hotel. Regional Historian John Hussey determined that the building was neither historically or architecturally significant from either a national, state, or local perspective. The building met none of the federal criteria (see Appendix 3.1), or those established by the NTHP.[14] This evaluation was not unexpected for a structure that was less than 15 years old and had few historical associations.

As Congress came to grips with a post war period of urban redevelopment, efforts to return the religious section of the skyscraper church and hotel to a spiritual function were debated in the late 1940s. Not only did the property house offices of various members of Congress after World War II, but the former sanctuary was also used by the Internal Revenue Service. Proponents of the retrocession of the church called upon a variety of both biblical and Cold War allusions to support their cause: Some questioned whether such use—the presence of "money counters" in a house of worship—was anything but sacrilegious, while others wanted to ensure that the church had not been unfairly acquired by the federal government, nor that the building's fabric had not been mistreated during federal management. Moral arguments and sentimentality notwithstanding, the federal government's property managers were under congressional mandate to ensure that surplus real estate was sold at fair market value, and only after it was certain that the subject holdings were in fact unneeded. In postwar San Francisco, downtown office space was at a premium—however, given the fact that, as a former hotel, the building was generally ill-suited for conversion to bureaucratic use, it was difficult to determine just what the government's plans were for the building's future.[15]

The search for alternative space available for the relocation of federal offices inevitably landed at the Old San Francisco Mint building, located nearby. At that time the Old Mint was "hardly being used" and thus, according to local advocates, was available for office conversion. As an old-fashioned and strongly constructed building, its cyclical maintenance was costly and its rehabilitation into office space had "never been justified." The Old San Francisco Mint, reflected the head of the Public Buildings Service, "has given us more problems than any other building in America."[16]

As with many large federally owned buildings located in downtown urban neighborhoods, the fate of the former Methodist Temple Church was long delayed. After the building was finally declared surplus property in the 1970s, the Hastings College of Law purchased it in 1978 and converted it for use as student housing. The building now comprises 252 apartments and related dormitory services. Wartime changes to the sanctuary were reversed and the interior was converted to a performance space that is used by local theater groups.[17]

Old Forts Bill

In order to facilitate the transition to a peacetime economy, Congress passed the Surplus Property Act in 1944 as a temporary measure to accommodate the disposition of numerous airports, buildings, factories, and other parcels acquired for the duration of World War II.[18] The legislation was generally considered successful except for the transfer of so-called old forts, where there was dissatisfaction over restrictions that prevented state and local agencies from acquiring these types of sites. After transferring several historic fortifications and battlefields to the NPS in 1933, the War Department was interested in disposing of additional disused garrisons, because over the last 50 years the nature of military training activities had significantly changed.[19] At the insistence of local proponents, Congress recognized that the historical significance or recreational values of a parcel might outweigh other considerations or uses: commercial or residential development was "frequently not in the public interest." To encourage such transfers, properties destined for recreational use were made available at 50 percent of fair market value, while those designated as historic sites were provided to local governments at no cost. In addition, proposed historical and recreational values were given a priority within the decision process for allocating these resources.[20] Following the Historic Sites Act, the Secretary of the Interior—acting through the National Park System Advisory Board (NPSAB) and the NPS—determined if surplus old forts and other properties were eligible for consideration as historic sites. Communities quickly took advantage of this new access to formerly used defense sites. For example, after Old Fort Moultrie (a harbor defense for Charleston, South Carolina) was closed by the U.S. Army in 1947, it was transferred to the city in 1949. Two years later, at least nine other historic properties in six states had been transferred to state agencies.[21]

As the United States entered the 1950s, efforts to identify and dispose of surplus federal buildings intensified as a matter of economic efficiency. To support this endeavor, the GSA embarked on a national survey of post offices, courthouses, custom houses, and general office buildings to determine which structures had "become obsolete from a current operating standpoint."[22] Presented with only a 90-day review period, the NPS was hard pressed to meet its obligations because of the paucity of comprehensive surveys of American historic sites. This lack of basic information on the distribution of historic sites led NPS planners to recommend and rely upon increased cooperation with state and local agencies on the identification of historic properties.[23] As with the consideration of urban renewal projects (see Chapter 4), here the data collected by the Historic Sites Survey and the Historic American Buildings Survey (HABS) was useful. However, most federal structures had never been studied from a historical perspective. The NPSAB Committee on Surplus Properties, frequently recommended that although a building was not deemed to be nationally significant, it was "suitable and desirable" for the GSA to transfer it to the local community (without cost) as a historical monument.[24] Former military installations, lighthouses, life-saving stations, and other maritime navigation and safety related infrastructure became increasingly subject to surplus property declarations (see Sidebar 3.2).

Sidebar 3.2   Disused and Repurposed

While surplus federal real estate and buildings presented a challenge to the broader land conservation and historic preservation communities, other property types offered unique opportunities for adaptive use. Where technological change over time created whole classes of disused properties such as lighthouses, local creativity and commitment engendered repurposing of historic properties. Despite their status as obsolete, lighthouses possessed compelling historical values as mementos of a heroic maritime history that was both inspirational and educational.

As navigational technology developed, lighthouses increasing became dysfunctional during the second half of the 20th century.[25] Lights and other signaling devices that previously required constant maintenance by a lighthouse keeper were replaced by more efficient automated systems.

With an estimated 1,000 lighthouse stations constructed from the late 18th through the early 20th centuries, this technological transformation found among all types of aids to navigation produced a significant surplus property issue. From time to time the NPSAB evaluated the historical significance of surplus lighthouses. In 1960 it "passed favorably" on the disposition of Old Macinaw Light Station in Michigan. A few years later, the NPSAB's Committee on Disposition of Surplus Historic Property disapproved a request to recommend the transfer of Minnesota's White River Light Station to the local government as a historic monument.[26]

The NTHP publication *Preservation News* covered a variety of lighthouse stories during the 1960s and 1970s. On Lake Michigan in 1965, the local historical society acquired a surplus 1858 lighthouse to serve as a city museum. Citizens in Lorain, Ohio worked to preserve a 56-year-old lighthouse praised for its scenic beauty that was threatened by wide-ranging improvements to the city's harbor. The 1883 Hooper's Strait Lighthouse was moved 60 miles and reinstalled at the Chesapeake Bay Maritime Museum in St. Michael's, Maryland. Lighthouses in Alabama, California, New York, Oregon, and Virginia were transformed from active service into historical monuments and museums. In 1977 *Preservation News* highlighted three lighthouse preservation success stories: Minot's Lodge in Cohassett, Maine; Round Island Lighthouse along the Straits of Mackinaw in Michigan; and the Split Rock Point Lighthouse in Minnesota. Efforts to preserve the picturesque Split Rock Point facility began in the late 1930s, as the completion of a highway opened up the remote area to automobile tourism. The state created a wayside that provided views toward the site's distinctive setting, perched on a cliff face more than 100 feet above Lake Superior. When the station was finally closed in 1969, after only 59 years of service, it was transferred as surplus property to Minnesota for use as a historic monument.[27]

The Bicentennial of the Declaration of Independence spurred the NTHP to focus on maritime heritage issues, but it was not until the mid-1980s that Congress directed the NPS to create a National Maritime Initiative to focus on the unique preservation issues found in historic vessels, shipwrecks, and maritime-related properties.[28] Two centuries after the Lighthouse Act of 1789 the last lighthouse keeper retired as improvements in aids to navigation supplanted the need for many installations. While the U.S. Coast Guard still operates around 500 lighthouses, more than 150 have been declared surplus. To address the issue of surplus lighthouses, in 2000 Congress passed the National Historic Lighthouse Preservation Act, which created a procedure for the regular transfer of disused National Register–listed or –eligible lighthouses to government agencies or nonprofit groups willing to undertake their long-term stewardship. As of 2015, more than 120 lighthouses have been repurposed via this system.[29]

Consideration of surplus federal property during the postwar period also led to the first codification of American historic preservation's so-called 50-year rule, which would become Criterion Consideration G of the National Register of Historic Places. As enacted, the Surplus Property Act of 1944 restricted the GSA from disposing of any property purchased after January 1900, a provision that was designed to prevent federal acquisition of parcels for the specific purpose of conveying them to state or local governments as a historic monument. Problems with this restriction were highlighted by the agency's inability to transfer Lillie Moore's home in Roseburg, Oregon to the Douglas County Historical Society.[30] In 1960 the Surplus Property Act adopted the guidance established by the NPSAB in 1948: "structures or sites of recent historical importance relating to events or persons within 50 years will not as a rule be eligible for consideration" as nationally significant historic sites. As a "well-considered requirement," the 50-year rule was calculated to ensure that historic matters were "considered in their proper perspective" as "assisted through the appropriate lapse of time."[31]

Two principles served as the foundation for the federal administration of surplus real estate: fair market value and highest and best use. As competition for recreational and other land uses increased during the 1960s, planners looked to surplus federal property as a potential source for new parklands. "In practice, park and recreation and esthetic land uses are generally not competitive with industrial and commercial development interests." From 1944 to 1967 a total of 265 surplus federal properties totaling 42,500 acres were conveyed to state and local governments for public park and recreation purposes. During that same period only 40 properties totaling 2,000 acres were conveyed as historic monuments.[32] Qualified market appraisals and competitive bidding processes ensured that the treasury was reimbursed as a result of land disposal. To promote additional transfers, prominent conservationists such as Laurance Rockefeller proposed that all surplus federal property be given to the states and local governments, rather than sold at 50 percent of fair market value. A variety of administrative and legislative proposals were considered during the Johnson administration that tried to ensure the federal government received a fair market value for its surplus property while still allowing for discounted access and preferential consideration for park, recreational, and historical uses.[33]

Can the GSA Dispose of History?

Completed in 1874 from a design by Alfred Mullet, the U.S. Mint in San Francisco, California functioned as such until 1937, after which it was adapted for use as general office space. Beginning in the mid-1950s, plans to redevelop the site sparked a decades-long campaign by local preservationists to find a new use for this significant building. Observing that the Old Mint's neighborhood was "due for redevelopment," the 1958 HABS report for the massively constructed 220-by-165-foot structure concluded: "Such a building of the historic past could do much to add scale and permanence to the design of any urban development in this area of the city."[34] The public value of the Old Mint was worth more than its architectural components scheduled for salvage: The building represented the noble idealism of the American people; it was a distinctive monument to the long history of the country's financial system; and it "personified the cosmopolitan city." In 1955, the NPSAB classified the building as nationally significant, which bolstered the NPS's proposal to convert the Old Mint to a regional headquarters and museum as part of its Mission 66 program of infrastructure development.[35]

A strong proponent of extensive urban renewal, San Francisco Mayor George Christopher was more than convinced that the U.S. Mint could be repurposed by the private sector. During the 1950s he marshalled political support in Congress to restrict the ability of the NPS to consider rehabilitation of the site for its own use. Congressman John Shelly threatened to withhold appropriations to the NPS that had been set aside for rehabilitation of the building.[36] Transforming the U.S. Mint into a museum was not universally applauded:

> I read with disgust this morning of the Interior Department's intention to spend $600,000 turning an ancient mint building in San Francisco into a museum. I protest most vigorously . . . this sort of blood-sucking boondoggle. I suggest that. . . you get rid of the people in your sprawling bureaucracy who are contributing so handsomely to the Russian design of spending our way into bankruptcy.[37]

The NPS countered such criticism by minimizing the museum aspects of the project. It was true that several rooms would include exhibits on the process and history of coinage, and one or two of the offices were slated to be restored to their 1874 appearance, but the Old Mint was not going to "stand simply as a 'dead' museum:" the rest of the building would be rehabilitated and adapted as the administrative offices of the NPS. "This is no time to demolish a useable existing building," noted a NPS administrator, which would cost upward of $250,000 to tear down.[38] In fact, the high cost of demolition was one of the factors that helped save the Old Mint from redevelopment pressure from the private sector because including those substantial costs made any new construction project economically unfeasible.

The GSA thought that the best interests of the government were to dispose of the building following surplus property statutes, which it considered paramount to the goals of the Historic Sites Act of 1935. From an economic perspective, the GSA was never fond of the Old Mint and it proposed to either sell or otherwise dispose of the property soon after it ceased to function as a mint.[39]

Because few other options were available for the adaptive use of the Old Mint, architects and preservationists across the country conspired and cooperated to help the NPS acquire the building in the late 1950s. In early 1959, the agency hosted a public hearing in San Francisco on the fate of the Old Mint, in the hopes that demonstrating a significant groundswell of local support would help secure the necessary maintenance and rehabilitation funding.[40] For its part, the National Trust for Historic Preservation (NTHP) focused its concern on the unfortunate precedent that the demolition of the Old Mint would set for the potential adaptive use of other examples of significant federal architecture.[41] Despite the apparent success of the public hearing in San Francisco and the nationwide publicity campaign, NPS Director Conrad Wirth remained somewhat uncertain about the fate of the property because Congress failed to fund its reconditioning as federal office space or provide even a very small appropriation necessary to maintain security at the mothballed building.[42]

Wary of GSA's intentions, the Department of the Interior took the highly unusual step of requesting confirmation from the Attorney General that federal agencies could take no adverse action against properties declared as nationally significant under the Historic Sites Act of 1935. For its part, GSA filed a counterargument that contended it was within its administrative rights to sell the building to private parties without restrictive covenants that ensured its long-term stewardship and use. On July 18, 1960 the U.S. Attorney General ruled that although the Old Mint was a historic building of national significance, such status did not preclude GSA from disposing of it through sale. Attorney General William Rogers' opinion hinged on the word demolition: The Historic Sites Act prevented GSA from demolishing nationally significant historic buildings, but did not prevent it from disposing of these surplus properties through sale. Despite NPS plans for adapting the Old Mint as its western regional offices, Congress remained singularly reluctant to fund such a proposal.[43]

This opinion effectively hindered the ability of NPS to use National Historic Site designation as a preservation tool. Absent any formal administrative means, preservationists retreated to mounting an information campaign, hoping to influence Mayor Christopher with evidence of successful urban adaptive use projects from across the country. Robert Sproul, the recently retired president of the University of California and a member of the NPSAB, was chosen to deliver a compendium of favorable newspaper coverage, annual reports, pamphlets, and other publications that illustrated successful examples of urban renewal projects that also preserved selected historic properties.[44] In addition, Ronald Lee sketched an optimistic view of the intersection of urban renewal, open space, and historic preservation programs:

> Sweeping programs of slum clearance, on the other hand, if they neglect historical values, may carelessly or ignorantly destroy important landmarks and valuable examples of historic architecture. There are mounting protests against the damaging effects on historic preservation of such slum clearance projects as that in Greenwich Village, New York City and elsewhere. A sense of conservation and discrimination needs to accompany slum clearance and urban renewal, not only out of respect for history, but also because of economic and social dislocation.[45]

At the same time, Lee convinced Department of the Interior leadership that a new type of federal designation was necessary—Registered National

Historic Landmarks—to reduce confusion among the public, who expected that every National Historic Site (a category created in 1935 with the Historic Sites Act) was owned and operated by the NPS. National Historic Landmark designation acknowledged that there were many more nationally significant historic properties in the country than could ever be incorporated into the national park system.[46] Moreover, a perceived benefit of formal designation by the Secretary of the Interior was that, through deference among presidential cabinet officials, other departments would avoid harming these unique historic places. As a class of historic properties, National Historic Landmarks also skirted the problem of securing presidential and congressional approval for the creation of new National Historic Sites. On Independence Day, 1961, the NPSAB declared the Old San Francisco Mint to be eligible for designation as a National Historic Landmark, a recognition that the GSA only reluctantly accepted.

During the mid-1960s the GSA took steps to remove architectural details—especially along the building's deteriorating cornice—that posed a potential safety hazard when fragments detached and fell to the sidewalk below. Architectural groups protested this defacement and argued that any funds spent on the building should go toward its rehabilitation, not its demolition. Invoking the language of President Johnson's 1965 message on natural beauty, the NPSAB deplored the "current mutilation" of the building and urged that it be quickly returned to "its original dignity and useful government purpose."[47] This despoilment led to the revitalization of local efforts to develop a plan for the building's reuse. The AIA's Northern California chapter urged John Shelley, now serving as San Francisco's mayor, to accept the building from the GSA. Local leaders tempered their efforts during 1966, thinking it "undesirable to make a big splash" because ongoing congressional debates regarding new national historic preservation legislation had the potential to "provide a better climate" for the continued use of such properties.[48]

Sidebar 3.3   Mullets in Maine

The fate of several buildings executed by the architect Alfred Mullett (1834–1890) in Maine illustrate characteristics of the life cycle of federal architecture during the mid-20th century: Portland's Post Office and Court House (1873–1965), U.S. Custom House (1872), and a more modest custom house and post office for the town of Wicasset (1870). Mullett, the supervising architect for the Treasury Department, designed Portland's Post Office and Court House in the classical revival style, similar to that found at the Old San Francisco Mint. The Custom House was built in the Second Empire style. Construction of two monumental federal buildings at the same time in Portland reflected the close relationship between the Maine congressional delegation and Treasury Department officials.[49]

Figure 3.2a U.S. Post Office and Courthouse, Portland, Maine. Completed in 1873, this federal building was declared surplus property by the GSA and demolished in 1965.

Source: LOC Prints and Photographs Division, HABS ME, 3-PORT, 11–1.

Figure 3.2b U.S. Customs House, Portland, Maine. Built in 1868–1872 from a design by Alfred Mullett, the U.S. Customs House is an excellent and well-preserved example of late 19th century federal architecture that survived potential classification as surplus during the 1960s and continues in active use.

Source: LOC Prints and Photographs Division, HABS ME, 3-PORT, 25–1.

With a less-complex design that was more suitable for a small maritime town, Wicasset's Custom House was executed in brick with a simple gable roof. Its custom house function abandoned in 1912, the building continued to serve as a post office until the early 1960s, when a new facility opened nearby. In 1963 the NPSAB recommended that the GSA turn over the building to the town to serve as a museum and library, a proposal the community rejected. In 1965, local artist and entrepreneur Charlotte Hodgman purchased the property at auction for $5,400 and transformed the building into a gift shop, art gallery, and residence. Listed on the National Register in 1970, the building had not only been saved, but it had been "constructively utilized."[50]

As in many other cities, Portland lost several important structures to urban renewal activities during the 1960s, including two train stations (built in 1888 and 1903) and the Falmouth Hotel. Demolition of Portland's Old Post Office in 1965 was typical of the impact of surplus property procedures, while in contrast, the city's Custom House continued to be utilized as a federal office building (and is now highlighted by the GSA as a stewardship success story). On May 1, 1964 the GSA notified the Secretary of the Interior that the Old Post Office had been declared surplus and was scheduled for demolition in order for the site to be converted into a parking lot. According to GSA, in addition to being "functionally obsolete and not adaptable" for continued use, the 1870s building was reportedly structurally unsound and a serious hazard to the public because of stonework dislodging from its façade.[51] At that point the NPS had only 90 days to determine if the building was nationally significant, a process that required, consultation with the membership of the NPSAB. The agency dispatched a recently hired historian, Daniel Kuehn, from Salem Maritime National Historical Park to Portland to visit the site, conduct research, and prepare his report over a weekend in late May.[52]

In his study, Kuehn's confidentially concluded that the building was not nationally significant because it did not illustrate any broad aspect of American history, making its preservation "difficult to justify." The site had not witnessed any events of state or national significance, nor was it associated with any important historical persons. It was however, "something of a town landmark, being in dramatic contrast architecturally with neighboring buildings," although Kuehn was generally unimpressed by the qualities of Alfred Mullett's design. As confirmation, he noted that the building had not been selected for documentation by the HABS.[53]

The threat to the Old Post Office was the first challenge for the newly formed Greater Portland Landmarks organization, which was concerned with the impact of urban renewal and other projects on historic buildings within the city. Kuehn noted that this 30-member group had proposed that the building be adaptively used either as a maritime history museum or a bank. A teenaged Earle Shettleworth, who would later serve as the Maine State Historic Preservation Officer, prepared a report describing the significant attributes of the Old Post Office. Without definite plans from local preservationists (especially financial models), Kuehn concluded that the NPS "not participate in or encourage the preservation" of Portland's Old Post Office.[54]

The Portland Post Office was not the only building designed by Alfred Mullett to be demolished by the GSA. The U.S. Custom House and Post Office in Rockland, Maine, was declared surplus and was taken down in 1969. In fact, buildings across the country were threatened: a post office (built 1914) and custom house (built 1856) in Mobile, Alabama, and a post office and custom house (built 1905) in Chicago, Illinois among others, were lost during the 1960s. The tool kit of the American preservation movement was limited during the first half of the decade. The focus of the NPS was restricted to sites of national significance, and few communities had access to comprehensive and accurate information on the scope of their historic built environments. In addition, there were only a handful of examples for the conversion of large federal buildings located in historic downtown districts. Enactment of the National Historic Preservation Act in 1966—with its mandate to identify, evaluate, and consider the impacts of federal undertakings on historic properties—significantly changed the process of disposing of reportedly outdated federal buildings. "Had the timing been a few years later," reflected Earle Shuttleworth, Portland's Old Post Office "would surely have been saved."[55]

Nixon Saves San Francisco's Old Mint[56]

On August 12, 1966 the GSA officially declared the Old Mint surplus, kicking off another episode in the long process of trying to identify a federal agency steward. The NPS, now under the leadership of George Hartzog, with the tepid support of the Department of the Interior, remained interested in the adapting the building as a regional headquarters. Another option was that the City of San Francisco could incorporate rehabilitation of the Old Mint as the keystone for a larger urban renewal project that would improve the "slightly skid-row" character of the neighborhood and address long-neglected maintenance issues with the building. Countering claims of imminent danger espoused by GSA, NPS architects (confidentially) provided the city of San Francisco with an entirely positive appraisal of the building's sound overall condition:[57]

> The preservation and use of old and/or historic buildings is a matter of increasing public and government concern. Their rate of loss during the last 20 years has been appalling; another twenty years and there will be none. Significant old buildings, treasured by their community, give

depth and roots to a community. They establish ties with the past which are all too easily lost in this day of rapid change. Invariably their loss is regretted. They are what we architects call the 'visual fabric' of the city; they form interesting contrasts with the new, as well as reminders of a bygone era.[58]

By the fall of 1968, as the nation focused on the upcoming presidential election campaign between Richard Nixon, Hubert Humphrey, and George Wallace, San Francisco officials announced that they were not able to use the building, even with the promise of substantial urban renewal funding.[59] With neither the NPS nor the city able to take on the complex project, in June 1969 the GSA unexpectedly assigned the building to the Department of Health, Education, and Welfare (HEW) for conveyance to San Francisco State College. President Nixon was apparently impressed with the steadfast resistance to ongoing student protests shown by the college's president, S. I. Hiyakawa. Nixon wanted to reward Hiyakawa by transferring the Old Mint to the school for redevelopment as a new satellite campus. Following Section 106 of the National Historic Preservation Act of 1966, this action triggered review of the proposed transfer by the newly established Advisory Council on Historic Preservation (ACHP).[60] Ernest Connally worried that the conflict between President Nixon's desire and the new regulatory system might be the "source of some embarrassment" to both the White House and the historic preservation community.[61] Despite California officials being sympathetic to the historic qualities of the Old Mint, prospects for its adaptive use seemed dim, as the NTHP carefully used its limited access within the Nixon administration to brief the president's domestic policy advisor, John Erlichmann.[62] "It is really a white elephant," noted the Smithsonian's Paul Schumacher, "too expensive to maintain, much too expensive to restore, and even very expensive to demolish."[63]

In early August 1969 the ACHP hosted its quarterly meeting in Washington, DC. On the agenda was a series of precedent-setting project reviews as the council gingerly exercised its new regulatory responsibilities. Given the presidential political pressure it was uncertain if GSA would even participate in the new Section 106 process. Support for retention and continued use of the Old Mint came from across the country.[64] At the NTHP, Hellen Bullock concluded that preservationists should be "rightly and fully committed to this fight," especially since there were alternative parcels available for the proposed college. The NPS prepared a detailed 40-page summary report that described the historical significance and architectural qualities of the Old Mint and recounted efforts since the mid-1950s to identify a suitable candidate to take on the future stewardship of this urban icon.[65]

Economic factors, however, weighed heavily at the ACHP meeting: while it was "extremely easy to attract sentimental support for the building," noted William Penn Mott, Jr., the California State Historic Preservation Officer, it was "considerably more difficult to attract public and private financial support" for its rehabilitation.[66] Mott concluded firmly stewardship of the Old Mint was wholly a federal responsibility. Despite the high cost of demolishing such a substantial building, applying the proposed $6 million budget for new campus construction toward rehabilitation of the Old Mint would result in only a fraction of the useable space possible with new construction. San Francisco State College president Hayakawa argued that the social value of the new campus took precedence over nostalgic value of the historic building. "'Significance' is a weak word with which to try to classify the noble and momentous things for which the Old Mint stands in the history of our Nation," testified Representative Phillip Burton, a longtime supporter of the expansion of the national park system.[67] In a telegram, the architect Lawrence Halprin concluded:

> In addition to the architectural values of the building, its retention could provide a visual, historical and architectural catalyst toward enrichment of the environmental quality of a neighborhood currently undergoing significant economic mobility. Restoration is structurally and economically feasible. Existing building offers potential for on-going use as identifiable core for downtown.[68]

On August 11, the ACHP delivered its recommendation to Robert Finch, the Secretary of Health, Education and Welfare. Saying that it was "not sufficient to merely advise you that the building should be preserved," Chairman Sylvester Stevens committed the ACHP to work toward finding a feasible alternative that would ensure the building's continued use. Uncertain how to proceed, GSA established a committee to again study the problem, an approach that allowed the NPS to craft, during 1970, its own ambitious proposal for how the federal government should manage such historic properties.[69]

New Preservation and Surplus Properties

The National Historic Preservation Act of 1966 was an administrative expression that reflected and accelerated changes occurring within the wider conservation movement during the postwar period. With the new preservation movement, the latest thinking emphasized "adaptive modern use as more justifiable and less costly than the traditional house museum approach." The NPS encouraged the GSA to allow utilitarian rehabilitation for surplus federal buildings, many of which were much too large to serve their communities only as museums. In addition, the GSA's rules prohibited recreational uses at surplus historic properties granted to states and localities, a restriction that was counter to the NPS's own practices at national historic sites. This disagreement became public in 1969 when Senator Henry Jackson recommended that properties proposed for parks and recreation should be provided to local governments free of charge.[70] Trying to minimize the parcels granted to states at no charge, GSA managers frequently disagreed with NPS historians regarding the extent of areas proposed for conveyance. As efforts to efficiently dispose of unneeded federal property accelerated during the 1960s, the NPS hoped to encourage the GSA to give "equal status to both social values and economic values" in determining the highest and best use for surplus buildings. In early 1970, President Nixon ordered a continuing and critical review of supply and demand for federal real estate, with the goal of establishing a uniform policy that promptly identified surplus property and secured its transfer to other owners. Executive Order 11508 required that each federal agency submit an annual real property survey to the newly established Property Review Board (a federal committee) that would then recommend actions regarding the disposal of excess properties.[71]

Responding to the Executive Order, Chief Historian Robert Utley developed a highly ambitious proposal in which the NPS would identify nationally significant federal buildings and incorporate them into a new administrative category of national park units:

> Such buildings would not, however, be managed and presented to the public like Gettysburg or Independence Hall. Rather the appropriate historic monument use is the continued presence of the monument in its environmental setting. Maximum adaptive use of the interior, compatible with architectural and decorative integrity, is to be sought. Many such uses would be revenue-producing. Since the principal object is to insure preservation and use, the conventional type of National Park Service interpretation would not be necessary. The monument in its setting speaks for itself.[72]

Formulated to address the fate of the Old San Francisco Mint, Utley's proposal acknowledged the impending and ongoing crisis regarding large federal buildings constructed in the 19th century that were now considered obsolete:

> Today, those Federal buildings that survive are deeply embedded in the public consciousness and the physical aspect of their respective cities. They contribute diversity and a sense of continuity to the urban texture. On both historical and environmental grounds, the preservation of the greatest of them becomes a matter of concern to the Government that built them. In the truest sense, they are national monuments.[73]

In this proposal, the NPS would act as landlord and technical advisor to local organizations that would oversee the day-to-day operations of these multi-use facilities. Because the cost of maintenance was beyond the capacity of most local organizations, the NPS would ensure the physical integrity of the exteriors and character-defining qualities of interior spaces. This fact alone meant that adoption of Utley's proposal would have necessitated an expansion of the agency's technical staff and annual appropriation. In August 1970 GSA officials met with a range of representatives from the Department of the Interior to discuss how this new imperative to dispose of surplus property would impact federally owned historic resources.[74] Both agencies adapted long-held policies and conventions to the new reality of well-funded urban renewal programs (see Appendix 3.1), the Section 106 review process, and the expansion of the National Register of Historic Places to contain properties eligible at the state and local level of significance. In the end, many components of Utley's expansive proposal were superseded by White House actions in 1971.

Great Big White Elephants

Just as it had in 1969, during the summer of 1970 the ACHP debated the fate of yet another large surplus federal office building (also designed by Alfred Mullett): the Old Custom House and Post Office located in downtown St. Louis, Missouri. Here, as in San Francisco, local preservationists had mounted a long campaign to secure the retention of this Second French Empire–style building that was scheduled for disposal and demolition. Analysis by activists such as Ada Louise Huxtable illuminated the conflict between surplus property and historic preservation mandates within the federal government.

Confronted with a variety of issues caused by the inability of federal agencies to know which resources it controlled were historically significant, President Nixon issued Executive Order 11593, "Protection and Enhancement of the Cultural Environment," in May 1971.[75] This Executive Order dramatically impacted the practice of historic preservation in the United States, establishing the convention that federal agencies had to identify historic properties eligible for the National Register of Historic Places as part of project planning for a wide range of federal undertakings. As Ernest Connally recounted on the 20th anniversary of the National Historic Preservation Act, Nixon's executive action was rooted in the problems presented by taking care of "some of these great, big, white elephant federal buildings."[76]

The ongoing controversy regarding restrictions on the continued use of large surplus federal buildings located in urban settings across the country was the foundation for legislative change to GSA's surplus property mandate in 1972. Preservationists in St. Louis and San Francisco successfully argued that it was impossible to ensure the long-term stewardship of buildings like the Old Custom House or the Old Mint given previous limitations on how historic monuments could be used after donation by the federal government to local authorities or organizations. This allowed revenue-producing activities at nationally significant historic properties if needed for the "preservation and proper observation of its historic features."[77] In effect, changes to the surplus property law operationalized Robert Utley's 1970 proposal that the NPS assist the stewardship of nationally significant inner-city federal office buildings, without the requirement that the agency take on actual ownership of the properties.

Spelling out additional duties for the NPS (as delegated by the Secretary of the Interior), Section 3 of Executive Order 11593 held important promise for the future of historic preservation in the United States. In addition to encouraging the identification and registration of historic places—especially those proposed for sale, transfer, demolition, or substantial alteration—the Executive Order required the NPS to develop and distribute guidance on "professional methods and techniques for preserving, improving, restoring and maintaining historic properties" and advise other federal agencies in the evaluation, identification, preservation, restoration, and maintenance of historic properties.[78]

Not by coincidence, one of the first applications of this new duty was when the NPS assisted in the rehabilitation of the Old San Francisco Mint. In July 1972 NPS representatives met with Mary Brooks, the director of the U.S. Mint, regarding the adaptive restoration of the property as a numismatic museum and a mail-order processing facility.[79] "Since an authentic restoration" would "require a degree of expertise not readily available," Connally offered the assistance of the NPS to provide professional architectural advice. However, the rehabilitation of the Old Mint was a substantially larger project than was found in the typical NPS portfolio of historic buildings.[80]

Almost immediately the NPS's role as advisor to the Bureau of the Mint came under fire. Kenneth Eisenberg, a restoration specialist whose company had unsuccessfully bid on the rehabilitation project for the Old Mint, raised serious concerns to the ACHP about how the building's character defining features were being treated. While Brooks defended her agency's management approach, the NPS defined its contribution as authorized under Executive Order 11593 and that the project was "consistent with the best preservation policy of our time."[81] Publicity surrounding charges that the project was dedicated to the "cheapest way possible" and possessed "no sensitivity or orientation to restoration" exacerbated attempts by the NPS and the ACHP to gauge and resolve any adverse effects on the Old Mint. Privately, Eisenberg described the project engineers as "butchers totally insensitive" to historic preservation practice and, from his perspective, Utley was concerned that the NPS, by showing public support for the Bureau of the Mint's undertaking, might fall into an "untenable professional position." Brooks was embarrassed by the controversy, especially its public disclosure, which, she felt, overlooked the fact that the adaptive use of the Old Mint was a pioneer effort.[82]

Reviewing the case of the Old Mint, John McDermott reflected:

> The particular method of preservation agreed upon—that of adaptive use—is an excellent one, and one that reflects the new preservation philosophy, which is based on the premise that a historic building will stand as long as it can serve a useful purpose, and that if it can contribute to

economic well-being as well as the quality of life in a community, its chances of survival will increase. By definition adaptive use involves a certain amount of change and modification. Such change and modification are permissible if they contribute to the life of the building but do not destroy its overall integrity, character, or esthetic quality. In reaching a balance, professional judgment is necessary and opinions will differ. It is clear that if the method of preservation for the Old Mint had not been adaptive use, the building would not be standing today.[83]

Retention and rehabilitation of the Old Mint in San Francisco and the Old Custom House and Post Office in St. Louis formalized the concept of adaptive use within federal infrastructure management when surplus property legislation was amended on August 4, 1972 to permit the no-cost transfer of historic buildings to local communities where compatible revenue producing activities were envisioned as part of a long-term stewardship plan. It was because of the Old Mint, Robert Garvey later reflected, that the ACHP "built consultation and explicit attention to alternatives" into Section 106 compliance procedures. By the mid-1970s the ACHP became independent of Department of the Interior oversight. At the same time the council's procedures under Section 106 had matured such that requirements for the Secretary of the Interior to review the historic status of surplus federal buildings had become duplicative and were abandoned. In June 1973 the renovated Old Mint was reopened to the public, serving as a museum until 1993.[84] In 2003 the city finally acquired the landmark building, but it has yet to find a steward that will ensure its continued viability within the San Francisco community.

The resiliency of the Old San Francisco Mint, as well as other old white elephant buildings, was a tribute to their design and construction, as well as to the substantial value that preservationists placed on their potential contribution to the civic life of urban environments. Once established, federal buildings and other infrastructure play an important role as anchors within communities (see Sidebars 3.2 and 3.3). Historic surplus federal architecture were coincidentally somewhat like the great white elephants found in the traditional Siamese tale—a present that was so large, burdensome, and expensive to maintain that it was no gift at all. Making the case for recycling old buildings to new uses was an important goal of the evolving preservation movement, one that was challenged by the federal system of surplus property, as well as by the impending onslaught that characterized post–World War II urban renewal.

Notes

1. Lois Craig, *The Federal Presence: Architecture, Politics, and Symbols in United States Government Building* (Cambridge, MA: MIT Press, 1978).
2. Antoinette Lee, *Architects to the Nation: The Rise and Decline of the Supervising Architect's Office* (New York: Oxford University Press, 2000), p. 7.

3. Robert Utley, "Proposal for Preservation of Federal Buildings as National Monuments," April 14, 1970, ACHP ED AF.

4. Melissa Houghton, *Architects in Historic Preservation: The Formal Role of the AIA, 1890–1990* (Washington, DC: The American Institute of Architects, February 1990).

5. Jennifer Perunko, Susan Salvatore, Stephanie Foell, Barbara Frederick, Emma Young, Zana Wolf, and Matthew McDaniel, *U.S. Custom Houses: A National Historic Landmark Theme Study* (Washington, DC: NPS, December 2008). In a curious bureaucratic experiment, from 1933 to 1939 the NPS was given responsibility for managing more than 20 million square feet of office space in 58 federally owned buildings in the capitol.

6. Richard Sellars, *Preserving Nature in the National Parks: A History* (New Haven: Yale University Press, 1997), p. 137. For a short period the agency was renamed: "Office of National Parks, Buildings and Reservations." Public Buildings Commission, *Annual Report of the Public Buildings Commission for the Calendar Year 1932* (Washington, DC: Government Printing Office, 1933), pp. 3–4, 45. "To Review the Proposed Demolition of the Old Post Office Building and Other Landmarks," Hearing before the Subcommittee on Public Buildings and Grounds of the Committee on Public Works, United States Senate, 92nd Congress, First Session, April 21, 1971. Subsequent threats to the Old Post Office during the 1970s became the catalyst for the creation of "Don't Tear It Down," a preservation organization that evolved into the District of Columbia Preservation League. For many years the building housed the offices of the ACHP until in 2015 GSA permitted its rehabilitation into a luxury hotel.

7. "An Act to Authorize the Sale of Federal Buildings," August 26, 1935. States and localities could purchase such property at 50 percent of fair market value.

8. Kimball also served on the NPSAB, a group also established by the Historic Site Act. See: John H. Sprinkle, Jr., *Crafting Preservation Criteria: The National Register of Historic Places and American Historic Preservation* (New York: Routledge, 2014), pp. 58–61.

9. Marilyn Harper, *World War II & the American Home Front: A National Historic Landmark Theme Study* (Washington, DC: NPS, 2007). Marilyn Harper, Lafayette Building (Washington, DC), National Historic Landmark Nomination, 2005. "Post-Defense Planning," Hearings before a Subcommittee of the Committee on Education and Labor, United States Senate, November 3–7, 1941, pp. 69–75.

10. "Government to Aid Postwar Sale of its Real Estate," *The Washington Post*, July 11, 1943; "Liquidation Program for Surplus U.S. Real Estate," *The Washington Post*, September 9, 1943; "U.S. Property Disposal Plan is Proposed," *The Washington Post*, December 19, 1943.

11. "Conveyance of Space in Federally Owned Building to Temple Methodist Church, San Francisco, California," Hearing before a Subcommittee of the Committee on Public Works, United States Senate Eighty-First Congress, First Session on S. 384, May 9, 1949, p. 12.

12. Michael Corbett, "Uptown Tenderloin Historic District," National Register of Historic Places Nomination, May 2008. See also: Hastings College of the Law, Parking Garage and Residential Upgrade, Draft Environmental Impact Report, January 16, 2002.

13. Frederick Harris to Senate Subcommittee on Public Buildings. "Conveyance of Space in Federally Owned Building to Temple Methodist Church, San Francisco, California," May 7, 1949, pp. 6–7.

14. John Hussey, "100 McAllister Building, Leavenworth and McAllister Streets, City and County of San Francisco, California," Report on a Review of Historic Federal Buildings Scheduled for Demolition. NPS, August 17, 1956. NPS PHP OSFM.

15. "Conveyance of Space in Federally Owned Building to Temple Methodist Church, San Francisco, California," p. 11.

16. "Conveyance of Space in Federally Owned Building to Temple Methodist Church, San Francisco, California," pp. 21–22.

17. This combination of church and skyscraper is a rare property type. In 1929, a 40-story "temple tower" with Art Deco styling and gothic details was proposed by the First Presbyterian Church for downtown Cincinnati, Ohio, but with the advent of the Great Depression, the building was never built. Jeff Suess, "'Never Built' Temple Tower Skyscraper Could Have Been a Companion to Carew Tower," *Cincinnati Enquirer*, February 1, 2015.
18. "Old Forts Bill to Save Historic Sites is Signed," *The Washington Post*, June 13, 1948. Surplus military properties at Fort Wayne, Michigan, Fort Schuyler, New York, For Douglas, Utah, Fort Moultrie, South Carolina, Fort Reno, Oklahoma, San Antonio Arsenal, Texas, Fort San Carolos and Fort Barrancas, Florida and the Marblehead Military Reservation, Rhode Island were highlighted.
19. Surplus military forts were the subject of discussion at the first meeting (April 1947) of the National Council for Historic Sites and Buildings, the predecessor group that led to the National Trust for Historic Preservation. David Doheny, *David Finley: Quiet Force for America's Arts* (Washington, DC: National Trust for Historic Preservation, 2006), p. 249. Ronald Lee noted former defense fortifications as an issue facing postwar preservationists. Ronald Lee, "The Effect of Postwar Conditions on the Preservation of Historic Sites and Buildings," American Association for State and Local History, October 26, 1946. HFC Lee Papers Box 6.
20. The administrative record is silent as to why communities had to pay half the value for recreational facilities while historic sites could be had at no cost. "Disposition of Certain Surplus Military Posts, Camps and Stations: A Study of Proposed Legislation to Amend Section 13 of the Surplus Property Act of 1944, as Amended, to Provide for the Disposition to States, Political Subdivisions and Municipalities of Surplus Real Property for Public Park, Recreational, or Historic Monument Purposes," February 2, 1948. Congress was inundated with 100 to 150 requests for special legislation to accommodate the transfer of parcels destined for monument and recreation uses.
21. The Historic Sites Act created an Advisory Board on National Parks, Historic Sites, Buildings, and Monuments which now operates as the National Park System Advisory Board. "Township buys Historic Old Fort Moultrie," *The Washington Post*, December 28, 1949. In 1960 the property was incorporated into Fort Sumter National Monument.
22. Associate Director to Regional Directors, "Review of Historic Federal Buildings Scheduled for Demolition," May 17, 1956. NPS PHP OSFM. "Belt Tightening: U.S. to Sell Unneeded Real Estate," *The Washington Post*, December 30, 1953.
23. The NPSAB frequently made recommendations regarding the national significance of surplus federal buildings and facilities. In March 1963, for example, the board concluded that California's Benicia Arsenal, which served as a military post from 1851 to the early 1960s, was not of exceptional value and recommended that the local community take steps to preserve its historic features. NPSAB, March 27, 1963. NPS, *Mission 66 Report* (Washington, DC: NPS, September 1955), p. 42.
24. From 1937 to 1970, the Surplus Property Committee of the NPSAB reviewed the historic status of at least 46 surplus properties found across 18 states. "Suggested Outline for Report Historic Federal Buildings Scheduled for Demolition," Attached to May 17, 1956 memorandum, Associate Director to Regional Directors, "Review of Historic Federal Buildings Scheduled for Demolition," NPS PHP OSFM.
25. James Delgado and Kevin Foster, *Guidelines for Evaluating and Documenting Historic Aids to Navigation* (Washington, DC: NPS, 1990).
26. NPSAB Minutes 42nd Meeting, March 21–23, 1960. NPSAB Minutes 52nd Meeting, April 12–15, 1965, p. 38. The committee felt that local government lacked both the experience and the funding to adequately maintain and operate the light station.
27. "On Lake Michigan Harbor," *Preservation News*, Vol. 5, No. 5, July 1965. "Local Citizens in Lorain, Ohio," *Preservation News*, Vol. 5, No. 11, October 1965; "Lighthouse

Rescued by Maritime Museum" *Preservation News*, July 1967; "Lighthouse Restored," *Preservation News*, August 1967; "Montauk Point Light, NY in Danger," *Preservation News*, June 1968; "Summer Study Made of Old Cape Henry Lighthouse," *Preservation News*, January 1968; "Mobile Bay Light No. 6639," *Preservation News*, Vol. 14, No. 3, March 1974; "Lighthouse Restored," *Preservation News*, Vol. 16, No 11, November 1976; "Lighthouses," *Preservation News*, Vol. 17, No. 12, November 1977.

28. Stephen Delgado, "The National Maritime Initiative: An Interdisciplinary Approach to Maritime Preservation," *The Public Historian*, Vol. 13, No. 3 (Summer 1991), pp. 75–84.

29. The NHLPA was passed as an amendment to the National Historic Preservation Act: 54 USC 305101–305106 (formerly 16 USC 470w-7). General Services Administration, "2015 NHLPA Program Highlights Report," 2016. Eight lighthouses were transferred to other federal agencies, 3 to state agencies, 22 went to local governments, 41 were granted to nonprofit groups, and 46 were sold to private citizens. See: Jennifer Leeds, *The New Lighthouse Keepers: A Comparative Analysis of Ownership Structures under the National Historic Lighthouse Preservation Act Program*, M.A. Thesis, Clemson University, 2017.

30. Lillie Moore had bequeathed her estate to the federal government with the intention of preserving her family's 1858 home in Roseburg, Oregon. After her death in 1940 the GSA sold her various properties in 1958. Although the home was purchased by local business interests, the historical society was unable to successfully move building and it was torn down. House Committee on Government Operations, Subcommittee on Government Activities, Hearing on H.R., 1310. April 27, 1960.

31. House of Representatives, "Amending Section 13(h)(2) of the Surplus Property Act of 1955 So to Eliminate the Requirement That Property Conveyed for Historic-Monument Purposes under Such Section Must Have Been Acquired by the United States on or before January 1, 1900," Report No. 2032, 86th Congress, Second Session, June 20, 1960. See also House Report No. 588, 87th Congress, First Session, June 21, 1961.

32. Mr. Visher to Mr. Allen, "Federal Surplus Real Property Disposal: Policy Questions Raised by Bills Introduced in the 90th Session of Congress and up for Review by Council Staff and GSA Task Force," April 4, 1967. RG 368 HCRS Councils & Committees Box 6. The federal government administered about one third of the nation's real estate; about three quarters of a billion acres distributed among 18,651 parcels.

33. Chief, Division of Council Services to Director, BOR, "Chronology of Recent Proposals to Modify Procedures for Making Conveyances of Surplus Federal Lands," June 13, 1967. RG 368 HCRS Councils and Committees Box 6.

34. Kenneth Cardwell, "United States Branch Mint, Cal-160," HABS documentation, August 1958.

35. Augustin Keane, "National Historical Significance of the Old Mint at San Francisco," February 28, 1959. NPS PHP OSFM. Keane was a prominent San Francisco attorney who had participated in the development of the city's Civic Center. NPSAB Minutes December 1–7, 1956 and Minutes, October 7–10, 1957. NPS NHL.

36. John Shelly represented San Francisco in Congress from 1949 to 1964, when he was elected as Mayor, serving until 1968. "Brief Fact Sheet on the Old Mint, San Francisco, California," n.d. [post June 30, 1963]. NPS PHP OSFM.

37. Herbert Whitman [Wilton, CT] to President Dwight Eisenhower, February 5, 1958. Herbert Whitman to SOI, February 5, 1958. NPS PHP OSFM.

38. NPS Associate Director to Herbert Whitman, February 21, 1958, NPS PHP OSFM.

39. Franklin Floete to Hatfield Chilson, August 23, 1957. NPSPHP OSFM. "Authorizing the Administrator of the Federal Works Agency to Transfer Certain Property in San Francisco, Calif. to the City and County of San Francisco for Street Purposes," House of Representatives Report No. 2337, 76th Congress, 3rd Session, May 29, 1940. See also Senate Report No. 1785, 76th Congress, 3rd Session, June 6, 1940.

40. Charles Pope [Preservation Officer, Northern California AIA] to Earl Reed [NPS Advisory Board and AIA Preservation Committee], January 18, 1958. NPS PHP OSFM. "Public Hearing to be Held in San Francisco February 18 on Proposal to Designate Old United States Mint Building as a National Historic Site." NPS PHP OSFM. Conrad Wirth to SOI, "Report on the Public Hearing, February 18, Old United States Mint, San Francisco, California," April 13, 1959. RG79 NPS General Records, Administrative Files, 1949–1971, L58 to L58, Box 2030, "L58, CA, Old Mint, Public Hearing, 1959."

41. David Finley to Franklin Floete, January 3, 1957. NPS' Chief of Interpretation, Ronald Lee drafted a letter of support for David Finley's consideration. Lee to Finley, December 31, 1956. LOC Finley, Box 51; "Draft of Order of Designation of National Historic Site: Old United States Mint Building, San Francisco, California," December 12, 1957. "Notice to General Services Administration Regarding Determination of National Significance for the Old United States Mint, San Francisco, CA." NPS PHP OSFM. Arthur Brown, a California architect, provided his congressional delegation with a copy of a bill establishing the historic Customhouse in Charleston, SC as National Historic Site. Brown to Senator William Knowland and Representative William Mailliard, June 22, 1956. LOC Finley Box 50. Stephen Jacobs, "Statement on Behalf of the National Trust for Historic Preservation Favoring the Restoration of the Old United States Mint in San Francisco," February 18, 1959. Conrad Wirth to Walter Huber, April 1, 1960, RG 79 Admin Files, 1949–1971, L58 to L58, Box 2090, Old Mint, Calif. Huber had sent Wirth a copy of a San Francisco Chronicle editorial ("Lunatic Cry for Razing Old Mint," February 18, 1960) that included a cartoon showing a worker from the "Willy Nilly Destruction Co., Inc." dreaming of taking a swing with a pick axe at the Old Mint's columns.

42. Fred Seaton (Secretary of the Interior) to Harold Bradley (President, Sierra Club), March 6, 1959. NPS PHP OSFM.

43. Conrad Wirth to Walter Huber, April 1, 1960, RG 79 Admin Files, 1949–1971, L58 to L58, Box 2090, Old Mint, Calif. Opinion of the Attorney General of the United States, "Old San Francisco Mint Building Disposition as Surplus Property," July 18, 1960. NPS PHP OSFM.

44. Acting Director E. T. Scoyen, to Robert Sproul, November 29, 1960. RG79, General Records, Admin Files, 1949–1971, L58 to L58, Box 2090, Old Mint, CA.

45. Ronald Lee to Director, NPS, "Discussion of United States Mint, San Francisco at the September Meeting of the Advisory Board," November 7, 1960. Lee was encouraged that changes in the Housing Act of 1954 "extended the scope" of urban renewal to permit the rehabilitation of older buildings and the "conservation of historic districts." RG79, General Records, Admin Files, 1949–1971, L58 to L58, Box 2090, Old Mint, CA.

46. Lee first proposed the creation of "National Historic Landmarks" as a class of federal designation in 1958. The program was established in early 1960. Director, NPS to Secretary of the Interior, "National Survey of Historic Sites and Buildings," June 30, 1959. Ronald Lee to Conrad Wirth (NPS Director), "Classification of Historic Sites and Buildings," April 2, 1958. NPS NHL CC.

47. NPSAB Minutes, April 18–21, 1966. "The Old Mint's New Face," *San Francisco Sunday Chronicle*, August 22, 1965; "AIA Unit Hits 'Defacement' of Old Mint," *Daily Pacific Builder*, September 7, 1965; "Architects Protest 'Defacement' of Old Mint," *San Francisco Chronicle*, September 7, 1965; "Architect's Plea: Save Old Mint," *San Francisco Examiner*, September 7, 1965.

48. Edward Hummel to Ronald Lee, March 25, 1966. Hummel thought that former congressman (now San Francisco Mayor) John Shelly might have some influence with Congressman Michael Kirwan, who oversaw the NPS's appropriations. HFC RL OSFM Roy Appleman to Chief, OAHP, "Hazardous Condition of Old Mint Building, San Francisco," February 5, 1968; Acting Western Regional Director to Director, "Old Mint Building—San Francisco," February 5, 1968. Privately, the NPS

considered the building to be in "no worse condition" than it had "been for some time." Handwritten note by Ernest Connally dated February 12, 1968 attached to these memoranda. NPS PHP OSFM. Robert Marquis to John Shelley, July 16, 1966. Charles Pope to William Scheick (Executive Director, AIA), July 15, 1966. Raymond Mulvany to Director, NPS, "Revised Interest in Preserving the Old Mint, San Francisco, California," July 22, 1966. NPS PHP OSFM.

49. Antoinette Lee, "Alfred B. Mullett, 1834–1890," in *A Biographical Dictionary of Architects in Maine* (August, Maine: Maine State Historic Preservation Office, 1985).

50. "Report of the Committee on Disposition of Surplus Property," NPSAB, 48th Meeting, 1963, p. 26; John Briggs, U.S. Custom House and Post Office, National Register Nomination, May 12, 1970; Susan Johns, "A Home, Again." *Wicasset Newspaper*, November 25, 2013. The Hodgman family also adaptively used a former automotive repair building, converting it to a restaurant called, "La Garage."

51. Bernard Boutin to Stewart Udall, May 1, 1964, NPS PHP OSFM.

52. Daniel Kuehn, "Study of the Historical Significance of the Old Post Office and Courthouse, Exchange and Middle Streets, Portland Maine," NPS, May 27, 1964, pp. 9–11. NPS PHP OSFM. Graduating with a bachelor's in history from the University of Minnesota in 1959, Kuehn (1931–2013) had joined the NPS in 1964. "Requiescat in Pace: Daniel R. Kuehn," *Arrowhead*: The Newsletter of the Employees and Alumni Association of the NPS, Vol. 20. No. 4 (Fall 2013), p. 9.

53. HABS documentation for the building was gathered several years after the building's demolition. See: Denys Peter Myers, "United States Post Office and Courthouse Building (Old), HABS No ME-120," Historical American Buildings Survey, December 31, 1968.

54. Daniel Kuehn, "Study of the Historical Significance of the Old Post Office and Courthouse, Exchange and Middle Streets, Portland Maine," NPS, May 27, 1964, p. 11. NPS PHP OSFM. Earle Shettleworth, "94 Year History of Old Post Office Reviewed," *Portland Maine Evening Express*, January 20, 1966.

55. Earle Shettleworth email to John Sprinkle, May 2, 2016.

56. "Nixon Saves S.F.'s Old Mint," *San Francisco Chronicle*, January 25, 1972.

57. John Waterson to Ernest Connally, "The Old San Francisco Mint," March 29, 1968. NPS PHP OSFM. George Hartzog to Stewart Udall, "Old Mint Building, 5th and Mission Streets, San Francisco, California," January 13, 1967. NPS PHP OSFM.

58. Joseph Watterson (Chief, NPS Division of Historic Architecture) to John Tolan (Deputy for Development, Office of the Mayor, San Francisco, CA), "The Old San Francisco Mint," March 26, 1968. NPS PHP OSFM.

59. Raymond Freeman to NPS Western Regional Director, "Old Mint Building, San Francisco," March 21, 1968; National Trust for Historic Preservation, "San Francisco Mint Still in Danger," *Preservation News*, May 1968. Congressman Philip Burton had introduced legislation to establish the building as a National Historic Site under NPS stewardship. NPS PHP OSFM. Regional Director John Rutter was directed to "take no active part in pressing for" National Historic Site legislation. Theodor Swem to John Rutter, "Old Mint Building," May 3, 1968. NPS PHP OSFM.

60. Frank Harrison to Thomas Holley, "San Francisco Mint," June 18, 1969. NPS PHP OSFM. Ernest Connally, Hosmer Interview, pp. 139–140. Sylvester K. Stevens (Chairman, ACHP) to Robert Finch (Secretary HEW), August 11, 1969. ACHP, "Comments Upon the Proposal to Transfer the Old Mint Building in San Francisco to the State of California for Use by San Francisco State College," June 13, 1969; Ross Holland to Robert Utley, "Old Mint, San Francisco," April 16, 1968. NPS PHP OSFM. From 1966 to 1976 the ACHP administratively fell under the NPS.

61. Connally was most probably worried about embarrassing the newly launched Nixon administration. Ernest Connally to Tom Holly, "San Francisco Mint," June 11, 1969. NPS PHP OSFM. Ernest Connally to Assistant to the Director,

Legislation, "Burton Bill San Francisco Mint," August 28, 1969, 91st Congress, First Session, H.R. 12343. Connally argued that NPS should make a "strong statement" before Congress favoring retention and use of the mint. NPS PHP OSFM. "Reaffirming Position of Board of Supervisors Urging Acquisition of the Old Mint Building for Preservation as an Historic Monument, Resolution No. 405–88," June 18, 1969. RG421 NTHP ACHP Box 5; "Burton Moves to Save Old Mint," *San Francisco Chronicle*, June 25, 1969.

62. "Summary of the National Trust for Historic Preservation's Involvement with the San Francisco Mint," June 24, 1969. James Biddle to John Erlichman, August 16, 1969. RG 421 NTHP ACHP Box 5. ACHP Deputy Executive Secretary to Executive Assistant to Director, NPS, "San Francisco Meeting on the Mint," June 25, 1969. NPS PHP OSFM. The school's existing downtown center was located in a "vintage building" dating from 1909 which was ill-suited for its mission. Harry Brakebill (California State College) to Mel Summers (HEW, Division of Surplus Property Utilization), May 28, 1969. RG 200 NTHP ACHP Box 5.

63. Paul Schumacher to Ernest Connally, "San Francisco Old Mint," June 16, 1969. The Smithsonian was interested in salvaging architectural elements from the building. NPS PHP OSFM. One observer noted that only "lobbying and horse trading at the Presidential level" might be able to stop the "diabolically clever scheme" that was designed to highlight claims for the administration's effective action on urban issues. Robert DeVelviss to Helen Bullock, June 26, 1969. RG 421 NTHP ACHP Box 5. Preservation of the mint was supported by the *San Francisco Chronicle*, but not by the *Examiner.*

64. "Agenda, Advisory Council on Historic Preservation, August 6–7, 1969." RG 421 NTHP ACHP Box 5. Also on the agenda was consideration of impacts from undertakings at the Vieux Carre District, New Orleans; Las Flores Adobe at Camp Pendleton, California; and the First Telephone Exchange, New Haven, Connecticut. "Discussion on San Francisco Mint, TBM with Dr. Connally, June 16, 1969." RG421 NTHP ACHP Box 5. Connally observed that both GSA and HEW were now mute on the issue—the White House was handling all communication. Charles Shumate, President, San Francisco Landmarks Preservation Board to Sylvester Stevens, Chair, President's Advisory Council on Historic Preservation, August 1, 1969. Rex Whitaker Allen (President, AIA) to Lawrence Halprin, August 4, 1969. Lawrence Halprin to Sylvester Stevens, Chairman, Advisory Council on History Preservation, August 4, 1969. RG 421 NTHP ACHP Box 5. Resolutions supporting the preservation of the Old Mint were recorded from seven local organizations, seven statewide associations, and 10 nationwide organizations.

65. Helen Bullock, "Hand Written Note on an NTHP Inter-Office Transmittal Memorandum," July 16, 1969. Her boss, James Biddle, replied, "Fight, Ok! But what's the next step you recommend: We've already hit the White House on it." RG 421 NTHP ACHP Box 5. S. Allen Chambers and Barbara Hochstetler, *The Old San Francisco Mint, 1869–1874: Summary Report for the Advisory Council on Historic Preservation* (Washington, DC: OAHP, July 1969).

66. William Penn Mott, Jr., California State Liaison Officer (now State Historic Preservation Officer) to Ira Whitlock, ACHP, August 1, 1969. RG 421 NTHP ACHP Box 5. Mott also expressed concern that the integrity of many of building's distinctive features would be compromised by any rehabilitation.

67. Diane Maddex, "Notes on Meeting of Advisory Council on Historic Preservation, Washington, DC, August 6." RG421 NTHP ACHP Box 5. Scott Blakey, "Demolition of Old Mint Urged by Hayakawa," San Francisco Chronicle, August 7, 1969. Phillip Burton, "Statement to the Advisory Council on Historic Preservation Meeting at Washington, DC, on Wednesday, August 6, 1959." RG 421 NTHP ACHP Box 5.

68. Lawrence Halprin to Sylvester Stevens, Chairman, Advisory Council on History Preservation, August 4, 1969. RG 421 NTHP ACHP Box 5.

69. Sylvester Stevens to Robert Finch, August 11, 1969. RG 421 NTHP ACHP Box 5. National Trust for Historic Preservation, "Council Offers Aid on Old San Francisco Mint," Preservation News, September 1969; Scott Blakey, "New Ally in Fight to Save the Old Mint," San Francisco Chronicle, August 8, 1969; "Up to Finch: U.S. Council for Keeping the Mint," San Francisco Chronicle, August 12, 1969.

70. Robert Utley to John Visher, BOR, "Historic Preservation and GSA," April 4, 1969. ACHP ED AF. Allowing the compatible recreational use of conveyed surplus federal property was one recommendation from "Utilization and Disposition of Federal Lands for Recreation," Bureau of Outdoor Recreation, August 28, 1968. Spencer Rich, "Parkland Bill Would Free Surplus Sites," *The Washington Post*, June 26, 1969. It was estimated that at least 12,000 acres of surplus federal lands were suitable for recreational purposes.

71. Louis Reid (Assistant Director, NPS) to Daniel Kingsley (Commissioner, GSA Property Management and Disposal Services), July 29, 1969. ACHP ED AF. EO 11508 was signed February 12, 1970. The Property Review Board comprised the heads of the General Services Administration, the Bureau of the Budget, the Council of Economic Advisory, and the Council on Environmental Quality.

72. Robert Utley, "Proposal for Preservation of Federal Buildings as National Monuments," April 14, 1970. ACHP ED AF.

73. Robert Utley, "Proposal for Preservation of Federal Buildings as National Monuments," April 14, 1970. ACHP ED AF.

74. The August 5, 1970 meeting included representatives from the GSA the ACHP, BOR, OAHP, and the DOI Solicitor's Office. ACHP ED AF.

75. See: "Eligible for Inclusion," in John Sprinkle, ed., *Crafting Preservation Criteria: The National Register of Historic Places and American Historic Preservation* (New York: Routledge, 2014), pp. 196–213.

76. Ernest Connally, "Creating a Federal Program," MCW, RTF, 1986.

77. Here the Department of the Interior had to approve the fiscal program, as well as the plan for repair, rehabilitation, restoration and maintenance of the historic property. P.L. 92–363. 92nd Congress, S. 1152, August 4, 1972.

78. Executive Order 11593, Section 3, May 1971.

79. "Nixon Saves S.F.'s Old Mint," *San Francisco Chronicle*, January 25, 1972. By early 1972, President Nixon had abandoned his plans to transfer the property for use by San Francisco State College. "Life Begins at 105 for San Francisco Mint: Other Surplus Buildings Traveling Rocky Roads," *Preservation News*, Vol. 12, No. May 5, 1972.

80. Thomas Crellin to Ernest Connally, "Old San Francisco Mint," July 26, 1972. Connally was concerned that Brooks, who had "some very curious ideas about what constitutes an accurate historic restoration," was receiving "all kinds of advice" about what to do with the building. Ernest Connally to Robert Utley, June 12, 1972. NPS PHP OSFM. As historical evidence suggested that the beige and white paint found in the principal rooms formerly had "a much more exciting color scheme," NPS staff undertook a comprehensive study of the building's original decorative treatments. Thomas Crellin to Director, OAHP, "Old San Francisco Mint," August 18, 1972. Mary Brooks to Ernest Connally, August 27, 1972. Brooks thought that the "paint job" would provide an "authentic touch" at the proposed reopening ceremony, at which President Nixon was scheduled to appear. Mary Brooks to Ernest Connally, August 27, 1972. NPS PHP OSFM.

81. Kenneth Eisenberg to Executive Secretary, ACHP, "Old San Francisco Mint, 5th and Mission Streets, San Francisco, California," November 20, 1972; Ernest Connally to Robert Utley, November 27, 1972; Ralph Craib, "Mint Chief Denies a Critic's Claims," *San Francisco Chronicle*, November 28, 1972. NPS PHP OSFM.

82. Kenneth Eisenberg to Thomas Crellin, November 28, 1972; Kenneth Eisenberg to Director, U.S. Mint, December 4, 1972; Robert Utley to Ernest Connally, December 5, 1972. Mary Brooks to Hon. Phillip Burton, December 12, 1972; Mary Brooks to Kenneth Eisenberg, December 12, 1972. NPS PHP OSFM.
83. John McDermott, ACHP, to Earl Darrah, Office of Management and Budget, January 3, 1972. NPS PHP OSFM.
84. Robert Garvey, "Foundations of Advisory Council Policy: Early Cases Under Section 106," n.d. NPS PHP OSFM. ACHP, *The National Historic Preservation Program Today* (Washington, DC: GPO, January 1976), pp. 59–60. "Old San Francisco Mint Reopens Today," *The Washington Post*, June 17, 1973.

4 Open Space for Urban America

On Memorial Day 1964, the City of Alexandria, Virginia commemorated the centennial of the American Civil War by opening a public park on the site of Fort Ward, one of the earthen fortifications designed to protect Washington, DC. The park comprised a rehabilitated earthen bastion, based on archaeological evidence; a new museum building, with an extensive collection of Civil War artifacts and memorabilia; and a memorial entrance gate authentically reconstructed by the Army Corps of Engineers. A mixed-use facility, it also included infrastructure designed to meet the growing recreational needs in the urban community. The success of Fort Ward was a widely recognized model of civic involvement that fostered Alexandria's designation as an "All American City."[1] At the foundation of this historic preservation project was financial assistance from a new federal program that fostered the preservation of open space within the urban United States.

Historic preservation, reflected Robert Weaver, who served as the Secretary of the Department of Housing and Urban Development (HUD), was one of the most complicated aspects of federal urban renewal programs during the third quarter of the 20th century.[2] With seemingly similar goals for improving the urban environment that resulted in widely divergent outcomes when it came to the revitalization of American cities and towns, the relationship between urban renewal and historic preservation advocates was often tense, and frequently spiced with controversy.[3] Each movement had a specific grammar and vocabulary that resulted in the inconsistent and perhaps ironic application of policy and procedure to urban redevelopment. Perhaps nowhere was this incongruity more visible than in the application of federal urban open space programs, which provided an opportunity for otherwise restricted renewal programs to promote historic preservation. Providing open space in the urban United States resulted in the:

- recognition that urban planning efforts were at risk because of the lack of comprehensive historic resource survey data within most urban areas;
- adoption of historic districts as a property type by the National Park Service (NPS); and,

- acknowledgment that the values inherent in historic neighborhoods
  were not at the core of most urban renewal projects.

Signed into law by President John F Kennedy on June 30, 1961, Title VII
of Public Law 87–70 contained important provisions with the potential to
protect historic properties.[4] Recognizing that a combination of forces had
caused the rapid expansion of metropolitan areas, which in turn, had created "severe problems of urban and suburban living," Congress directed
the Urban Renewal Administration (URA) to distribute up to $50 million
annually in matching funds to support local communities in acquiring open
space. The goal was to help prevent the spread of blight and deterioration
by preserving predominately open land in urban areas having either "recreational values; conservation value in protecting natural resources; or historic
and scenic values."[5] The acquisition of open space had broad political support, but Maryland Congressman Charles Mathias thought that it did not go
far enough: he accurately predicted that without cooperation at the highest
levels, uncoordinated federal programs would "run the risk of colliding plans
and bureaucratic competition." As a new mandate set within an existing
administrative framework, federal support for the acquisition of open space
land must be viewed within the context of urban renewal programs after
World War II.[6]

Figure 4.1 Denver Colorado Skyline. Taken from the roof of the Tivoli–Union Brewery,
this photo shows the area slated for slum clearance through building demolition,
followed by urban renewal.

Source: LOC Prints and Photographs Division, HABS COLO, 16-DENV, 17–1.

The Rise of the Renewalists

During the early 20th century, urban planners believed that development was cyclical, where "living accommodations" in cities became "antiquated and consumed by decay," only to be abandoned in favor of "undeveloped frontiers."[7] Some architects saw the Great Depression as an opportunity to employ out-of-work laborers, craftsmen, and professionals by replacing "old, uninhabitable, or unsanitary" houses and replacing them with a diversity of housing stock.[8] After World War II that pattern was transformed through the adoption of urban renewal as an active form of public policy that integrated free enterprise and market forces with increased government control, as seen in an expanded role for professional planners in guiding the development process at all levels of government. Congress addressed the increasing need for federal assistance within the urban United States at several points in the postwar period.[9] The Housing Act of 1949 was designed to assist local communities with slum clearance by fostering the identification of blighted areas and the demolition of older buildings, thus allowing private enterprise to establish new housing in the cleared areas (at that time, federal support for new construction was prohibited). Within a decade, more than 1,130 projects were funded at the request of local institutions. This limited program was enhanced in 1954 with the addition of conservation and rehabilitation to the existing slum clearance approach, and in 1959 further amendments encouraged community planning in preparation for urban renewal.[10]

After the 1954 Berman v. Parker Supreme Court decision, allowing government to take private property for redevelopment or other public purposes, urban renewal focused on community development rather than housing. Federal guidelines clearly influenced local renewal plans, but there were few avenues for individuals or community groups, such as those interested in historic preservation, to impact proposals from local planning agencies. In the decades after World War II, the complexity of American urban renewal undertakings increased with the ever-expanding federal role in financing local projects.[11] By the mid-1960s a variety of urban issues had exploded in the United States, resulting in the creation of the Department of Housing and Urban Development (HUD) in 1965.

Federal sponsorship of urban renewal efforts met with criticism and controversy during the late 1950s and early 1960s. In *The Exploding Metropolis* (1959), *Fortune* magazine's William Whyte (see Sidebar 6.1) attacked urban renewal's proclivity for large high-rise structures seated within manicured landscapes meant to deter human use rather than encourage it. Whyte's support for the work of that "crazy dame" Jane Jacobs helped her to challenge the movement's basic assumptions and impact with *The Death and Life of Great American Cities*.[12] Jacobs' attack on urban renewal's sterile designs and separation of uses—where projects are segmented into solely housing, transportation, or commercial developments—saw urban neighborhoods as layered tapestries of mixed uses. Yet, as with most proposals for redevelopment, widespread opposition to urban renewal came primarily from those immediately and most directly impacted by a given project—although most urban poor were unable to participate in this opposition. While the rehabilitation of existing buildings was included as an option under federal housing programs, it was hardly ever used. Local planning agencies considered the attractiveness of a property in its project formulations, but the economic impact of rehabilitation (increased rents and/or property values as neighborhoods became more desirable) resulted in additional relocation of less-affluent residents who could not afford to remain in redeveloped areas—a process that URA called intergroup relations but that was soon labeled gentrification.[13]

Many urban reformers posited a comprehensive approach to redevelopment, arguing for a larger scale that would "comprehend not merely the surroundings of a historic building, or a housing group, or a shopping center, but a whole district of the town itself."[14] However, it was apparent that urban renewal during the third quarter of the 20th century, like so many experiments in social policy, was afflicted by the disconnection of policy, process, and product. Warren Lehman lamented:

> The failure to recognize the absence of clear purpose in urban renewal programming may be explained, at least in part, by the emphasis on the motivation for renewal rather than its results. There are slogans a-plenty, all of which prove the intentions of renewalists—the preservation of home and hearth—are beyond reproach. . . . The response to any criticism of renewal is a full page spread of slum photos.[15]

Figure 4.2 Gadsby Commercial Urban Redevelopment Project. This six-block area urban renewal project in Alexandria, Virginia, created a large Market Square adjacent to City Hall in 1964. While Gadsby's Tavern (visible in the center of the photograph) was preserved, the adjacent Belvoir Hotel (ca. 1792) was demolished, as was nearby Arell's Tavern.

Source: Office of Historic Alexandria

Preservationists React to Urban Renewal

In response to passage of the Housing Act of 1961, Charles Peterson (see Sidebar 4.1) wrote to Robert Garvey, the Executive Director of the National Trust for Historic Preservation (NTHP) in Washington, DC:

> I believe that one of the greatest missions the National Trust could undertake (at a time when increased urban renewal appropriations multiply the hazards to city landmarks) is to intervene on the national level by influencing bureau heads in Washington and in encouraging the passing of legislation which might make historic preservation easier. It's hard enough to accomplish when the legal lights are green. Many—if not most—of our Philadelphia problems stem from official indifference in Washington and clumsy laws or regulations set up there.[16]

From a variety of perspectives, the historic preservation movement was ill-equipped to handle the challenges presented by urban renewal in the 1950s and early 1960s. To many Americans in 1961, preservation meant efforts to save monumental Egyptian temples from the flooding caused by construction of the Aswan Dam, as documented in the pages of *Life* magazine. Hometown American heritage deserved equal consideration, but the movement was hampered by a lack of administrative recognition for properties of less-than-national significance. When confronted in late 1961 with an aggressive proposal to remove 110 feet from the crest of Cameron Hill (overlooking Chattanooga, Tennessee) to provide fill material for a new interstate highway and housing development, the National Trust could only climb the bully pulpit and complain: "To revitalize a city at the expense of its important scenic and historic landmarks seems counter to the best planning." Revitalization proposals that move forward "without the sacrifice of scenic beauty and historic and architectural values . . . bring prestige to the city and eventually a greater economic return than when landmarks are destroyed."[17] Chattanooga's planners and political leadership were unimpressed with the significance of Cameron Hill and the project was soon completed.

Sidebar 4.1   Charles Peterson Retires

Although he never served as the program's director, Charles E. Peterson is most well-known within the American historic preservation movement as the father of the Historic American Buildings Survey (HABS).[18] In 1933, during the height of the Great Depression, Peterson proposed the creation of HABS as a way to employ out-of-work architects, draftsmen, and photographers. He defined the goals of the architectural documentation program as:

> Our architectural heritage of buildings from the last four centuries diminishes daily at an alarming rate. The ravages of fire and

Figure 4.3 Kings' Mill, Alleghany County, Virginia. Charles Peterson took this photo in June 1937 as part of the Historic American Buildings Survey, a program that he created in 1933 to compile create a comprehensive collection of the builder's art in the United States.

Source: LOC Prints and Photographs Division, HABS VA-1373–1.

the natural elements together with the demolition and alterations caused by real estate "improvements" form an inexorable tide of destruction destined to wipe out the great majority of the buildings which knew the beginning and first flourish of the nation. . . . It is the responsibility of the American people that if the great number of our antique buildings must disappear through economic causes; they should not pass into unrecorded oblivion.[19]

Restarted after World War II as part of the agency's Mission 66 expansion, HABS was "carried out as a kind of neglected step-child" by the NPS.[20] Yet the pressure and pace of urban demolition seen in the pre-war years only accelerated after World War II. As Peterson noted in 1961, the "decades of the 50's and 60's will be remembered more for what we have re-developed than for what we have preserved."[21]

With more than a 30-year NPS career that was often seated within urban settings, Peterson had a front-row seat from which to view the demolition that was associated with federally supported urban renew programs, especially in his Society Hill neighborhood of Philadelphia.[22] Early in 1962, he crafted a long memorandum on the future of historic structures work within the NPS in which he confessed to being tired and frustrated with the modernist direction of architectural work generated by the agency's Mission 66 program. From his perspective, in the postwar period historic buildings had become a "dirty word" within the agency.[23]

Having privately vented his frustrations with the NPS, Peterson felt free to publically attack projects sponsored by the URA at several venues during 1962. His early January presentation in the Georgetown district of Washington, DC, generated considerable negative publicity back home in Philadelphia. Undeterred—and more likely encouraged—by the controversy, he continued his campaign at a conference in Annapolis, Maryland, where preservationists expressed their "concern over the failure thus far of urban redevelopment programs to contribute to area preservation in historic American cities."[24] The urban planner Fritz Gutheim (see Sidebar 2.1) set the stage with opening remarks that decried the absence of any mention of historic preservation within the agency's administrative manuals. In an after-dinner speech, Peterson described the rehabilitation of Philadelphia's Society Hill in a "tirade" filled with "rabble-rousing tactics."[25] Asserting that not only were many significant examples of historic architecture being demolished, but also those buildings that remained were the subject of rampant vandalism of their architectural elements. In York, Pennsylvania, for example, eight buildings that postdated 1800 were demolished as part of an open space grant on a half-acre lot in order to improve the setting of the Gates House and Plough Tavern.[26]

With the provocative title: "Urban Renewal a la Mode: Can the Patient Survive?" Peterson's presentation to the Baltimore Chapter of the American Institute of Architects (AIA) at Hampton National Historic Site in July was specifically designed to provoke a response from leadership of both the preservation movement and the URA. Armed with his list of practical solutions for the problems of urban renewal (see Appendix 4.3), Peterson added Lewis Mumford's recent criticism of the Society Hill redevelopment:

> From the moment I saw the model of the 'removal' projects I realized that all that was valuable there had been surrendered without a struggle to the avaricious developers in order to get their quite nominal support; their high-rise structures destroy the scale of the historic buildings even worse than the office buildings on Independence Square. I gave a sharp "crit" of these projects for a group of students; but by then the damage was done.[27]

The impact of urban programs on historic neighborhoods received national attention that summer in *The Magazine Antiques*.[28] At the same time, Richard Steiner, who worked at Baltimore's local planning agency, carried the issue to his URA partners in Washington, DC. Following his suggestion, the AIA hosted a "closed luncheon" during the fall of 1962 at the Octagon House in Washington, DC, to discuss the possible public condemnation of the entire urban renewal program.[29]

In October 1962, Charles Peterson retired from the NPS. As noted by Ethan Carr, many of the professionals who had joined the agency during the 1930s were slated for retirement in the early 1960s, including landscape architect Thomas Vint and historian Ronald Lee, and, perhaps most controversially, the early departure of Director Conrad Wirth, who had championed the agency's Mission 66 program. Afterwards, Peterson continued efforts to raise public awareness regarding the conflict between historic preservation and urban renewal, while at the same time advertising his planning and preservation consulting services to cities and towns considering federal grants.[30] Presented with the NTHP's Crowninshield award in 1965 for his significant contributions to the historic preservation movement, Peterson remained critical of the "Slayton Colossus", a reference to the influence of the URA administrator William Slayton, throughout the 1960s primarily because the agency refused to fund historic resource surveys. The bureaucrats, concluded Peterson, think that "the business of research must be so fascinating that historians should be grateful to do it for free."[31]

Renewal projects attacked the infrastructure of blighted areas through the demolition of dilapidated buildings and structures, generally without consideration of existing resources "destroyed in favor of the new beauty." In cities across the country photo-illustrated publications, as well as some short films, documented the physical decline of neighborhoods—pictures of shabbiness and decay that cried out for and justified demolition. Perhaps the most famous of these photo-jeremiads was *God's Own Junkyard: The Planned Deterioration of America's Landscape.*[32]

Renewalists were active across the country. The process in Syracuse, New York, a city labeled by *Fortune* magazine as typically American, was characteristic of other urban areas. In 1963, the work of the city's Metropolitan Development Association was described as "the awakening of a city":

> Now the shack, the junkyards, the hovels on the Near East Side are being bulldozed into the ground, along with the better structures in the area, to make room for a community plaza and for a giant Urban Renewal development which is just about to flower into apartment houses, office buildings, and other modern facilities.[33]

A year later, after the publication of *Architecture worth Saving in Onondaga County*, the architectural critic Ada Louise Huxtable attacked plans for the wholesale demolition of existing structures.[34] Fearful that the city would be left with a "bulldozed wasteland at its heart," Huxtable described how Syracuse planners and architects were outfitted with "those particular renewal blinders" that prevented consideration of rehabilitating historic structures to new uses, such as the then-threatened Third Onondaga Courthouse. As long as we "reject the past and fail to deal in continuity," opined Huxtable, urban centers would certainly become a nightmare of lost architectural values.[35] A week later, the head of Syracuse's Metropolitan Development Association, John Searles, counterattacked, arguing that Huxtable's condemnation of the proposed renewal of the Clinton Square area might "give comfort to the hand wringers and finger pointers who plead for historic preservation" but:

> How many cities can expect a Williamsburg treatment or have the opportunity to enjoy a Georgetown rehabilitation movement? Owners of obsolescent but historic property cannot be expected to let sentiment outweigh economic considerations for any substantial period of time.[36]

Acknowledging the emotional, psychological, and cultural values embodied by historic properties, Syracuse's 1964 general neighborhood renewal plan for its urban core emphasized the preservation of a few extraordinary structures and original architectural details.[37]

Certain historically minded communities tried to "resist yet accommodate" the challenges of urban renewal: local citizens did not want to replace slums and blight with a "neon and asphalt horror."[38] Efforts to save the "jumbled diversity, antique 'charm,' and narrow streets for visual adventure and aesthetic pleasure" and criticism of sterile high-rise encroachment was designed to save certain neighborhoods for tourists and more affluent residents, who appreciated such environmental qualities.[39] By the late 1950s and early 1960s

Figure 4.4 Third Onondaga Courthouse, Syracuse, New York. Completed in 1858, this
        courthouse was documented by the Historic American Buildings Survey in
        1962 prior to its eventual demolition in 1968.

Source: LOC Prints and Photographs Division, HABS NY, 34-SYRA, 13–1.

architecturally distinctive buildings in urban neighborhoods were so sought
after by "'taste-makers,' artists, artisans, intellectuals, and camp-followers," that
renovation was becoming a booming business.[40] This housing stock had obvious values: "individuality, convenience of location, [and] charming settings."
Despite ample evidence that there was a market for housing rehabilitation, the
renewalists continued to demolish significant buildings, "casting their poor
occupants upon the uncharted sea of urban progress."[41]

Homework for Preservationists

One fundamental problem that confronted the renewalists and the preservationists was a general lack of authoritative information on the number,
nature, and distribution of historic and architecturally important buildings
within urban communities large and small. Preservationists like Huxtable and
Harley McKee, the Syracuse University architecture professor who sponsored
Architecture worth Saving, agreed that identifying the properties that contained
valued historical and aesthetic qualities was the first step in planning for
urban renewal. McKee sorted Syracuse's built environment into four categories: 1) particularly distinguished buildings, 2) representative buildings, 3)
buildings of historical interest, and 4) examples of adaptive use.[42] Following

in the footsteps of the National Council for Historic Sites and Buildings (the predecessor of the National Trust), Wilbur Hunter argued in Annapolis, Maryland that historic properties should be judged according to their "aesthetic quality," "economic utility," and "symbolic importance." For areas of urban blight, he asserted that the only relevant criterion was economic utility and the "harmonious continuity" of the entire city.[43] Recognizing the need for comprehensive data, the NTHP organized a model statewide architectural survey in Virginia conducted by a host of volunteers. It inventoried 3,200 buildings, of which 76 (2.4 percent) were of national significance and nearly 200 (6.2 percent) of importance to Virginia's heritage. At least those buildings that had been spared "more by accident than by intent" within the Commonwealth were now enumerated so that they might be considered in renewalist plans.[44]

Federal urban renewal planners also recognized the utility of conducting surveys to identify distinctive historical and architectural components of a city's built environment. Countering the critics who decried urban redevelopment as decimating the country's architectural and historical heritage, the commissioner of the URA, William Slayton, considered historic preservation projects as a very important aspect of the agency's activities.[45] He highlighted the 1959 report on the College Hill Demonstration Project in Providence, Rhode Island, as a classic in the field that had stimulated and guided a number of similar efforts across the country. By the mid-1960s more than 100 communities had embraced federally funded historic preservation projects, where "concern for the aesthetics of residential living also extends to spiritual values of the American tradition."[46] But as urban renewal programs progressed with their assault on blight, it became increasingly apparent that slum clearance had unanticipated consequences when it came to the historic character of urban neighborhoods. Despite their appearance, it appeared, to some, that slums had their own inherent values—perhaps hidden or poorly understood—within urban society. "It may seem implausible to argue that anything is lost when a slum is destroyed," noted one critic, "but certainly something is."[47]

Since the mid-1930s the standard response to the impending demise of an architecturally significant building was to engage in some level of historical documentation:[48]

> The buildings were classified by architects and architectural historians according to the treatment they were to receive—which were to be photographed and measured, which to be raped of decorative detail (interior or exterior), and which to be preserved entirely (curiously, none were considered quite worthy of preservation). The ornaments were removed by teams from the urban renewal project office, often under the shadow of the wrecking ball. The photographer took his pictures. Measurements and descriptions were 'recorded on standard forms' and copies placed in various public depositories.[49]

Figure 4.5 View of Benefit Street, facing northwest from Bowen Street, College Hill
Historic District, Providence, Rhode Island, 1997. Development pressures from
local institutions, especially Brown University, threatened the integrity of this
historic community after World War II.

Source: LOC Prints and Photographs Division, HABS RI,4-PROV,197-.

Standardized forms, photographs, and "shards of beautiful buildings no
longer with us" were somehow considered an adequate substitute for the
buildings themselves.[50] Recognizing the need for additional baseline data,
in 1952, the NTHP joined with the Historic American Buildings Survey
(HABS) partnership—the NPS, American Institute of Architects (AIA), and
the Library of Congress—to create a comprehensive inventory of historic
architecture that was to guide the selection of those buildings worthy of
HABS documentation.[51]

Acknowledging that documentation was a poor form of preservation,
despite rabble rousing among some of its members, the newly appointed
leader of the NTHP, Gordon Gray, was unwilling in the fall of 1962 to "take
a slap at urban renewal" in light of President Kennedy's endorsement of
preservation goals at Lafayette Square, immediately adjacent to the White
House.[52] The AIA was also conflicted in its response to urban renewal activities. Too few of its membership were appropriately trained or interested in
either the history of American architecture or the challenges of rehabilitating

older buildings, and, moreover, a majority appeared to be more attracted to the promise of significant design commissions for new construction projects that often followed slum clearance. At their discretion, individual architects became actively involved in local preservation battles, while the national AIA Committee on Historic Resources focused on influencing federal policy.[53]

Recognizing the seriousness of this professional criticism, URA Commissioner Slayton presented an address at the 1962 annual meeting of the NTHP in an attempt to diffuse the "intermittent pressure to lead a holy war" against his agency.[54] The problem, as articulated by Slayton, was a matter of homework:

> One of the most effective ways of assuring successful blending of old and new that is both pleasing and economical is to do enough homework— homework that is diligently pursued before a project is initiated, when it is being planned, and during the execution state. Every community should have carefully prepared surveys of structures and other elements of historical or architectural significance that could be placed in the hands of all local officials—not only renewal officials—with responsibilities likely to affect properties.[55]

Members of the AIA, the Society of Architectural Historians (SAH), and the NTHP knew that most communities did not possess any form of comprehensive inventory of historic properties worthy of preservation—but, unfortunately, the URA was unable to fund these studies.[56] After a request for assistance from the Pittsburgh Architectural Club, the URA responded:

> Neither detailed architectural and historic research, nor the design, improvement or reconstruction of buildings can be undertaken with project funds. . . . Federal urban renewal funds would not be available for any general survey of the buildings in a community which might be of historical-architectural worth or for similar general research projects. We definitely believe in the value of such activities even though we cannot provide Federal assistance for them.[57]

As evidenced by the pathbreaking late-1950s study of the College Hill neighborhood of Providence, Rhode Island, this URA position was inconsistently applied. [58]

Historic Preservation through Urban Renewal

The first public copy of *Historic Preservation through Urban Renewal* was delivered to the White House on May 8, 1963, prompting President Kennedy to remark:

> I am highly pleased to see the Federal government's help successfully applied to preserving our historic past. This book demonstrates how local initiative, through local public and private groups, can use Federal urban

renewal assistance to restore to our historic sites and structures much of their original charm and, beauty, proud character.[59]

Margaret Carroll, an URA planner, had developed the 28-page document as a response to complaints that the agency was not doing enough to support the aspirations of historic preservation. URA's mantra that projects were "locally initiated, locally administered, and locally planned and carried out," kept the agency at a bureaucratically acceptable distance from the ultimate impact of its funding, as did strictly held restrictions that no funding was available for historic restoration activities.[60] However, preservationists continued to be concerned about the "considerable variance in practice" from the theories put forward in the guidance. Upon reviewing the publication, Robert Kerr, the Director of Historic Annapolis, Inc., concluded that federally assisted urban renewal undertakings were not designed to accomplish the goals of historic preservation. The true function was the elimination of dilapidation, deterioration, and "the all too apparent ugliness of our cities." URA Commissioner Slayton agreed: the focus of both pursuits was the conservation of beauty through the application of good design.[61]

Publication of *Historic Preservation through Urban Renewal* increased the visibility of URA programs. As URA officials noted, interest in the relationship between urban renewal and historic preservation had become increasingly significant during the early 1960s.[62] Community leaders in Atlanta, Georgia; Cape May, New Jersey; Annapolis, Maryland; Chattanooga, Tennessee, Philadelphia, Pittsburgh and Germantown, Pennsylvania; San Gabriel, California; Richmond and Alexandria, Virginia; Salem, Massachusetts, Winston-Salem, North Carolina, and Middlesex, Connecticut, each wrote to the URA headquarters during 1963 for clarification of how urban renewal programs could support historic preservation efforts. In Baltimore, Maryland, for example, the Women's Civic League, a group that was the principal sponsor of an annual flower market within the city's Mount Vernon Square historic district, kept close track of urban renewal efforts, heralding creation of the city Commission on Architectural and Historic Preservation.[63]

Urban renewal's impact on historic properties was one of the principal themes discussed at the *Seminar on Preservation and Restoration* held at Colonial Williamsburg in September 1963.[64] Many participants thought that the URA had previously ignored historic preservation's potential to contribute to a revitalized urban environment and that the agency's delegation of decision making put control in the hands of those least able or least qualified to make smart preservation choices.[65] Focusing on what William Murtagh called the "knotty problems" of area preservation, Christopher Tunnard described the middle-aged suburbs that surrounded most cities as vastly more suitable for wholesale architectural clearance programs, rather than their older and more distinctive urban cores.[66] Quoting descriptions of urban decay from Edgar Allen Poe and Sinclair Lewis to provide some historical context on the decline of cities, he put forward, from a design perspective, the consideration of historical areas and axes (linear development along roads or rivers), and the need for protected open space to give old and new construction a sense of definition.[67] In the end, while urban renewal programs were seen as "both helpmate and foe of the preservation cause," the URA leadership was encouraged by the growing knowledge of the significant role urban renewal can play in what, after passage of the National Historic Preservation Act in 1966, became known as the "new preservation."[68]

> Modern preservation is, therefore, directed toward perpetuating architectural and aesthetic as well as historic and patriotic values; historic districts as well as individually notable buildings; 'living monuments' as well as historic house museums; grounds and settings, including historic gardens, town squares, and traditional open space as well as historic architecture; open air museums and historic villages including characteristic architecture which cannot be preserved in place; archaeological sites, including prehistoric villages, earthen mounds, pueblos and other ancient ruins, as well as historic sites with foundations and artifacts of successive periods; and objects and interior furnishings from the decorative arts including books and documents, which illuminate our past and inspire the present.[69]

Recognition of Historic Districts

During the summer of 1961, the NPS, because of its expertise in the identification, evaluation, and recognition of historic properties, and its experience in providing park planning guidance to state and localities, worked with URA staff to develop policies, procedures, and standards for grants to local agencies that would foster acquisition of open space parcels. NPS Regional Director Ronald Lee saw the open space program as an important opportunity to address an acute need for preservation of historic sites in connection with urban renewal projects, which were often located in the oldest and most historic portions of cities and towns.[70] Lee easily identified more than a dozen cities in the northeastern United States where urban renewal projects had adversely impacted historic communities.

In October 1961, NPS forwarded two documents to the URA: One described appropriate criteria for evaluating applications for open space grants (see Appendix 4.1); and the other outlined the agency's historical programs that could provide current and accurate information regarding historic sites in urban areas.[71] The criteria were adapted from contemporary NPS guidance on the characteristics of potential units of the national park system. Sites might possess outstanding value if they depicted events that best illustrated the broad history of the state, county, or municipality; key historic persons; or an important idea or ideal of the American people. Historic structures might embody the distinguishing characteristics of an architectural type specimen, and archaeological sites were considered significant if they had yielded information of major scientific importance to the state or locality. Historic properties also had to retain the integrity of location and authenticity of materials, as well as the difficult-to-define concepts of feeling and association. The focus on urban areas stretched traditional NPS characterization of historic sites to include, for the first time, the concept of historic districts, such as those found at Old Georgetown (Washington, DC) or the Vieux Carre (New Orleans, Louisiana). These standards served as the foundation for the criteria adopted by the NPS with the expansion of the National Register of Historic Places in 1966.

In addition to the historical significance criterion, the NPS recommended that open space parcels had to be suitable for federal assistance. This meant that the properties had to possess "distinctive values in quality and quantity of physical remains, and in terms of events and personalities." Mimicking its own congressional mandate, the NPS suggested that that funding should support the creation of a "well-rounded pageant" of state or community history—without emphasis on one period—an approach that argued for the mixed use diversity of urban spaces. The agency also cautioned against funding projects that would require extensive reconstruction of missing elements or those where the encroachment of industrial, residential, or other land uses had compromised the property's historic surroundings. This last point was ironic, given that the focus of most urban renewal projects was the removal of blight and unsightly conditions, as was the assumption by NPS planners that state and local communities would adopt the mandate for a system of parks that provided a comprehensive panorama of historic sites.[72]

For its part, the URA was generally unimpressed by the NPS guidance on grant-making criteria, but it did appreciate the potential value of the agency's store of information on historic resources. The work of the HABS, the Historic Sites Survey, and the recently created National Historic Landmark designation program each had the potential to assist local planning agencies in the identification of the most important historical and architectural sites within urban redevelopment zones. The problem here was one of coordination and access: Many of the buildings documented by the HABS program had been previously demolished, and the records of the Historic Sites Survey, which included numerous sites of less-than-national significance, were located only in Washington, DC.[73] Finally, there was the issue of mandate and funding, in that NPS officials thought that any assistance to the URA—since it was beyond the scope of the agency's traditional portfolio—warranted financial compensation for the staff time involved.[74] In 1963, for example, it recommended amending the National Housing Act to require that URA consult with the NPS, on a reimbursable basis, regarding which properties were historically significant within a particular project area.[75]

By 1964, after the success of *Historic Preservation through Urban Renewal* in ameliorating some of the concerns within the historic preservation

community, the leadership of URA and NPS worked on increased cooperation on urban undertakings.[76] NPS historian Robert Utley was given
the task of negotiating how his agency could contribute to URA-funded
projects "without diluting or relaxing" the criteria of national significance
and in the process incorporated historic districts as a property type into federal recognition programs. Since passage of the 1935 Historic Sites Act, the
NPS had developed and applied standards that sought to recognize historic
properties suitable for inclusion as part of a system of national parks. Already
encumbered by too many sites supported by too little funding, the criteria
were designed to deny, deter, and defer consideration of new historical units,
constituting an administrative definition that might be more restrictive than
required by Congress. Few individual sites within areas proposed for urban
renewal met the NPS standards for national significance; the value of these
assemblages of buildings lay in their "collective capacity to recall the ways
and forms of the past" that provided visual continuity between the past and
the present. Referencing the statement of principles and guidelines developed at the Seminar on Preservation and Restoration in 1963, Utley proposed that the NPS criteria adapt to changing conditions to provide a new
dimension to the definition of national significance:

> When preserved or restored as integral parts of the modern urban environ-
> ment, historic buildings not individually significant by reason of historical
> association or architectural merit may collectively assume significance to
> the nation in illustrating a way of life in its developing culture.[77]

Utley's administrative patch would allow the NPS to work with URA
grant makers, but more importantly, it forced official federal acknowledgment of historic districts as a type of historic property worthy of stewardship.
In some of its earliest deliberations during the 1930s, the NPSAB considered the recognition of La Villita, a historic neighborhood in San Antonio,
Texas, without ultimately designating the area.[78] During the late 1950s the
NPSAB's Consulting Committee debated the concept of historic districts
and its application to federal recognition programs. While the members saw
the need for a clear definition of historic communities, they declined to
recommend the creation of a new criterion (see Appendix 4.4). Adoption
of historic districts as a property type was clearly influenced more by the
expansion of urban renewal grant programs during the 1960s than by the
locally based creation of historic preservation zoning ordinances on either
side of World War II.[79] For example, recognizing that Old Sacramento, California, retained the largest collection of Gold Rush–era buildings, in 1964 the
NPSAB commended the city's urban renewal agency for its attempts to preserve this historic district. By the mid-1960s, historic districts had become
an increasingly important aspect of the NPS's Historic Sites Survey, urban
renewal projects, and the overall national preservation movement.[80]

Perhaps the most important historic district defined during the mid-1960s was that seated along Pennsylvania Avenue in Washington, DC. During his 1961 inaugural parade, President Kennedy observed that the area between the capitol building and the White House had become dilapidated and unattractive. Initial studies for the redevelopment of the area were augmented and accelerated in the aftermath of Kennedy's assassination, such that Secretary of the Interior Stewart Udall designated the Pennsylvania Avenue Historic District in September 1965, despite some internal administrative controversy regarding the individual significance of some of the extant buildings and the proposed aggressive program of demolition and new construction along the avenue.[81] Udall's application of the rarely used authority under the Historic Sites Act of 1935 to unilaterally designate a National Historic Site provided ample evidence that this recognition was clearly motivated by Criterion P, wherein power, politics, and persons of influence trumped any administrative frameworks devised by bureaucrats trying to impartially implement congressional laws and executive policies.[82]

In many ways the NPS viewed the impact of urban renewal to be similar to that caused by numerous federally sponsored reservoir projects that had

Figure 4.6 U.S. post office, 1100 Pennsylvania Avenue, NW, Washington, DC. Designed by Willoughby Edbrooke, the Old Post Office was constructed between 1892 and 1899. It is one of the city's few examples of Richardsonian Romanesque style buildings. The building is 200 by 305 feet in area and boasts a 315-foot tall picturesque tower. Long a focus of federal surplus property efforts, this building was a prominent historic feature located within the Pennsylvania Avenue National Historic Site.

Source: LOC Prints and Photographs Division, HABS DC, WASH, 533A-1.

been ongoing across the trans–Mississippi since the end of World War II. Partnering with the Smithsonian Institution, the NPS had conducted extensive archaeological excavations to salvage important scientific information before sites were demolished by dam construction or inundation. From the mid-1950s onward it became increasingly apparent that open spaces, as well as historic sites, were rapidly disappearing in urban neighborhoods. Nearly half of the buildings documented as part of the HABS since the mid-1930s had been destroyed by the mid-1960s. As federally assisted urban renewal programs expanded, not only was archaeological salvage warranted, but also structures of historic or unique architectural interest deserved to be recorded, measured, and photographed for posterity before it was too late.[83] Preservation-minded architects hoped to build upon the success of the archaeological salvage program before Congress and obtain improved funding for the documentation of a wide range of doomed buildings, while others decried the "opportunism and improvisation" that led to minor vernacular structures, traditionally viewed as unimportant, being recorded as valued historic resources.[84]

Open Space Land Program Results

Somewhat ironically, the first assessment of the URA's open space program appeared in *A Place to Live: The Yearbook of Agriculture, 1963*. Interest in the new grant program was wide ranging, as were the types of lands put forward for open space grants. Arthur Davis, the program's administrator, reported support for the acquisition of disued railroad rights-of-way, former battlefields, and parcels that buffered historic site from modern encroachments.[85] "Clearly," Davis remarked, "there is an unmet need of substantial proportions to acquire open space lands while they are still available." From 1962 to 1964 the URA awarded more than 200 open space grants to 177 communities located in 31 states, providing for the protection of more than 100,000 acres of predominately urban parcels.[86] While most of the grants supported the establishment or improvement of regional parks and greenbelts, eight grants were specifically designed to assist in the preservation of historic sites. Davis took special care to report to Laurance Rockefeller on the success of the open space land program and noted the close working relationship between the URA and the newly established Bureau of Outdoor Recreation (BOR). For its part, the NPS devoted the lead article in its April 1965 issue of *Trends in Parks and Recreation* magazine to the preservation of open space and the urban environment. Reflecting an emerging paradigm shift within the wider conservation movement toward a concern toward the "total environment," the Audubon Society published *Open Land for Urban America: Acquisition, Safekeeping, and the Use* in 1971.[87]

As the program gained in popularity and the URA became more experienced in its implementation, the open space grant administrators began clarifying several important aspects of its operation. First, the requirement that grants support the acquisition of a minimum of 10 acres was set aside as being an unrealistic expectation for most urban settings. Given the intensive use and relatively small size of many historic lots, this factor limited the number of individual buildings that qualified for acquisition. Second, the agency defined the concept of predominately undeveloped land to account for historic buildings seated on urban lots.[88] In addition, historic buildings were exempted from a general restriction applied to other open space grants that constrained the value of buildings to be acquired to less than $15,000. In many cases, the "inclusion of high value structures" in open space grant applications had proved to be a troublesome problem. This policy sometimes encouraged local project proponents to overestimate the historic qualities of structures found on proposed open space parcels. Due to its inexperience and the lack of local surveys, the URA was frequently hard pressed to estimate or evaluate the authenticity and historical or architectural value of the buildings.[89]

In 1965, as a result of an inquiry by Senator Henry Jackson regarding the role of the open space land program in preserving historic properties, the URA surveyed its regional offices to develop an accurate and current list of all federally sponsored historic preservation projects (see Appendix 4.2). The resulting list provided a comprehensive view of the agency's involvement with historic preservation. In response to the congressional request for information, the URA highlighted six projects:[90]

1. Ainsley Hall in Columbia, South Carolina, a unique example of the architecture of Robert Mills, the designer of the Washington Monument;
2. Fort Ward in Alexandria, Virginia, one of the series of forts built to protect Washington during the Civil War;
3. Monmouth Battlefield in New Jersey, the scene of the creation of the famous Molly Pitcher legend during the Revolutionary War;
4. Fort Snelling in Minnesota, built to defend part of the northwest frontier in 1819;
5. Pittock Estate in Portland, Oregon, part of a park chain overlooking the city and the Cascade peaks in the distance; and
6. Old St. Hilary's Church site in Marin County, California, an example of "Carpenters' Gothic" architecture built in 1888.

After five years of operation, the URA's historic preservation projects accounted for less than 2 percent of open space grant projects. Thus, despite some administrative accommodations that encouraged the incorporation of historic properties within open space grant applications, the effort was only minimally successful at helping communities conserve historic spaces. By 1969 the agency had expanded its support for historic preservation related projects, announcing $2.8 million in grants to projects in 12 states over a two-year period, including Lloyd House in Alexandria, Virginia (see Sidebar 4.2).[91]

Sidebar 4.2 The Long Name Commission Finds a Home

Figure 4.7 Lloyd House, 220 North Washington Street, Alexandria, VA, 1959. This late-Georgian-styled house was built in 1796. The Alexandria Historical Restoration and Preservation Commission acquired the property and its adjoining lots through HUD's open space land program in 1968.

Source: LOC Prints and Photographs Division, HABS VA, 7-ALEX, 15–2.

Chartered by the Virginia legislature in 1962 as an activist response to urban renewal programs, the Alexandria Historical Restoration and Preservation Commission (AHRPC) was known locally as "the long-name commission." The composition of the AHRPC was unusual in that it included two gubernatorial appointments along with the members appointed by the city council. Its mission was broader than the regulatory focus of the Old and Historic District Board of Architecture Review (another long name), which provided limited design and demolition control within the historic core of the city. The AHRPC's mandate included the ability to acquire and rehabilitate historic properties across the entire city.[92]

As Alexandria engaged in a range of urban renewal activities around its city hall, one focus of the AHRPC and other preservation-minded groups was the Lloyd House, which was the subject of a 15-year preservation campaign. Built in 1796 by Alexandria's "tavern king," John Wise, the Lloyd House takes its name from its association with the family of John Lloyd, who lived there during the second half of the 19th century. By early 1950s the disused and dilapidated home was proposed for demolition, which kicked off a year-long good-faith effort by the owners (as required by local zoning) to secure a new, preservation-minded steward for the property. The demise of the substantial brick structure was delayed until 1956, when Robert New, a petroleum engineer from California, purchased the building, sight unseen, after reading about its plight in a local newspaper while waiting for a flight at the nearby Washington National Airport. The subsequent rehabilitation removed most of the post-1800 fabric from the home and installed reproductions of lost elements, such as the plaster cornices in the principal rooms.

When adapting the home for use as an office building in 1963, New enraged local preservationists by proposing the construction of a nine-story office complex on the L-shaped lot behind the building. After a two-year battle with local officials over the size, scale, and design of the proposed office tower, a frustrated New threatened to demolish Lloyd House. A consortium of local preservation groups, led by Robert Montague and others, then sought to combine private, local, state, and federal funds to acquire the building from its previous savior. In 1968, the AHRPC received a $200,000 open space acquisition grant from HUD and acquired the property. HUD's Dwight Rettie highlighted the Lloyd House acquisition as one of 40 historic properties that the agency's open space program had supported that year.[93] Once again rehabilitated, the building served as part of the city library system until its collections were transferred to a newly expanded local history research facility. Since 2000 the long-name commission has rented the building to the Office of Historic Alexandria for use as office and meeting space. As with all federally funded open space grant properties, restrictions on the conversion of the Lloyd House lots were removed in the early 1980s, and for a time the property was unknowingly unprotected. Subsequent grants for garden landscape rehabilitation through the Save America's Treasures program came with easement restrictions that now ensure that the open setting of the home will never be compromised.

Criticism of urban renewal's impact on cities led to new legislation, the Housing and Urban Development Act of 1965, which significantly altered the federal government's approach to both housing and renewal. "Increasing the tax base, saving the central business district, historic preservation, good urban design, and real estate investment opportunities" were major themes addressed by urban critics. Congressional debate prior to this legislation included consideration of a future for the past.[94] The concern for open space was often paired with urban beautification such that the City of Philadelphia, Pennsylvania might plan for creating 250 "vest-pocket" parks on publically owned vacant lots. By mid-decade more than 60 cities in 17 states had carried out beautification projects at a total cost of nearly $10 million. Following HUD's lead, the National Endowment for the Arts (NEA) sponsored open space studies in 11 communities across the country as part of a $17 million architecture and environmental arts grant program funded from 1966 to 1977. For example a $10,000 grant allowed Milton, Massachusetts, to preserve the historic roadbed of an early horse-drawn railway associated with the construction of the Bunker Hill Monument.[95] In one estimate, in 1967 HUD assisted 277 communities to purchase 41,000 acres of open land in 35 states—for a total of more than 220,000 acres in 40 states though 777 grants with a federal investment of $106 million. Despite this success haphazard growth had taken its toll. Parcels with unique scenic and historic value were decimated as urban and suburban growth claimed 3,000 acres a day, leaving communities several million acres short of an adequate supply of open spaces during the last quarter of the 20th century. As noted by historian David Louter: "Suburbs offered a connection to open space and quiet achieved, ironically, by cutting down trees and turning fields into asphalt streets."[96]

Open Space Conversions

One of the principles underlying the federal open space grant program was that parcels acquired with federal funding would remain undeveloped for the foreseeable future. Within 10 years the open space grant program had worked with more than 1,000 local governments to acquire 380,000 acres of open space, which represented about 2.6 percent of urban lands in 1970. By the early 1970s, as communities changed and expanded (growing by 8 million acres since 1950), local development pressure began to argue for the repurposing of some of these open areas. With HUD approval, local governments could convert preserved open spaces to other uses; however, analysis by the General Accounting Office found that frequently the agency's monitoring of these grant conditions was less than adequate.[97]

These conversions usually involved the substitution of feasibly equivalent property that replaced (in size, quality, and utility) the parcels originally purchased with federal funds. In Norwalk, Connecticut, for example, local preservation advocates brought suit in early 1970s over conversion of portions of the Gallaher Estate that had been acquired with an open space grant. Initial HUD approval of a proposal to transform 15 percent of the 196-acre designed landscape into a community college campus was challenged when it became clear that the agency had not executed an administrative process that included review by the Secretary of Housing and Urban Development, George Romney.[98] Although the open space grant program was terminated in 1975 with the advent of the Community Development Block Grant (CDBG) approach to urban program funding, requirements that conversions be reviewed by the HUD secretary remained in effect until 1983. In order to "decentralize the decision making process," "remove cumbersome restrictions," and give localities the greatest discretion in land-use decisions, all restrictions on open space conversions were quietly repealed during the Reagan administration.[99] Since that time, urban communities have had the unfettered option to convert open spaces purchased with federal funds to alternative uses without oversight or review. The full impact of this substantial policy change has yet to be measured, as communities generally become aware of this planning freedom only when they request HUD's permission to convert an open space parcel.[100] Unless protected by some other instrument, such as local zoning controls or an easement, it would appear that vast areas of open space within American cities remain unprotected and subject to potential conversion and development.

Attempts to help local communities conserve open space during the 1960s addressed the growing need for recreational infrastructure in metropolitan areas. As with other urban renewal programs, the historic preservation community tried to shape the direction of grant funding away from wholesale demolition and toward stewardship of existing resources. In 1976, on the 10th anniversary of the National Historic Preservation Act, Robert Rettig reflected on the status of the federal approach to historic preservation. "All in all," he noted, "the confrontation between national historic preservation directives and existing urban renewal and housing programs was not a success story." Different challenges, based upon new legislation, would continue HUD's muddled relationship with the historic preservation community throughout the 1970s.[101] Most importantly, the urban open space grant program laid an important administrative foundation for a new and more extensive federal program: the Land and Water Conservation Fund.

Notes

1. Krystyn Moon, "Finding the Fort: A History of an African American Neighborhood in Northern Virginia, 1860s–1960s," Office of Historic Alexandria, September 2014. Adoption of the Fort Ward as the city's official Civil War centennial project was ironic on several levels.
2. Weaver was quoted in "The Department of Housing and Urban Development," *Preservation News*, Vol. 6, May 1966.
3. Richard Longstreth aptly describes how urban renewal is "fraught with more pejoratives connotations" than any other term in the history of planning. "The Difficult Legacy of Urban Renewal," *CRM: The Journal of Heritage Stewardship*, Vol. 3, No. 1 (Winter 2006), pp. 6–23.
4. "Bill Will Seek U.S. Aid to Save Parks in Cities," *The Washington Post*, February 9, 1961. The open space legislation was introduced by New Jersey Senator Harrison Williams.
5. Public Law 87–70, June 30, 1961. Initially, open space grants covered 20 to 30 percent of the project costs, by mid-decade the federal share had been raised to 50 percent.
6. URA, "Specific Articles Implementing and Accelerating URA Programs since January 20, 1961," July 26, 1961. RG 207 URA Subject 61–63, Box 719. Early in the Kennedy administration, URA programs approved more than $250 million in new and ongoing projects in order to increase economic activity in urban areas. Charles McC. Mathias, "Ill Fares the Land: Statement on the Floor of the House of Representative on June 15, 1961," RG 79 Administrative Files 49–71, Box 333. See: Robert Weaver, *Dilemmas of Urban America* (Cambridge: Harvard University Press, 1965); James Wilson, ed., *Urban Renewal: The Record and the Controversy* (Cambridge: MIT Press, 1967); Jewel Bellush and Murray Hausknecht, eds., *Urban Renewal: People, Politics, and Planning* (New York: Anchor Books, 1967); John Willmann, *The Department of Housing and Urban Development* (New York: Frederick Praeger Publishers, 1967); John C. Weicher, *Urban Renewal: National Program for Local Problems* (Washington, DC: American Enterprise Institute, 1972).

7. Eugene Morris, "The Role of Administrative Agencies in Urban Renewal," *Fordham Law Review*, Vol. 29 (1960–1961), pp. 707–728; Maxine Kurtz, "Urban Renewal: Partnership of Public and Private Interests for Urban Betterment," *Dicta*, Vol. 39 (1962), pp. 291–298.

8. Victor Abel, "Slums: Whose Responsibility?" *The Octagon: A Journal of the American Institute of Architects*, Vol. 5, No. 11 (November 1933), pp. 3–6. Coincidentally the same issue included an announcement of another Depression era make-work project, the Historic American Buildings Survey, a collaborative effort between the NPS, the AIA, and the LOC that was established to document some of the buildings being torn down during slum clearance.

9. Andrew Rouse and Kurt Wehbring, "Housing as a National Priority," *George Washington Law Review*, Vol. 39 (1970–1971), pp. 674–690.

10. Edward J. Wynne, Jr., "Ensuring Proper Land Re-Use in Urban Renewal: An Analysis of Present Federal and Local Policies and Practices," *New York University Law Review*, Vol. 37 (1962), pp. 882–915. These were projects funded out of Title I of the Housing Act. Eugene Morris, "The Role of Administrative Agencies in Urban Renewal," *Fordham Law Review*, Vol. 29 (1960–1961), pp. 707–728.

11. State laws added another wrinkle in the implementation of federal urban renewal programs: only total clearance of slum areas was permitted in some jurisdictions. Howard Wharton to Edward Braswell, December 26, 1963. RG 207 HUD URA Box 736. Edward J. Wynne, Jr., "Ensuring Proper Land Re-Use in Urban Renewal: An Analysis of Present Federal and Local Policies and Practices," *New York University Law Review*, Vol. 37 (1962), pp. 882–915.

12. William Whyte, "Urban Sprawl, and Are Cities Un-American?" *The Exploding Metropolis* (Garden City, NY: Fortune Magazine, 1957); William Whyte, "C. D. Jackson Meets Jane Jacobs," Preface to a reprint of *The Exploding Metropolis* (Berkeley: University of California Press), 1993. Jane Jacobs, "Downtown Is for People," in *The Exploding Metropolis* (Garden City, New York: Fortune Magazine, 1957); *The Death and Life of Great American Cities* (New York: Random House, 1961). While not embracing historic preservation's goals entirely, Jacobs saw a great "need for aged buildings." For a different perspective, see: Martin Anderson, *The Federal Bulldozer: A Critical Analysis of Urban Renewal, 1942–1962* (Cambridge: MIT Press, 1964), which was reportedly timed to impact the 1964 presidential election.

13. Warren Lehman, "Thinking Small about Urban Renewal," *Washington University Law Quarterly*, Vol. 1965 (1965), pp. 396–428. Martin Anderson, *The Federal Bulldozer: A Critical Analysis of Urban Renewal, 1942–1962* (Cambridge: MIT Press, 1964), pp. 147–160. In 1962, the URA reported that only 16.9 percent of all housing unit work had involved rehabilitation. The term "gentrification" was created as pejorative in 1964 by the English sociologist Ruth Glass to describe the demographic and economic transformation of certain London neighborhoods.

14. William Holford, "Plans and Programs," *Annals of the American Academy of Political and Social Science*, Vol. 314 (1957), pp. 94–100.

15. Warren Lehman, "Thinking Small about Urban Renewal," *Washington University Law Quarterly*, Vol. 1965 (1965), pp. 396–428.

16. Charles Peterson to Robert Garvey, July 27, 1961, LOC DEF, Box 49.

17. Robert Garvey to Hon. P.R. Olgiati, December 1, 1961. RG 207 HUD URA Box 736.

18. Catherine C. Lavoie, "Architectural Plans and Visions: The Early HABS Program and Its Documentation of Vernacular Architecture," *Perspectives in Vernacular Architecture*, Vol. 12, No. 2, Special 25th Anniversary Issues (2006/2007); Virginia Price, "Drawing Details: Taking Measure of the HABS Collection," *Preservation Education and Research*, Vol. 4 (2011).

19. Charles E. Peterson, "Memorandum," November 13, 1933, handwritten memo, NARA RG 515, HABS/HAER. In 1969 the HABS model was expanded to include

properties associated with engineering, with the creation of the Historic American Engineering Record (HAER) and the belated recognition of landscapes with the establishment of the Historic American Landscape Survey (HALS) in 2000.

20. Ernest Connally, "Creating a Federal Program," MCW, RTF.
21. CEP to Mrs. George Stuart Patterson, December 11, 1961, UMCP CEP, Box 172.
22. Joining the NPS in early 1929, Peterson served the NPS staff architect on large-scale urban projects at the Jefferson Expansion National Memorial in St. Louis, Missouri (1936–1942 and 1946–1948), and at Independence Hall National Historical Site in Philadelphia, Pennsylvania (1948–1962). See: Nancy Love, "Report from Society Hill," *Greater Philadelphia*, June 1956.
23. Charles Peterson to NPS Director Conrad Wirth, February 14, 1962. He promised that if nothing were done to address the issues raised in this memo, he would retire in October 1962.
24. CEP to Grant Simon (Chairman, Philadelphia Historical Commission), January 31, 1962. UMCP CEP Box 430. "Society Hill Critic is Wrong, Redevelopment Chief Says," *The Evening Bulletin*, January 16, 1962. Soon after, URA dispatched Margaret Carroll to reassure Georgetown residents. "Planner to Discuss Urban Renewal Use," *The Washington Post*, February 6, 1962. Historic Annapolis Foundation, "A Digest of Growth of Historic Towns: An Annapolis Roundtable Conference," May 1962.
25. Margaret Carroll to Urban Renewal Commissioner, "Digest of Annapolis Roundtable Conference, the Growth of Historic Towns," July 19, 1962. William Slayton to Robert Kerr, August 6, 1962. RG 207, HUD URA Box 736. Peterson was distrustful of Caroll's "optimistic pitch" for URA projects, noting that "lovely sketches pale in front of the results." Charles Peterson to Robert Kerr, May 24, 1962, UMCP CEP 307.
26. Margaret Carrol, "Note to Mr. Slayton," October 8, 1962. Carroll investigated Peterson's claims and reported that the NPS's development of Independence National Historical Park had decimated a far greater percentage of period buildings than the ongoing renewal work. "History Preserved," *The Washington Post*, May 5, 1962.
27. Lewis Mumford to Charles Peterson, April 29, 1962, UMCP CEP Box 430.
28. Barbara Snow, "Urban Renewal: Wolf in Sheep's Clothing?" *The Magazine Antiques* (July 1962).
29. Richard Steiner to CEP, July 13, 1962, UMCP CEP Box 196. John Forbes to William Slayton, October 11, 1962. William Slayton to John Forbes, November 27, 1962. RG207 HUD URA Box 736. From the URA perspective the problem was twofold: First, its congressional authorization did not specifically include consideration of architectural and historic values; and, consequently, the agency's operating manuals could not include historic preservation as worthy goal. Second, without such mandate, local planning agencies were reluctant to put forward preservation projects, fearing unwarranted delays and additional fiscal oversight.
30. Ethan Carr, *Mission 66: Modernism and the National Park Dilemma* (Amherst: University of Massachusetts Press, 2007), pp. 306–315. See the picture on p. 303. Peterson's constant criticism began to resonate with NTHP Chairman Gordon Gray, prompting him to ask Executive Director Robert Garvey "is there anything we ought to do which we are not doing with respect to urban renewal." Gordon Gray to Robert Garvey, March 12, 1963, UNC GG.
31. Charles Peterson to Hellen Bullock, October 10, 1964, UMCP CEP Box 359. Charles Peterson to Robert Montague, March 26, 1968, UMCP CEP Box 361.
32. Warren Lehman, "Thinking Small about Urban Renewal," *Washington University Law Quarterly*, Vol. 1965 (1965), pp. 396–428. Peter Blake, *God's Own Junkyard: The Planned Deterioration of America's Landscape* (New York: Holt, Rinehart and Winston, 1964).
33. "The Awakening of a City: Syracuse Faces Dynamic Future," *The Post-Standard*, January 13, 1963. Urban renewal in Syracuse was directed by John Searles, who had previously overseen a program of extensive slum clearance in southwest Washington,

DC. Mark Schudel, "John R. Searles, Jr. Dies: Oversaw Renewal in SW," *The Washington Post*, October 30, 2005.

34. Syracuse School of Architecture, *Architecture worth Saving in Onondaga County* (Syracuse: New York State Council on the Arts, 1964). This work was spearheaded by Harley McKee (1905–1976), who taught architecture at Syracuse University for 21 years beginning in 1946.

35. Ada Louise Huxtable, "Ugly Cities and How They Grow," *The New York Times*, March 15, 1964.

36. John Searles, "To the Editor, *The New York Times*." Reprinted in *The Post-Standard*, March 28, 1964.

37. Central Syracuse, *A General Neighborhood Renewal Plan, Part 1: Development Policies and Objectives* (Syracuse, New York: Syracuse Urban Renewal Agency, October 1964). The plan devoted one page out of 67 to historic preservation issues, which were grouped with eight other "principles of design."

38. Robert Kerr, "Annapolis: A Look to the Future," *Architects' Report*, Vol. 3 (1961), pp. 12–13.

39. Herbert Gans, "The Failure of Urban Renewal: A Critique and Some Proposals," *Commentary* (April 1965), pp. 29–37.

40. For example: Orin Bullock, *The Restoration Manual: An Illustrated Guide to the Preservation and Restoration of Old Buildings* (Norwalk, CT: Silvermine Publishers, 1966). Begin in 1961, this book was a project of the AIA's Committee on Historic Resources and lists several contemporary practical guides to historic property rehabilitation.

41. Warren Lehman, "Thinking Small about Urban Renewal," *Washington University Law Quarterly*, Vol. 1965 (1965), pp. 396–428.

42. See: Harley McKee, *Manual of the Historic American Buildings Survey, Part II: Criteria* (Philadelphia, Pennsylvania: NPS, Eastern Office Division of Design and Construction, October 1961).

43. Wilbur Harvey, "Preservation for What?" *Architects' Report*, Vol. 3 (1961), pp. 5 and 20. The Society for Architectural Historians praised the Maryland governor and legislature for sponsoring an architectural study of the city's waterfront. Constance W. Werner, "Architectural Research in the Annapolis Dock Space," *Journal of the Society for Architectural Historians*, Vol. 21, No. 3 (October 1962), pp. 140–145.

44. Orin Bullock, "Virginia's Heritage Inventory: A Step to Protect History," *Architects' Report*, Vol. 3 (1961), pp. 8–9.

45. William Slayton, "The Operation and Achievements of the Urban Renewal Program," in James Wilson, ed., *Urban Renewal: The Record and the Controversy* (Cambridge: MIT Press, 1967), pp. 217–218. Slayton's essay was an edited version of congressional testimony delivered in 1963.

46. John Willmann, *The Department of Housing and Urban Development* (New York: Praeger Publishers, 1967), p. 151. Willmann referenced redevelopment in Plymouth, Massachusetts, as an example of HUD funded preservation.

47. Warren Lehman, "Thinking Small about Urban Renewal," *Washington University Law Quarterly*, Vol. 1965 (1965), pp. 396–428.

48. See: "Relief Employment: Recording Historic Buildings," *The Octagon: A Journal of the American Institute of Architects* (November 1933); Charles Peterson, "H.A.B.S. Redivivus," *The Octagon: A Journal of the American Institute of Architects* (November 1934); "Our National Archives of Historic Architecture," *The Octagon: A Journal of the American Institute of Architects* (July 1936).

49. Warren Lehman, "Thinking Small about Urban Renewal," *Washington University Law Quarterly*, Vol. 1965 (1965), pp. 396–428.

50. Ibid.

51. The Historic American Building Inventory (HABI) was merged with HABS in 1962, and continued to operate until 1986. NPS, "Historic American Buildings Survey Inventory: First Preliminary Draft, October 24, 1962. UMCP CEP Box 34.

52. G. G. (Gordon Gray), "Memorandum for the File," October 17, 1962; "National Trust Endorses New Plan for Lafayette Square," October 18, 1962. UNC GG. Following the example shown at Lafayette Square, President Kennedy hoped that other federal renewal projects would harmonize preservation goals with the "requirements of growth" though quality design and effective planning.

53. Melissa Houghton, *Architects in Historic Preservation: The Formal Role of the AIA, 1890–1990* (Washington, DC: The American Institute of Architects, February 1990), pp. 42–56. Charles Peterson was appointed to the American Institute of Architects' historic preservation committee in December 1961.

54. Slayton, NTHP presentation, San Francisco, CA, 1962. John Forbes to William Slayton, November 30, 1962.

55. William Slayton to Barbara Snow, August 15, 1963.

56. Likewise, the Historic Sites Survey conducted by the NPS was of little help to state and local governments, as it focused only on nationally significant sites. Chief, National Survey of Historic Sites and Buildings to Assistant Director, Resource Studies, "Comments on the Director's Query about What We Do about Sites of State Importance in the Survey," November 9, 1965. NPS PHP.

57. Robert Weaver to Rep. Richard Schweiker, October 22, 1963, responding to a request for assistance from Thomas Morgan, publisher of the *Pittsburgh Charrette*, the journal of the Pittsburgh Architectural Club.

58. Robert Utley to Assistant Director, Resource Studies, "State Historic Sites Surveys," November 24, 1964. NPS NHL CC.

59. Housing and Home Finance Agency, Press Release, May 8, 1963. HFC RFL.

60. In 1962 John Searles had suggested to William Slayton that the URA prepare a "LPA [local planning agency] letter on the positive encouragement of historic preservation" in order to facilitate the elimination of administrative "roadblocks." Searles to Slayton, October 26, 1962. RG 207, HUD URA Box 736. Margaret Carroll, *Historic Preservation through Urban Renewal* (Washington, DC: URA, 1963). Case studies included Portsmouth, New Hampshire; Mobile, Alabama; Monterey, California; Bethlehem, Philadelphia, and York, Pennsylvania; New Haven, Connecticut; Little Rock, Arkansas; San Francisco, California; Washington, DC; Norfolk, Virginia; San Juan, Puerto Rico; Providence, Rhode Island; and Wilmington, North Carolina.

61. Alexander Smith to William Slayton, May 10, 1963. RG207 HUD URA Box 736. Robert Kerr to William Slayton, May 8, 1963. William Slayton to Robert Kerr, June 10, 1963. RG207 HUD URA Box 736.

62. Dorn McGrath, a URA planner, noted that the report had proven "very reassuring" to historic preservation groups concerned about urban renewal's impact on historic resources. McGrath to Harvey Poe, October 30, 1964. RG 207 HUD URA Box 736. Howard Wharton to Edward Braswell, December 26, 1963. RG 207 HUD URA Box 736. Wharton was the acting Commissioner for the URA and Braswell was the President of the Old Town Civic Association in Alexandria, Virginia.

63. *Women's Civil League News*, Vol. 45, No. 9 (May 1964) and Vol. 46, No. 9 (May 1965). In addition to reporting on urban renewal developments, these publications served as the programs for the association's annual Flower Market held on the Mount Vernon Square since 1912, location of the city's "Washington Monument" and the center of an ongoing urban renewal project.

64. NTHP and Colonial Williamsburg, Historic Preservation Today, Essays Presented to the Seminar on Preservation and Restoration, Williamsburg, Virginia, September 8–11, 1963 (Charlottesville: University Press of Virginia, 1966). With copies of *Historic Preservation through Urban Renewal* in hand, Margaret Carroll represented the URA at the conference.

65. James Short, "Preface," pp. v–viii in *National Trust for Historic Preservation and Colonial Williamsburg, Historic Preservation Today, Essays Presented to the Seminar on*

Preservation and Restoration, Williamsburg, Virginia, September 8–11, 1963 (Charlottesville: University Press of Virginia, 1966).

66. William Murtagh, "Comment," p. 146 and Christopher Tunnard, "Urban Rehabilitation and Adaptive Use in the United States," pp. 225–237 in *Historic Preservation Today, Essays Presented to the Seminar on Preservation and Restoration, Williamsburg, Virginia, September 8–11, 1963* (Charlottesville: University Press of Virginia, 1966). Tunnard used Frank Lloyd Wright's Robie House and the Oak Park neighborhood of Chicago, Illinois, as examples of suburban areas now subject to blight.

67. Christopher Tunnard, "Urban Rehabilitation and Adaptive Use in the United States," in *Historic Preservation Today, Essays Presented to the Seminar on Preservation and Restoration, Williamsburg, Virginia, September 8–11, 1963* (Charlottesville: University Press of Virginia, 1966), pp. 225–237.

68. Lachlan Blair to William Slayton, September 13, 1963. William Slayton to Lachlan Blair, October 29, 1963. RG 207 HUD URA Box 736.

69. "Appendix: A Report on Principles and Guidelines for Historic Preservation in the United States," in *Historic Preservation Today, Essays Presented to the Seminar on Preservation and Restoration, Williamsburg, Virginia, September 8–11, 1963* (Charlottesville: University Press of Virginia, 1966), pp. 243–256. This appendix was completed in October 1964 under direction of NPS Regional Director Ronald Lee.

70. Director, NPS to Legislative Counsel, Office of the Solicitor, "Housing Act of 1961." RG 79 Administrative Files 49–71, Box 333. Stewart Udall to Robert S. McNamara, "Outline for Joint Interior-Housing and Home Finance Agency Study: A Long Range Program and Policy for Open Space and Orderly Development in Urban Areas." RG 79 Administrative Files 49–71, Box 333. URA was a division of the Housing and Home Finance Agency (HHFA) until the creation of the Department of Housing and Urban Development in 1965. The NPS had previous experience in urban renewal projects—in the development of the Jefferson Expansion Memorial in St. Louis, Missouri and at Independence National Historical Park in Philadelphia, Pennsylvania. Ronald Lee to Conrad Wirth, "Historic Sites in Relation to the Housing Act of 1961," July 19, 1961. RG 79 Administrative Files 49–71, Box 333.

71. Herbert Kahler to Chief, Branch of Recreational Studies, "Statement on Historical Programs and Criteria Useful in the Planning Procedures under the 'Open Space' Legislation." RG 79 Administrative Files 49–71, Box 333.

72. Herbert Kahler to Chief, Branch of Recreational Studies, "Statement on Historical Programs and Criteria Useful in the Planning Procedures under the 'Open Space' Legislation." RG 79 Administrative Files 49–71, Box 333.

73. Margaret Carroll, "Meeting with Officials of the National Park Service on Historic Preservation," August 23, 1962; "Note to Mr. Slayton," October 5, 1962.

74. Conrad Wirth to Regional Directors, "Relationship of Recreation Planning and Historic Site and Building Preservation to Urban Development," March 19, 1962. NPS Director Wirth saw potential cooperation in the area of urban renewal open space land, highways, and other community facilities. In the memo he requested information on prior NPS collaboration on urban projects. RG 207, HUD URA Box 736.

75. NPS Director to Legislative Council, Office of the Solicitor, Department of the Interior, "S.2031: To Extend and Amend Laws Relating to Urban Conservation and Development," October 15, 1963. RG79 Admin Files 49–71, Box 333.

76. During the spring, NPS and URA officials met to identify how the NPS might assist in urban renewal projects. Hartzog spelled out his agency's commitments to provide information regarding known historic properties to regional URA offices and to review justifications of historical significance for buildings included as part of local planning agency proposals. George Hartzog to All Regional Directors, "Implementation of Thoughts Expressed at the Joint Meeting with the Urban

Renewal Administration, March 4," March 12, 1964. RG 79 Admin Files 49–71 Box 334. William Slayton to George Hartzog, February 24, 1964. RG 207 HUD URA Box 736. URA agreed to allow local project proponents to contract with NPS to identify historic preservation issues associated with urban projects.

77. Robert Utley to Chief, Division of History Studies, "A Program of Professional Assistance in Urban Renewal Projects," November 4, 1964. Utley noted that URA had not shown "any disposition to reimburse" NPS for its services.

78. John H. Sprinkle, Jr., *Crafting Preservation Criteria: The National Register of Historic Places and American Historic Preservation* (New York: Routledge, 2014), pp. 154–156.

79. NPSAB CC Minutes, September 16 and 17, 1959. Boundaries were seen as an essential component of any historic community, regardless of whether local government had applied preservation zoning ordinances to an area.

80. NPSAB Minutes, October 5–14, 1964, p. 58. Robert Utley, "Professional Assistance in Historic Preservation in Urban Renewal Districts," January 27, 1965; NPS Director to All Regional Directors, "National Survey of Historic Sites and Buildings: Revision of Administrative Criteria of National Significance," May 18, 1965. NPSAB CC.

81. Utley, *Custer and Me: A Historian's Memoir* (Norman: University of Oklahoma Press, 2004), pp. 98–99. NPSAB CC Minutes, August 30–31, 1965.

82. Use of the Historic Sites Act authority also raised the question as to whether the LWCF could be used to "finance historic sites" along the avenue. Director, BOR to Executive Staff, "Preparation for Budget Hearings," November 4, 1965. RG 368 HCRS BOR LWCF 68–68 Box 2.

83. NPS, "Historical Preservation in the Urban Community: A Joint Program by Housing and Home Finance Agency, Urban Renewal Administration and United States Department of the Interior, National Park Service." RG 79 Historic Subject Files 26–70, OAHP Entry 139, Box 22. This draft was prepared by the NPS, as evidenced that sections relating to URA programs were only outlined.

84. Earl Reed to Nathaniel Owings, December 27, 1965. John Cabot (NPS Chief Architect) to Earl Reed, December 10, 1965. LOC NAO Box 28.

85. Arthur Davis, "The Uses and Values of Open Space," in Alfred Stefferud, ed., *A Place to Live: The Yearbook of Agriculture, 1963* (Washington, DC: U.S. Department of Agriculture, 1963), pp. 330–336. By June 1963 the program had provided $18 million to 110 local agencies that acquired 57,000 acres.

86. Arthur Davis to Pat Healy, June 21, 1963. RG207 HUD URA Box 736. After a year of full time operation, Davis initially reported that his agency had committed $13 million on 75 projects—with other 25 grant applications in hand. "Preserving Urban Open space Land: The First Three Years," Housing and Home Finance Agency, URA, August 1964. The 219 grants totaled $32 million, which funded 20 to 30 percent of the total acquisition costs. RG79 Admin Files 49–71, Box 334. See: "Open Space Grants Aid 177 Places," *The Washington Post*, August 30, 1964. Among the projects highlighted was a $26,000 grant to acquire property at Fort Ward in Alexandria, Virginia.

87. Arthur Davis to Laurance Rockefeller, November 12, 1963. RG207 HUD URA Box 736. Before coming to URA, Davis had served as the chief of programs and policies for the Outdoor Recreation Resources Review Commission. Robert Weaver, "Open Space and the Urban Environment," Trends in Parks and Recreation, Vol. 2, No. 2 (April 1965). From 1961 through 1964, the open space land program had made 277 grants in 32 states that resulted in the protection of 111,360 acres of open land. The federal share totaled $32 million, matched with more than $100 million of state and local funds. Joseph Shomon, *Open Land for Urban America: Acquisition, Safekeeping, and Use* (Baltimore: Johns Hopkins University Press, 1971).

88. William Slayton, "Open Space Land Program," April 9, 1963. RG 207 HUD URA Box 736. Historic buildings could be acquired if their value was less than 50 percent of the land value, or one third of the total acquisition cost.

89. Bruce Wedge to William Slayton, "Open Space Land Program: Historic Sites," November 5, 1964; Edward Baxter to Bruce Wedge, "Open space Land Program: Historic Sites," December 14, 1964. RG 207 HUD URA Box 736. URA officials had "little doubt" that the "Corner of Celebrities" area in Frankfort, Kentucky, was an authentic and valuable site (see Appendix 4.2).

90. Senator Henry Jackson to William Slayton, May 28, 1965. Jackson included a NPS-prepared "Fact Sheet on Historical Preservation" that cited the URA's open space land program as a source of funding to support historic preservation projects. Urban Renewal Commissioner to Regional Directors, June 7, 1965. RG 207 HUD URA Box 736. William Slayton to Senator Henry Jackson, July 20, 1965. In a subsequent letter, the agency provided additional information on the program's operation, again referencing the College Hill Demonstration project as well as a more recent study of the Vieux Carre section of New Orleans. RG 207 HUD URA Box 736. Howard Wharton to Senator Henry Jackson, July 16, 1965. URA reported that more than 100 communities had included historic preservation as one objective in their urban renewal projects.

91. "Open Space Land Grants Awarded by HUD for Preservation of Historic Settings," *Preservation News*, May 1, 1969. One grant helped a local government in Maryland acquire the stables that were the birthplace of "Nashua," a famous racehorse from the mid-1950s.

92. The authoritative source on the history of the Lloyd House is Timothy Denee, *Lloyd House Historic Structures Report* (Alexandria, Virginia: Department of General Services, February 2001). Documented by the HABS before its rehabilitation by Robert New in the late 1950s, the property was listed on the National Register of Historic Places in 1971 and is located within the Alexandria National Historic Landmark District.

93. *American Association for State and Local History, Committee on Federal Programs in History, First Annual Meeting* (Washington, DC: NPS, 1968), pp. 60–61, 66.

94. Andrew Rouse and Kurt Wehbring, "Housing as a National Priority," George Washington Law Review, Vol. 39 (1970–1971), pp. 674–690. Housing and Urban Development Act of 1965, Hearings before the Subcommittee on Housing of the Committee on Banking and Currency, House of Representatives, April 1965.

95. National Endowment for the Arts, Revitalization by Design, FY 1966–FY 1977 (Washington, DC: National Endowment for the Arts, 1978). John Willmann, *The Department of Housing and Urban Development* (New York: Praeger Publishers, 1967), pp. 88–89, 103–105. After 1965, Cities could use federal funding for up to 50 percent of beautification projects or open space acquisition.

96. Arthur Davis, "Reserving Open Space So Cities May Breathe," Outdoors USA: The Year Book of Agriculture 1967, 90th Congress, First Session, House Document No. 29, pp. 308–311. David Louter, *Windshield Wilderness: Cars, Roads, and Nature in Washington's National Parks* (Seattle: University of Washington Press, 2006), pp. 117–119.

97. In 1971 HUD's open space land program, urban beautification and improvement program, and historic preservation program were consolidated into the Legacy of Parks Program. General Accounting Office, "Improvements Needed in Administration of the Open-Space Land Program," General Accounting Office Report 096646, March 8, 1972. In 1950 urban land (in cities with more than 100,000 residents) included 5.8 million acres; by 1960 it had grown to 10.8 million acres; and in 1970 it was 14.5 million acres.

98. *Schicke v. Romney*, U.S. Court of Appeals, Second Circuit, February 20, 1972. HUD could not document the administrative process, mandated by Section 1500 of the Housing Act of 1961, by which its Secretary had reviewed the conversion proposal.

99. For a review of the program's history see: *Louisiana Landmarks Society, Inc. v. City of New Orleans*, U.S. Court of Appeals, Fifth Circuit, June 7, 1996. See PL. 98–181, November 30, 1983.

100. For example, in 1996 New Orleans learned of the change in practice when it requested HUD approval for the conversion of uses at Washington Artillery Park. Henry Cisneros to Marc Morial, November 1, 1996.

101. Robert Rettig, Conserving the Man-Made Environment: Planning for the Protection of Historic and Cultural Resources in the United States (Washington, DC: NPS, September 1, 1975), p. 53. This study was prepared in association with the 10th anniversary of the National Historic Preservation Act of 1966. See, for example, John H. Sprinkle, Jr., "Now That the Slums Are Fashionable: Origins of Section 104 of the National Historic Preservation Act," *National Trust for Historic Preservation Forum Journal*, Vol. 31, No. 1–2 (Fall 2016/Winter 2017), pp. 25–32.

5   The Recreation Movement

In 1962, toward the end of his long and distinguished career with the National Park Service (NPS), Conrad Wirth prepared a memorandum that described a creative funding source for a new federal program to assist states in acquiring lands for recreational purposes (Appendix 5.1). Established in 1964, the Land and Water Conservation Fund (LWCF) has since provided more than $4 billion in funding to states and local governments, preserving 2.6 million acres for outdoor recreation in perpetuity, with an even greater amount ($7 billion) set aside for the federal acquisition of protected lands.[1] The LWCF was the culmination of a 30-year campaign designed to address a perceived national deficiency in access to affordable recreational facilities across the United States.

Beginning with President Franklin D. Roosevelt's New Deal, the NPS, through programs like the Recreational Demonstration Areas, added substantial emphasis on assisting states and local governments in the design, construction, and operation of parklands large and small (see Sidebar 5.1).[2] Wirth was at the center of this altered approach, one focusing on aesthetics and design of park infrastructure in a pattern that would be enhanced after 1956 with the agency's Mission 66 program. Ironically, responsibility for coordinating nationwide recreation programs would be cut from the NPS in the early 1960s, just as Wirth was retiring from federal service, with the creation of the Bureau of Outdoor Recreation (BOR).

The LWCF illustrated ongoing tensions between federal, state, and local governments regarding the desire for unfettered support for parkland planning, acquisition, and development. Implementation of the LWCF provided an important administrative precedent for the new federal grants-in-aid partnership programs created by the National Historic Preservation Act in 1966. Cautiously optimistic at the start of the program, the historic preservation movement was ultimately unable to foster the adoption of its adaptive use conventions as part of the LWCF guidance. This failure to significantly capture LWCF land acquisition funding was mitigated by the creation of the Historic Preservation Fund (HPF) in 1976, which supported restoration and rehabilitation work on historic properties.

For the Profitable Employment of Leisure Time

"You've got trouble," declared Professor Harold Hill in *The Music Man*, because the young men of small-town America were "frittern away their noontime, suppertime, choretime too!"[3] Recalling his Iowa childhood, the composer Meredith Wilson vividly captured one of the most pressing post–World War II social problems found among certain economic strata: the growing amount of leisure time. The 20th century economic transformation that came with increasing urbanism and industrialization led to an expansion of leisure time— time that might be more profitably spent, according to the proponents of the recreation movement, enjoying the benefits of the out-of-doors (rather than wasting time hanging around a certain pool hall in River City, Iowa). The potential crisis in productive recreation was illustrated during the 1920s and 1930s by works such as *The Threat of Leisure* and *The Challenge of Leisure*.[4] Although the American recreation movement was well established by the onset of the Great Depression, it was augmented by the expansion of available leisure time that came with the widespread adoption of the 40-hour work week and the two-day weekend institutionalized by the Fair Labor Standards Act in 1937.[5] The Great Depression itself, due to significant levels of unemployment, provided an ironic opportunity for productive leisure activities.[6] Not surprisingly, the benefits of this social movement were not fairly distributed among all classes or ethnic groups in American society, even as "recreation for all" became the movement's slogan during the late 1950s.[7]

As cities, towns, and counties across the country recognized their collective recreation responsibility, they sought out the expertise found within the federal government for technical and advisory services.[8] Assisting state and local governments was at the heart of the federal support system, principally because this helped to alleviate the mounting pressure on existing national parks and monuments, and the opportunistic attempts to create new units within the park system. Interior Secretary Harold Ickes even recommended presidential declarations under the Antiquities Act of 1906 be expanded to include the creation of National Recreation Areas.[9] The outdoor recreation movement gained substantial federal support with the enactment of the Parks, Parkway, and Recreational Area Study Act in 1936. Designed to "compliment the public service rendered" by the national parks, this bill established a new relationship between the NPS and the states, directing the agency, for the first time, to undertake a comprehensive survey of parks, parkways, and recreational programs throughout the United States.[10] The proposed study was considered far-reaching:

> Few present-day undertakings possess such social importance to the Nation as a whole as those designed to provide increased opportunity for healthful and profitable employment of leisure time. The park systems of today—national, state, and local—are making a magnificent contribution to the "leisure time" problem.[11]

While the magnitude of the leisure time problem for most levels of society during the middle of the Great Depression might be questioned, the idea was to provide data helpful to states in developing plans for coordinated and adequate public facilities. Trained as a landscape architect, Conrad Wirth designed and executed reports on conditions within more than 30 states prior to the publication of *A Study of the Park and Recreation Problem in the United States* in 1941. Federal action on many of the report's recommendations were put on hold for the duration of World War II, and yet park visitation contributed to the war effort by inspiring patriotism and maintaining morale, with recreational activities seen as vital to both civilians and the military.[12]

During this period, the emphasis was on planning for growth and the expansion of cities as the population became more urban during the mid-20th century. As metropolitan areas grew after 1900, there had been a failure to reserve sufficient open spaces within and adjacent to cities and towns, or to consider the preservation of notable historic sites. What properties remained often had been "despoiled of their recreational value."[13] The first step in addressing these concerns was to identify the state of the field: to compile an estimate of the nature and scope of publically owned parks and recreational areas, one that would set the stage for cooperation between all levels of government.

Such collaboration revealed two fundamental questions that lay at the foundation of the land conservation movement: How much open space is necessary to meet society's needs? And how many acres of protected spaces can our communities afford to acquire? Any enumeration of requirements envisioned a time when no new parks would be needed within a jurisdiction. This concept—that at some point in the future there would no longer be any gaps in the system of parklands—flows throughout the language of the historic preservation and land conservation movements during the 20th century. Despite the emphasis on the values inherent in the out-of-doors, the actual qualities of parks and recreation resisted quantification. "So long as any cultural and recreative factor in our historical and natural resources [were] being needlessly destroyed it is a challenge to Federal, State and local governments to take appropriate steps for its preservation."[14]

The foundation for postwar efforts in land conservation was presented in *A Park and Recreational Land Plan for the United States*. While rural areas also needed access to spaces for public recreation, the greatest need for parklands was within urban areas and their growing suburban belts. Larger parcels seated within easy driving distances to metropolitan areas provided a sense of freedom and separation from urban crowds during weekends and holidays. Even larger tracks—characterized by forests, rugged terrain, lakes and streams—were necessary for family vacations, and it was prudent to provide these experiences within reasonably easy reach of those families "who need them and who cannot afford to seek them at a distance." This service was provided by the NPS's Recreational Demonstration Areas (see Sidebar 5.1).[15]

Certain kinds of landscapes were viewed as being particularly important for conservation actions. Ocean, lake, and river frontages were highlighted because of the perceived ability of land and water settings to refresh both the body and the spirit. Areas with exceptionally beautiful and striking scenery were also sought after by park planners because of their inspirational values. Provisions for parkways, waysides, and trails enhanced these qualities, as did controls on outside advertising and provisions for the protection of roadside beauty.

Sidebar 5.1   Recreational Demonstration Areas

In theory, the goal of Recreational Demonstration Areas was a good one, an experiment that was part of President Franklin D. Roosevelt's "great recreational and educational project."[16] Across the country, the federal government would design and construct several dozen experimental facilities located close to urban areas to show the value of regional parks that provided accessible and affordable recreational opportunities to lower-income families. This effort was begun in the early 1930s, and by the start of World War II the NPS had established 46 public parks and waysides encompassing almost 400,000 acres in 24 states. Funding and labor came from a variety of agencies, including the Civilian Conservation Corps, Works Progress Administration, and the Resettlement Administration. In some cases, the government acquired large parcels of what was classified as marginal farmland, with the previous occupants removed to alternative sites. The mandate was clear:

> In developing these 46 projects in an effort to alleviate in some small degree, a long-felt need for increased recreational facilities— particularly among the lower income groups—an important objective has been that of demonstrating the practicability of such a program to the various State and local governments with the belief that they, in turn, might profit from the foundations laid by the Federal Government.[17]

Designed to address a variety of social, economic, and recreational needs, Recreational Demonstration Areas represented a departure from traditional NPS activities that led to criticism from a variety of conservation organizations. Newton Drury (who would become the agency's director in 1938) complained that the NPS was becoming a "Super-Department of Recreation."[18]

Recreational Demonstration Areas were conceived of as experiments, and once the development was completed, title to the vacation area, wayside, or extension of an extant state park was to be transferred a state or local government for permanent administration.[19] Recognizing

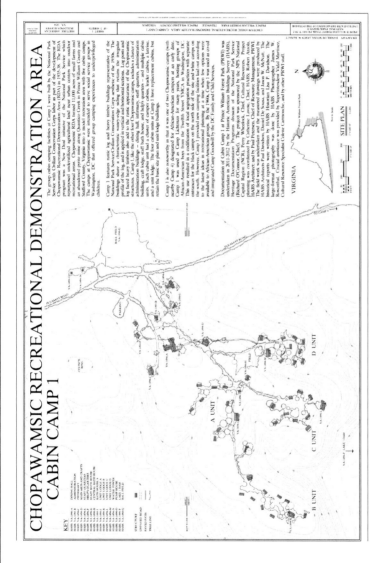

Figure 5.1 Chopawamsic Recreational Demonstration Area. Located south of Washington, DC near Quantico, Virginia, the Chopawamsic project comprised 11,000 acres of small farms and abandoned mines. Five camping areas, like this one, were developed to provide recreational facilities for organized groups such as the YWCA. Cabin Camp 1 was designated for African-American campers.

Source: Historic American Buildings Survey.

another opportunity to expand its contribution to the country's economic recovery, NPS leadership implemented the Recreational Demonstration Area program with enthusiasm, especially because the undertaking also expanded the boundaries at seven existing park units. As shown by historian Angela Sirna and others, Recreational Demonstration Areas transformed the existing rural collection of historic farmsteads and woodlots into designed park landscapes (using labor from a variety of federal make-work programs) that had social reform in mind. Oral histories document that the removal and resettlement of existing residents was often a painful, disruptive process—evidence that contrasts with official claims that local farm families voluntarily participated in the program. Although most Recreational Demonstration Areas were successfully transferred before the end of World War II, several—such as Maryland's Catoctin Mountain Park and Virginia's Prince William Forest Park—were retained within NPS stewardship.[20]

Recreational Demonstration Areas followed comprehensive park designs that called for the removal of old buildings, structures, roads, trails, fields, and fence lines—to be replaced on a vast scale by artificial recreational landscapes. They illustrated the transition from the naturally scenic parks of the first third of the 20th century to multipurpose recreational parks set within manipulated natural settings during the middle third of the century. The success of these experiments codified the idea that outdoor recreation should be affordable and accessible to every American.[21] Recreational Demonstration Areas also provided a bureaucratic precedence for federal fiscal support for the acquisition of parklands that would be managed by state and local governments—an idea that foreshadowed the operations of the LWCF.

Historic properties also had the power to inspire and educate an American public with more leisure time on its hands, a fact that was recognized by recreational planners. In the mid-1930s the NPS was delegated increasing responsibilities for the preservation and presentation of nationally significant historic sites across the country. The Historic Sites Act of 1935 required that the agency survey, classify, and formally recognize important places that illustrated a consensus-based comprehensive panorama of the American story. Here as well, the emphasis was on planning: there were simply too many potential historic sites that local boosters wanted to be included in the system of national parks. The federal government needed an administrative mechanism through which to determine which places were worthy of conservation. In the nationalistic language of the time, Secretary of the Interior Ickes considered that the goal of his agency's new role was consequential:

> With this step has come a still broader conception of America as a whole. We cannot honor our heroes and sages or visit the places hallowed by

them without deepening our own consciousness of what true patriotism means. It is good for us all to pause now and then to recall some of the costs and sacrifices that have gone into the making of America.[22]

From a recreational standpoint, historic properties had the added attraction of diversity. As the nation became more and more homogeneous, planners assumed that the different recreational desires exhibited within racial or national characteristics and traditions would diminish and that the best qualities of each group would become incorporated into the recreational movement. Historically themed pageants, such as coastal North Carolina's long-running "Lost Colony" drama, first performed in 1937, illustrated the process of incorporating diverse traditions within a nationalistic and heroic context. Within the context of a recreational melting pot, historic sites preserved the physical evidence of the various cultural traditions exhibited by the American people.[23]

In many ways historical and archaeological sites were on the same plane as scenic beauty—an inspirational resource that would refresh the visitor's mind and spirit. Both scenic views and historic properties warranted conservation to prevent unsightly encroachment or physical impairment. But while beautiful vistas might have been inherently awe inspiring, historical sites needed interpretation in order for their true value to be readily apparent. Despite this, due to the increasing availability of automobiles, the impact of a growing market in heritage tourism was well understood as a component of the recreation movement.[24]

Studies by the NPS on either side of World War II expanded the meaning of recreation to include intellectual and aesthetic pursuits that included the interpretation of historic sites and the appreciation of scenery. Educational, cultural, and recreational services were linked in their support of desirable activities that enhanced the stability of postwar communities. As physical reminders of important traditions, historic sites were respected, but only if they were found in an appropriate setting. "Preservation must be based upon a re-examination of the use of the land in relation to present and future needs of the community."[25] Poorly seated buildings, those impaired by the encroachment of modern developments, could be moved, gathered together, and adaptively used within a more authentic setting. Such approaches to historic preservation—moving buildings to preserve them in re-created artificial landscapes—reflected techniques practiced before World War II and foreshadowed some of the approaches utilized by federal agencies as part of urban renewal and highway construction projects during the third quarter of the 20th century.

The rise of the outdoor recreation movement confronted one of the primary dilemmas faced by land management agencies: the dual mandates of conservation and enjoyment. As defined in the post–World War II period, a great diversity of recreational activities were possible within the range of protected areas. The scope of the recreational planning and design work completed for state and local governments also challenged the portfolio of NPS

Figure 5.2 Excavations by the Archeological Society of Maryland at Iglehart Rock Shelter, Baltimore County, Maryland, early 1960s. On either side of World War II, avocational archaeology grew in scope and interest as a recreational activity that ensured the profitable pursuit of leisure time.

architects, engineers, and landscape architects.[26] For its part, however, the NPS consistently maintained that the inspirational qualities of the natural, scientific, or historic values it safeguarded were paramount: provisions for physical recreation were permissible only when they did not adversely impact those qualities.

Seizing the opportunities provided by the federal response to the Great Depression, the NPS heartily embraced its role in the specialized area of national recreation planning, overseeing $100 million in park and recreation grants to state agencies as part of its contribution to stimulating employment and economic activity across the country. This shift in emphasis led to a spirited fight within the agency and among its supporters regarding how much emphasis should be placed on recreational planning.[27]

One problem that confronted the diverse advocates for the recreation movement was the fact that no one federal agency was charged with developing and implementing a nationwide policy or framework. Organized in 1946 and disbanded in 1963, the Federal Inter-Agency Committee on Recreation included representatives from more than a dozen federal agencies. It served as a forum for the development of a national recreation policy, but it had no powers to direct federal activities. Another issue, exacerbated by the diffuse federal leadership during the 1950s, was the paucity of comprehensive data on the distribution, characteristics, and use of recreational lands within the United

States. In 1952 the establishment of Resources for the Future, Inc., the first nonprofit research organization devoted to natural resource and environmental issues, was a turning point in the history of recreation.[28] Marion Clawson and others at the organization were able to lay the groundwork for understanding patterns in the acquisition and use of public lands, forecasting trends and challenges in conservation. With former NPS director Horace Albright as one of its founders, Resources for the Future sponsored a critical review of NPS policies. One mid-century trend, espoused by the recreation pundits, was the "willingness to look to government for aid but not for controls of any sort."[29]

Mission 66

Outdoor recreation was an important, if conflicted, theme within Mission 66, the ambitious decade-long infrastructure development program created by NPS Director Conrad Wirth in the mid-1950s.[30] In planning for Mission 66, the focus was on the use and protection of scenic, scientific, and historical units, not on recreational facilities—although much of the substantial building program was designed to increase the use of the parks in support of an expanding tourism industry. Initial analysis suggested that not only was it inappropriate for the agency to provide recreational features primarily used by local residents, but also, the visiting public did not expect, nor did it approve of, "artificial types of recreation" that required extensive facilities, such as ski lifts. For its part, the NPS saw its own efforts at comprehensive planning for the national park system would complement any national recreation plan.[31]

Recognizing that much of American history happened out-of-doors, the NPS wanted the country to "embrace the broad outlines of our outdoor heritage" as it decided which new historical areas to consider for permanent conservation. Coordination with state and local governments was key, a function NPS compared to the local extension service offered by the Department of Agriculture's Soil Conservation Service. As noted by Richard Sellars, Mission 66 had its critics among the conservation movement: to some, the infrastructure construction and development undertaken within the parks was "too extensive, too modern, and too intrusive."[32] In addition, it primarily focused on the internal workings of the NPS. Mission 66's involvement with outdoor recreational planning would be supplanted by other forces in the late 1950s.

Outdoor Recreation Resources Review Commission

The work of the Outdoor Recreation Resources Review Commission (ORRRC)—an "awful acronym we lived with" noted the conservationist Henry Diamond—was a watershed in the post–World War II recreation movement.[33] Although it was headed by a highly significant patron of the NPS, Laurance Rockefeller, ORRRC, which operated between 1958 and 1962, minimized the agency's participation and recommended the creation of a brand new agency within the Department of the Interior to serve as the nationwide leader for recreational planning and implementation. In fact, as Harlean James argued before Congress, a competent survey of recreational resources had already begun as part of the NPS's Mission 66 operation, work that included investigation of proposed shoreline parks along the Atlantic and Gulf coasts. In addition, 16 out of 23 states with comprehensive planning efforts funded by the Urban Renewal Administration (URA) had already included recreational components in their statewide plans. For the land conservation movement, one irony was that the ORRRC studies identified "pleasure driving" as the most popular form of outdoor recreation in 1962.[34]

Notable for its bipartisanship and comprehensiveness, ORRRC was prolific in the sponsorship and production of detailed studies that were outlined in its final report: *Outdoor Recreation for America.*[35] It cast a wide thematic net in order to firmly establish a significant federal role in the planning and development of recreational infrastructure. Describing the significance of open space and unspoiled vistas within American culture, the anthropologist Margaret Mead noted the connection between conservation and recovery and recreation as leisure pursuits. Among the Commission's primary conclusions was that outdoor recreation was often compatible with the conservation and stewardship of other goals, such as wildlife and watershed management, as well as, "in some cases, historic preservation, timber harvesting and hunting."[36] Congress took the ORRRC recommendations to heart, enacting four major pieces of conservation legislation during the Johnson administration, including the LWCF and the Wilderness Act in 1964 (see Sidebar 5.2). The ORRRC report prompted congressional proposals for the creation of a similar commission to study historic preservation practice, an idea that bore fruit in the National Historic Preservation Act of 1966.[37] From a planning perspective, advocates for outdoor recreation, like historic preservationists, saw their pursuits as the cure-all for a wide range of society's problems in the 1960s.

Extraction of the recreational planning aspects of the NPS mandate was a substantial professional blow for NPS Director Conrad Wirth, who had fostered NPS leadership in outdoor recreation since the mid-1930s. His inability to embrace certain aspects of the Kennedy administration's new conservation, as promoted by Secretary of the Interior Stewart Udall, eventually led to Wirth's replacement by George Hartzog in early 1964. In 1952, when Conrad Wirth had assumed leadership of the NPS, annual appropriations stood at $28 million. Ten years later, in fiscal year 1963, funding had grown by more than $100 million due to Mission 66, despite the allocation of more than $1.1 million carved out for the BOR. All that was about to change: in 1964, the first year of Director George Hartzog's tenure, the agency's appropriation saw its first reduction in a more than a decade.[38]

In some ways the NPS would have the last laugh. While the BOR was created by Secretary Udall in April 1962 and was codified by the Outdoor Recreation Act of 1963 (Public Law 89–29, May 1963), in 1977 the agency was absorbed by the new Heritage Conservation and Recreation Service

(HCRS or "Hookers"), which itself was abolished in 1981 by the Reagan administration. The responsibility for nationwide recreational planning was then returned to the NPS's portfolio. BOR lasted only 15 years. [39]

Sidebar 5.2   Wilderness

In 1970, the historian Roderick Nash argued that the invention of the national park idea was one of outstanding contributions of the American system to modern civilization.[40] Nash, the author of *Wilderness and the American Mind*, traced the origins of this concept to the spring of 1832 when two events laid the ideological and bureaucratic foundation for the perpetual conservation of public lands. Writing near what would become Pierre, South Dakota, the artist George Catlin, after observing the degradation of Native Americans and the decimated buffalo herds they hunted on the prairie, wrote that the country must preserve a "magnificent park," a "nation's park" to ensure that some part of the wilderness would survive the onslaught of civilization.

At the same time, a thousand miles to the south and east, in the Arkansas territory, the federal government set aside more than 2,500 acres of public lands that contained numerous health-enhancing mineral hot springs. This reservation was the first of its kind in the United States, where the federal government established the administrative principle that public lands should be conserved for the benefit of future generations. At both places, it was perceived threats to the resources and values within that helped elucidate the need for publicly protected parklands. Ironically, argued Nash, it was the national economic engine fueled by the exploitation of wilderness areas that funded the country's ability to preserve vast areas, and it was individuals living furthest afield from these wide open spaces that were the most supportive of their protection. In the late 19th century Frederick Jackson Turner posited the end of the frontier and its subsequent impact on American character and culture from downtown Chicago, not from the Utah territory.

As a concept for land conservation, wilderness became increasingly important as the 20th century progressed.[41] During the 1930s the NPS had loosely defined the idea of a wilderness park, but the need for improvements to ensure public enjoyment conflicted with the desire for protecting truly untouched natural environments. Concerned about congressional enthusiasm for the construction of skyline drives, several conservationists organized the Wilderness Society in 1934. After World War II, it became commonplace among the NPS leadership to recognize the paradox of providing public access while trying to maintain wilderness qualities. In Mission 66 publications like *The National Park Wilderness*, the agency described the qualities such as "roadside wilderness" that conflicted with a vision of a primeval landscape untouched by human intervention.[42]

Led by Howard Zahniser and other purists, the nationwide campaign for the creation of a separate wilderness system began in earnest in the mid-1950s, but it was not until the new conservation in 1964 that the National Wilderness Preservation System was established by Congress. Federally designated wilderness areas grew from an initial 9 million acres to more than 100 million acres of public lands. President Lyndon B. Johnson signed the Wilderness Act the same day (September 15, 1964) as the same time that he executed the LWCF. At the time, most conservationists considered the LWCF as an afterthought relative to the significance of the Wilderness Act, which presented additional difficulties for the NPS.[43]

> Of all the federal bureaus the NPS operated under a mandate that was by far the most closely allied with the goals expressed in the Wilderness Act. Logically, then, the Service might have been expected to seize this opportunity to advance the principle of preserving huge tracts of public land in a wilderness, or unimpaired, condition, whether or not in national parks. . . . The NPS chose to be territorial rather than to commit to the principle of greater wilderness preservation. In truth, its deepest commitment was to another principle: to ensure public enjoyment of the parks.[44]

Bureau of Outdoor Recreation

As conceived of and created in 1962, the BOR had pan-agency responsibilities for the planning, coordination, and research associated with the creation of a National Recreation Plan.[45] It served as staff to the Recreation Advisory Council (RAC), established by Executive Order 11017, and endeavored to devise a separate and distinct mission as a non-land management agency from that of the NPS, which had a "primary purpose" management approach, or its traditional rival in the public recreation field, the U.S. Forest Service, with its "multiple use" approach to landscape conservation. At its first meeting in 1962, the RAC focused on diverse topics, such as user fees for federal facilities, the public health benefits of recreation, the availability of surplus military property, and the impact of scenic parkway construction.[46]

The RAC worked to define the characteristics of National Recreation Areas, which, in theory, were to be easily accessible to large urban centers and comprise 10,000 to 25,000 acres with a high recreational carrying capacity.[47] Late in the process, the NPS unsuccessfully challenged the definition, arguing that certain proposed areas, such as at Whiskeytown, California, were user and population focused, while other areas, like at Oregon Dunes, Oregon were more resource and conservation oriented. Outstanding recreational areas—like historic sites and areas of natural and scenic beauty—were not always located conveniently to population centers or interstate highways.[48] Here, the NPS attempted to preserve the distinctiveness of its own management approach, which enabled public enjoyment without impairment of the nationally significant resources. Logical additions to existing national parks and the URA's open space grant program were excluded from consideration as National Recreation Areas. In fact, as the first director of the BOR, Edward Crafts, revealed at the1963 meeting of the National Park System Advisory Board (NPSAB): "The creation of this Bureau did not come easily, I do not think the National Park Service was too happy to have it created, and I know the Forest Service was most unhappy about it." Not surprisingly, administrators within the two bureaus disagreed strongly regarding the criteria for establishing new National Recreation Areas.[49]

Never an enthusiast for outdoor recreation, except for sailing and shoreline stewardship, President John Kennedy relied on Secretary of the Interior Stewart Udall to help define the shape of the "New Frontier" in conservation. Following the principal recommendation from the ORRRC reports, the administration worked with Congress to craft a new mechanism for funding the acquisition of park lands and other protected spaces.[50] Conrad Wirth's 1962 memorandum (Appendix 5.1) set forth the basic premise that those families who enjoyed the inspirational and invigorating benefits of public recreational areas and other open spaces would be willing to help fund their stewardship. Support for the fund would come from congressional appropriations and from the profits from the sale of surplus federal property, entrance fees at certain federal recreation areas, and a surcharge on motorboat fuel sales. To demonstrate their support for conservation, individuals could display a LWCF sticker (purchased for $7 annually) on their automobile that would permit entrance to recreational areas. As originally designed, the LWCF was a temporary federal assistance program that would sunset in 25 years, with 60 percent of the monies targeted for states and the remainder set aside for certain federal agencies. Once created by the Congress, the BOR immediately began to publicize components of the LWCF, which was predicted to generate about $140 million each year.[51]

In 1965 the sticker program raised $2 million, surplus property sales added $27 million, and the motorboat fuel tax produced almost $17 million in funds, for a total of less than $50 million, less than one third of the projected income. Clearly new sources of funding were necessary if the LWCF were to successfully support land acquisition programs at the federal, state, and local levels. Since 1970 revenues from extractive mineral leases on sections of the country's outer continental shelf have provided more than 80 percent of the appropriated LWCF funds.[52]

Land and Water Conservation Fund

Implementation of the LWCF had the immediate impact of creating potential conflict with the Urban Renewal Administration's existing program of urban open space acquisition (see Chapter 4).[53] The obvious solution was to define the administrative priorities for each program—a process that involved establishing boundaries, whether urban, suburban, or rural spaces. The URA was directed to focus on squares, malls, and playgrounds, as well as smaller parks, recreation areas, historic sites, and scenic open spaces. The new LWCF program would work on "lands for larger regional parks, historic sites, and recreational and scenic areas" for use in urban, suburban, and rural areas. One third of these grant funds were set aside for the physical development of existing recreational resources, while the remaining two thirds supported the acquisition of new properties and the augmentation of existing protected areas. Initially the two agencies agreed to share information about incoming grant proposals from state and local governments and to coordinate their reviews. Signed in mid-1965, Executive Order 11237, directed BOR and URA administrators to cooperate, rather than compete, in channeling federal funds to local communities. In fact, President Johnson gave both programs an administrative back door, allowing them to depart from the general restrictions of the executive order if unusual circumstances presented an opportunity to better serve local interests.[54]

To assist states in the mandatory preparation of Statewide Comprehensive Outdoor Recreation Plans (SCORPs), the BOR created a land classification system with six categories (Appendix 5.1). Although all 50 states prepared SCORPs from 1965–1981, the conservation of historic properties was clearly not the focus of the LWCF. Class VI lands, areas of historic, scientific or archaeological significance, were seated on the periphery in the program's criteria for acquisition. While the identification, acquisition, and development of nationally significant historic sites was specifically enumerated as a federal responsibility, no such mandate was handed down to state and local government for less significant sites. The focus was on open space, shorelines and undeveloped parcels. Funding could be used to acquire buildings, but only if they were going to be used primarily to support outdoor recreation activities, or were slated for demolition or removal. Moreover, purchasing historic properties was specifically called out as inappropriate and unacceptable if the principal interest was in the architectural or historical values and the building could not otherwise contribute to outdoor recreation activities. On the federal side of the LWCF, Class VI lands (3,314 acres) accounted for 6.9 percent of acquisitions by the NPS, which totaled 48,000 acres proposed in fiscal year 1967 and only 1.2 percent of all federal land acquisitions.[55]

By the early 1970s, the BOR land classification system was considered outdated and confusing, especially because of complications generated by the Wilderness Act in 1964. In 1973 proposals called for dropping Class VI: Historical and Cultural Sites because these types of properties were already enumerated by the NPS and were outside of the natural scheme of things. Class VI was renamed "Non-recreational Lands" with no outdoor recreational uses, a label that surely reflected a pejorative attitude toward historic properties in recreational land-use decision making.[56]

In the early 1960s American historic preservation practice was not so well developed that the concept of creative adaptive uses for historic properties could extend to the repurposing of extant buildings to support outdoor recreation activities. BOR guidance acknowledged the need for signage and interpretive structures to identify historic features, and it permitted the construction of "simple exhibit rooms" to display outstanding natural, historical, or scientific artifacts. The rules also permitted the renovation of impaired or outmoded facilities to an appropriate standard of suitable quality and attractiveness, but adaptive use of historic buildings was not highlighted or encouraged.[57] Despite these administrative limitations, the funding potential represented by the LWCF was so attractive that the national historic preservation movement tried to creatively access this line of grant support for state and local projects.

Consideration of Historic Sites

Embracing the mandate as the principal federal historic preservation agency since the early 1930s, the NPS faced a variety of challenges during the early 1960s as programs directed by other agencies began to severely impact historic properties across the country. At a special conference on historic preservation in 1964, Ronald Lee devoted a half day to the activities of other federal agencies: leading off with the question: "Is the BOR involved in historic preservation?" BOR grants were never designed to directly support historic preservation projects, though the "protection of the environment of historic properties" was an eligible activity.[58] The BOR refused to evaluate values associated with historical and archaeological sites found within proposed National Recreation Areas, leaving that task, as a matter of courtesy, to the NPS. The BOR also questioned the mandate for the NPS to offer technical advice and assistance for historic preservation projects.[59] For its part the NPS fought the BOR's attempts to consider historic properties as second-class recreational assets. Recreation at historic sites was generally a passive activity of observation, interpretation, and inspiration—poorly suited for the active and profitable leisure envisioned by the recreation movement. Perhaps naively, given contemporary problems with convincing the URA of the value of historic preservation, private-sector preservation groups were enthusiastic about including historic properties as an essential component of recreation area planning. In 1963, noting that initial reports "gave history a good place" within the new program, the recently retired NPS architect Charles Peterson mobilized the American Institute of Architects historic preservation committee to offer its support for the BOR.[60]

The NPS worked to ensure that historical resources were not forgotten as the states began to develop recreational plans during the mid-1960s in response to funding available through the LWCF. NPS historian Robert Utley saw the LWCF as a potential funding mechanism for historic preservation projects—the Department of the Interior recommended that states enumerate historical and archaeological sites as part of their statewide recreational plans.

Figure 5.3 Betterton Beach, Kent County, Maryland. At parks and playgrounds across the country, signs like this one in Kent County, Maryland illustrate the wide range of agencies at all levels of government involved in the creation of recreational infrastructure. Installation of such signs was an important part of recognizing the important role of the LWCF.

Source: Kent County Parks and Recreation

NPS planners did review Statewide Comprehensive Outdoor Recreation Plans as part of the LWCF grant process but requests to highlight (or even recognize) the presence of National Historic and Natural Landmarks were never implemented (Sidebar 5.3). With the expansion of the National Register of Historic Places in 1966, the BOR agreed to require that all future statewide recreation plans include a list of National Register–listed properties.[61]

In the late 1960s, Ronald Lee, in his role as a special assistant to NPS Director George Hartzog, looked back at parts of the ORRRC reports and was impressed with the emphasis that had been given to cultural properties, both natural and historic. "Wouldn't there be ample justification," reflected Lee, "for expending Land and Water Conservation Fund money for acquisition of historic properties?[62] The issue, of course, was how to include historic properties within the definition of outdoor recreation. While the legal experts at the BOR were certain that the acquisition and rehabilitation of historic buildings was not a legitimate expense for LWCF support, the historic preservation community believed that it was more of a question of policy rather than of law. Clearly there was some room for compromise. As noted by Fred Jones,

> In the past we [at BOR were] . . . pretty liberal in interpreting historic sites for preservation in terms of outdoor recreation attributes. We

dressed some purely historical projects up with picnic tables, etc., so that there would be outdoor recreation benefits.[63]

Like NPS officials, the wider historic preservation community embraced the LWCF's potential, both as a source of funding and as a model for what would become the Historic Preservation Fund (HPF). Grants to communities in nine states were highlighted in the May 1, 1969 issue of the National Trust for Historic Preservation's (NTHP) *Preservation News*.[64] Dinosaur State Park, Connecticut, a National Natural Landmark received funding to preserve an 80-acre parcel where more than 250 species of Mesozoic dinosaurs had left footprints, which had been recently discovered as the result of a construction project. At Whitestone Hill, North Dakota, where in 1863 the U.S. Army attacked a village occupied by Yanktonai, Santee, and Teton (Lakota) Sioux Indians, the state historical society used a LWCF grant to construct picnic shelters and bathrooms. Federal funding helped purchase six acres of land that provided improved access to the Chief Plenty Coups State Park in Pryor, Montana. In most cases the historic qualities of the grant recipients were ancillary to the property's recreational potential. In the first five years of its operation, only 1 percent of the $250 million in LWCF funding distributed to the states had gone to historical and cultural properties.[65]

Sidebar 5.3   National Natural Landmarks

"Taking a leaf" from the recently enhanced National Historic Landmark program, in 1964 Secretary Udall established a National Natural Landmark program.[66] In 1965, at the same meeting in which it redefined the criteria for National Historic Landmarks, the NPSAB set forth its vision and policy for the identification, evaluation and recognition of natural landmarks. As the program got started, more than 100 sites were evaluated as meeting the designation criteria. The National Natural Landmark program was a consequence of the growing vision of park and other protected areas as laboratories for long-term research in the natural sciences. As with the identification of historic landmarks, the program followed a thematic framework that presented a comprehensive view of the continent's natural history.[67] Once the criteria were approved (see Appendix 5.3), the first group of designated National Natural Landmarks (NNLs) included Corkscrew Swamp Sanctuary, Florida (6,080 acres); Rancho La Brea–Hancock Park, California; Elder Creek, California (3,000 acres); Fontenelle Forest, Nebraska (1,500 acres); and Ramsey Canyon, Arizona (280 acres). Illustrating the growing interest in ecology and landscapes, this program was followed by NEED (National Environmental Education Development) in 1968 and by NEEL (National Environmental Education Landmarks) in 1971. Both were shot lived endeavors.[68]

The historic preservation movement was recast with the passage of the National Historic Preservation Act in 1966. Prior to the Act there had been no federal agency charged with providing financial assistance to state or local community historic preservation projects.[69] An example of President Johnson's creative federalism, the National Historic Preservation Act expanded the mandate for the National Register of Historic Places to include sites of state and local historical significance, as well as those of national importance, and it established a grants-in-aid program to restore historic properties within their jurisdictions. With two sources of potential funding, the bureaucrats in the BOR and the NPS had to develop criteria covering how each agency would view projects that had both recreational and historical value.[70]

The National Historic Preservation Act grant program was initially funded on an annual basis, from 1967 to 1976, and many of the early grants went to the NTHP. In 1977 grants-in-aid to State Historic Preservation Offices were supported through the HPF, which, like the LWCF, also used monies generated through receipts from oil and natural gas leases on the outer continental shelf. Pressure to use LWCF funds to support preservation projects relaxed after 1976, although the congressional appropriation (or authorization) for the HPF has never approached the levels established for the LWCF. Unlike the LWCF, HPF grants could not be used to acquire historic properties—the focus was on preservation, restoration, or rehabilitation.[71]

Expanding America's Outdoor Recreation Estate

The LWCF had considerable success during its first three years of operation (January 1965–January 1968). As the end of the Johnson administration approached, the BOR published *Expanding America's Outdoor Recreation Estate*.[72] More than $214 million of federal funding had been matched by the states to acquire recreational lands, and more than $130 million had been allocated for the use by federal agencies to purchase parcels (more than 300,000 acres in total) at national parks, forests, and refuges. Reflecting bureaucratic cooperation with the URA, less than one third of the 3,319 state and local government grants funded projects in urban areas. Only 5 percent of the funding was used to assist in developing on-site, historical, natural, and cultural programs. Less than 1 percent of the state and local property acquisition grants were used for "interpretive" properties, such as historic sites. Amendments in the late 1960s and early 1970s expanded the overall LWCF appropriation to $200 million annually.[73]

The administrators who created the LWCF borrowed a land use planning concept the URA's urban open space grant program: conversions. Section 6(f) of the Land and Water Conservation Fund Act contained provisions to protect federal investments in the acquisition and development of recreational resources. Although not formally protected by legal instruments such as easements, any site that had been acquired, developed, or improved using LWCF funds had to be open to the general public and maintained in perpetuity for public outdoor recreation. LWCF properties could be converted to other uses only if the Department of the Interior approved the substitution of "reasonably equivalent recreational facilities."[74] For example, 207 acres of the Creve Coeur Memorial Lake Park in St. Louis, Missouri were converted for use by the extension of Page Avenue (Route MO-364, a 10-lane-wide limited access highway) across the parklands. Originally conceived in the late 1960s, this controversial project impacted the oldest public park in St. Louis and included the construction of a large bridge across the southern end of the park and lake area. From 1971 to 1983 $2.3 million from the LWCF had been used to acquire 744 acres of parkland. Initially, Secretary of the Interior Bruce Babbit felt that the substitute parcels offered by the project proponents met the "reasonably equivalent usefulness and location" standard, but further analysis and negotiations increased the replacement property area to more than 720 acres valued at about $3.4 million. The project was completed in 2003 after a complex plan of activities that mitigated the impacts of the proposed highway were approved by a variety of consulting parties.[75] As the LWCF program passed its 50th anniversary, the land-use conversion process was further complicated now that the parklands preserved (in perpetuity) by early program grants have themselves reached possible historic status.

Although the LWCF had been conceived of by Congress as a temporary program, by 1981 some $2.45 billion had been obligated for state and federal land acquisition projects and statewide planning activities, providing funding over 27,000 separate projects.[76] In 1990, at the quarter-century mark—when it was supposed to sunset—the LWCF had had provided $7.3 billion for the acquisition of 3.5 million acres of new federally owned recreational lands that comprised the core of more than 50 new national park units. Nearly three quarters of a million acres had been added to the national wildlife refuge program. Through the execution of some 35,000 grants, state and local governments received funding for the protection of 2.3 million recreational acres.[77]

Supporters of the LWCF took advantage of the program's quarter century of operation to reflect on its accomplishments, as well as its future challenges. Henry Diamond, who had worked on the ORRRC and served as the executive director of the 1965 White House Conference on Natural Beauty recalled the "series of ironies" that had shaped the program's success: the continuing crisis of adequate funding, the federal/state apportionment competition, and the absence of a sustained political constituency. From Diamond's perspective, for good and bad, the focus of this conservation program was on the land: "if we had done right by the land in the first place, if we had a broader land acquisition program and a modest land use control program" many of the environmental problems facing the United States at the end of the 20th century would have been reduced in scope and severity. Statistics that elucidate the success of the LWCF abound; but in the final analysis, not enough land was set aside to ensure that the country's growing urban population would have viable access to sufficient recreational facilities.[78]

Recreation and Restoration

The word "recreation" is defined as "to refresh or enliven" the mind, spirit, or person by some pastime, amusement, or occupation. Given this, the human need for recreation suggests that there has been a declension in one's mind, body, or spirit. In much the same way, the historic preservation concept of restoration elicits the idea of retuning an object, interior, building, structure, or landscape to its former unimpaired state.[79] As noted by Margaret Mead, perhaps recreation and the historic preservation practice of rehabilitation are more closely aligned, in that they envision the continuing use of a space toward new utility: a floodplain along a river is transformed into soccer or baseball fields, or a canal-side lock keeper's cottage lives on as a gift shop. Despite these similarities, the post–World War II recreation movement rarely embraced the historic preservation movement that emerged with the establishment of the NTHP in the late 1940s. The educational and inspirational values of historic properties were not viewed as central to the recreational activities that were designed to address the profitable use of an expanding leisure culture. Although both were bureaucratically transformed with advent of the new conservation of the 1960s, the LWCF and what would later become the HPF supported fundamentally different systems of protected lands management. Where LWCF acquired ballfields that could be converted to other uses, as the needs of a community changed over time, one rehabilitated historic property could not be exchanged for another. As applied by the stateside portion of the LWCF program, this approach might be considered generational, as opposed to the perpetual uses mandated for properties managed by the NPS. Perpetual stewardship follows the agency's mandate to preserve resources unimpaired for future generations as well as the frozen-in-time approach to the restoration of historic properties and their use as house museums, which dominated the preservation movement until the 1960s. Of course, the adaptive use conventions of the new preservation embraced the concept of conversion, to a limited degree, while retaining a property's historical characteristics. Seated within the new administrative structure that was the BOR, the LWCF would face fiscal challenges, as would its less-well-funded cousin the HPF, which would point toward new forms of limited ownership (easements) that were designed to enhance the perpetual protection of the American landscape.

Notes

1. For descriptive summary statistics of the LWCF program see: Donald Helmann, "The National Park Service at 100," *Akron Law Review*, Vol. 50 (June 2017), p. 28. Since 1965, more than $3.6 billion in grants for the acquisition and development of local and regional facilities (contained within 40,000 projects) were matched dollar for dollar from state and local sources. In addition, $4.5 billion was directed to the acquisition of new lands incorporated into the national park system. Total investment for the recreational estate over five decades was $11.7 billion.

2. Raleigh Barlowe and Milton H. Steinmueller, "Trends in Outdoor Recreation," in *A Place to Live: 1963 Yearbook of Agriculture* (Washington, DC: GPO, 1963), pp. 299–303.
3. Meredith Wilson began work on *The Music Man* in 1948, with a Broadway debut in 1957, followed by a film version in 1962.
4. George Cutten, *The Threat of Leisure* (New Haven: Yale University Press, 1929); Arthur Pack, *The Challenge of Leisure* (New York: Macmillan, 1936).
5. See: Abbie Condit, "A National Congress," *The Journal of Education*, Vol. 96, No. 1 (2387) (July 6, 1922), p. 8. Review: "The Recreation Movement," *The School Review*, Vol. 28, No. 5 (May 1920), p. 394. See Richard Knapp and Charles Hartsoe, *Play for America: The National Recreation Association, 1906–1965* (Arlington, Virginia: National Recreation and Park Association, 1979). For more on the increase in leisure time and the subsequent growth in tourism in the postwar period, see Cindy Aron, *Working at Play: A History of Vacations in the United States* (New York: Oxford University Press, 1999); Hal Rothman, *Devil's Bargain: Tourism in the Twentieth-Century American West* (Lawrence: University Press of Kansas, 2000); Susan Sessions Rugh, *Are We There Yet? The Golden Age of American Family Vacation* (Lawrence: University Press of Kansas, 2008).
6. Rupert Hughes, "You Can Cure Your Own Unemployment by Using Leisure for Self-Improvement." *New York American,* February 8, 1931. Hughes recommended that the unemployed could "use slack times to read, study, [and] widen your mental horizons" thus turning "idleness into profit."
7. Verna Rensvold, Beatrice H. Hill, Elizabeth M. Boggs, and Martin W. Meyer, "Therapeutic Recreation," *The Annals of the American Academy of Political and Social Science*, Vol. 313, Recreation in the Age of Automation (September 1957), pp. 87–91; Jeffrey Pilz, "The Beginnings of Organized Play for Black America: E.T. Attwell and the PRAA," *The Journal of Negro History*, Vol. 70, No. 3/4 (Summer–Autumn 1985), pp. 59–72; Eva Mitchel, "Adult Health Education and Recreational Programs: National, State, and Local," *The Journal of Negro Education*, Vol. 14, No. 3, Adult Education for Negroes in the United States (Summer 1945), pp. 363–373.
8. Ott Romney, "What Place Should the Federal Government Assume in the Total Recreation Program?" *The Journal of Educational Sociology*, Vol. 21, No. 5 (January 1948), pp. 301–307.
9. T.H. Watkins, *Righteous Pilgrim: The Life and Times of Harold L. Ickes, 1874–1953* (New York: Harvey Holt & Co., 1990), p. 583.
10. An Act to Authorize a Study of the Park, Parkway and Recreational Area Programs in the United States, and for other purposes, Approved June 23, 1936 (49 Stat. 1894). Established in June 1934 by President Franklin Roosevelt's Executive Order 6777, the National Resources Board issued "Recreational Use of Land in the United States" in November 1934. See: Linda McCelland, *Building the National Parks: Historic Landscape Design and Construction* (Baltimore: Johns Hopkins University Press, 1998), pp. 421–424.
11. "Aid in Providing the People of the United States with Adequate Facilities for Park, Parkway and Recreational-Area Purposes, etc.," House Report No. 486, April 4, 1935. The report consists of a letter from Secretary of the Interior Harold Ickes to Representative Rene DeRouen, April 3, 1935. See also: "Public Parks, Parkways, and Recreational Areas," Senate Report No. 1547, January 16, 1936, which contains a letter from Secretary Ickes to Senator Robert Wagner, March 2, 1935; "Aid in Providing the People of the United States with Adequate Facilities for Park, Parkway and Recreational-Area Purposes and to Provide for the Transfer of Certain Lands Chiefly Valuable for such Purposes to States and Political Subdivisions thereof," House Report 1914, January 15, 1936; "Public Parks, Parkways and Recreational Areas," Senate Report No. 1694, February 24, 1936.
12. Harlan D. Unrau and G. Frank Williss, *Administrative History: Expansion of the National Park Service in the 1930s,* NPS, September 1983. Chapter 4, "New Initiatives in the Field of Recreation and Recreational Area Development," details the nationwide

study of recreational services. Janet McDonnell, "Far-Reaching Effects: The United States Military and the National Parks during World War II," *The George Wright Forum*, Vol. 32, No. 1 (2015).

13. NPS, *A Study of Park and Recreation Problem of the United States* (Washington, DC: NPS, 1941), pp. 7, 22: "On the other hand, the development of suburbs, of satellite cities, of garden cities, is somewhat modifying the ill effects of too intensive urban development."

14. *A Study of Park and Recreation Problem of the United States* (NPS, 1941), pp. 123-130

15. The plan was included in: A Study of Park and Recreation Problem of the United States (NPS, 1941). Harlan D. Unrau and G. Frank Williss, *Administrative History: Expansion of the National Park Service in the 1930s,* NPS, September 1983. Chapter 4, "New Initiatives in the Field of Recreation and Recreational Area Development."

16. "Speech by Roosevelt, Two Medicine Chalet, Glacier National Park, August 5, 1934," in Edgar Nixon, ed., *Franklin D. Roosevelt & Conservation, 1911–1945* (Hyde Park: Franklin D. Roosevelt Library, 1957), pp. 321–324.

17. NPS, *Administration Manual for Recreational Demonstration Areas* (Washington, DC: NPS, 1941).

18. Quoted in: Richard Sellars, *Preserving Nature in the National Parks: A History* (New Haven: Yale University Press, 1997), p. 143.

19. *Expansion of the National Park Service in the 1930s: Administrative History.* Chapter 4: "New Initiatives in the Field of Recreation and Recreational Area Development."

20. Located less than 35 miles south of Washington, DC, and encompassing more than 14,000 acres, Chopawamsic Recreational Demonstration Area was created to support organizational camping by a variety of religious, social, and educational groups. Angela Sirna, "Tracing a Lineage of Social Reform Programs at Catoctin Mountain Park," *The Public Historian*, Vol. 38, No. 4 (November 2016), pp. 167–189.

21. Linda McClelland, *Building the National Parks: Historic Landscape Design and Construction* (Baltimore: Johns Hopkins University Press, 1998), pp. 414–420.

22. NPS, *A Study of Park and Recreation Problem of the United States* (Washington, DC: NPS, 1941), p. 52.

23. NPS, *A Study of Park and Recreation Problem of the United States* (Washington, DC: NPS, 1941), p. 9.

24. NPS, *A Study of Park and Recreation Problem of the United States* (Washington, DC: NPS, 1941), p. 18. Hal Rothman, ed., *The Culture of Tourism, the Tourism of Culture: Selling the Past to the Present in the American Southwest* (Albuquerque: University of New Mexico Press, 2003), Rothman distinguishes between cultural tourism and recreational and entertainment tourism.

25. Linda McClelland, *Building the National Parks: Historic Landscape Design and Construction* (Baltimore: Johns Hopkins University Press, 1998), p. 422. Reginald Isaacs, "Educational, Cultural, and Recreational Services," *The Annals of the American Academy of Political and Social Science*, Vol. 242, Building the Future City (November 1945), pp. 129–138.

26. Linda McClelland, *Building the National Parks: Historic Landscape Design and Construction* (Baltimore, Maryland: Johns Hopkins University Press, 1998), pp. 414–420.

27. Donald Swain, "The National Park Service and the New Deal, 1933–1940," *Pacific Historical Review*, Vol. 41, No. 3 (August 1972), pp. 324–325.

28. Roy Wolfe, "Perspective on Outdoor Recreation: A Bibliographical Survey," *Geographical Review*, Vol. 54, No. 2 (April 1964), pp. 203–238. Robert Gotlieb, *Forcing the Spring: The Transformation of the American Environmental Movement* (Washington, DC: Island Press, 2005), pp. 73–76; Mark Dowie, *Losing Ground: American Environmentalism at the Close of the Twentieth Century* (Cambridge: The MIT Press, 1995).

29. Russell Whitaker, Review of: *The Nation Looks at Its Resources: Report of the Mid-Century Conference on Resources for the Future* (Washington, DC: Resources for the Future, 1954) in *The Annals of the American Academy of Political and Social Science*, Vol. 299 (May 1955), pp. 165–166. Marion Clawson, *The Federal Lands since 1956* (Washington,

DC: Resources for the Future, 1968); Marion Clawson and Burnell Held, *The Federal Lands: Their Use and Management* (Washington, DC: Resources for the Future, 1957); *The Nation Looks at Its Resources: Report of the Mid-Century Conference on Resources for the Future* (Washington, DC: Resources for the Future, 1954). John Ise, *Our National Park Policy: A Critical History* (Baltimore: Resources for the Future, 1961).

30. Ethan Carr, *Mission 66: Modernism and the National Park Dilemma* (Amherst: University of Massachusetts Press, 2007).

31. Roy Appleman, *A History of the National Park Service Mission 66 Program* (Washington, DC: NPS, January 1958), pp. 28–29, 31–32. NPS, *Mission Progress Report* (Washington, DC: NPS, March 1966), p. 2. The NPS saw any national recreation plan as the fulfillment of the 1936 Parks, Parkway, and Recreation Area Study Act.

32. NPS, Mission 66 Report (Washington, DC: NPS, September 1955), pp. 40–43. While the agency admitted that some segments of American history were "too generously represented" or "lacked sufficient justification for retention" within the park system, but it was unwilling to recommend the disposal of existing parks. Richard Sellars, *Preserving Nature in the National Parks: A History* (New Haven: Yale University Press, 1997), p. 203.

33. Ethan Carr, *Mission 66: Modernism and the National Park Dilemma* (Amherst: University of Massachusetts Press, 2007), pp. 303–310. "A Bill for the Establishment of a National Outdoor Recreation Resources Review Commission," Hearing before the Senate Committee on Interior and Insular Affairs, 85th Congress, First Session, May 15, 1957. The NPS testified (pg. 14) that the mandate to prepare a comprehensive survey of existing recreational resources was in line with the goals of the Historic Sites Act of 1935 and the Parks, Parkways and Recreational Areas Study Act of 1936. *America's Heritage: Proceedings of a Symposium on the 25th Anniversary of the Land and Water Conservation Fund* (Washington, DC: National Recreation and Park Association, 1990), p. 15.

34. George Siehl, "The Policy Path to the Great Outdoors: A History of the Outdoor Recreation Review Commissions," Resources for the Future, October 2008. "Statement of Miss Harlean James, Secretary, American Planning and Civic Association," pp. 43–48 in "A Bill for the Establishment of a National Outdoor Recreation Resources Review Commission," Hearing before the Senate Committee on Interior and Insular Affairs, 85th Congress, First Session, May 15, 1957. Conrad Wirth, "Foreword," in NPS, *Our Vanishing Shoreline* (Washington, DC: Government Printing Office, 1955). Summary Minutes, Recreation Advisory Council, December 18, 1962. RG 268 HCRS General Correspondence, 1962–1971, Box 1. Paul Sutter, *Driven Wild: How the Fight against Automobiles Launched the Modern Wilderness Movement* (Seattle: University of Washington Press, 2002), pp. 258–259.

35. ORRRC, *Outdoor Recreation for America* (Washington, DC: GPO, 1962). For coverage of the ORRRC report and creation of BOR in *The Washington Post* see: "Vast Park Expansion Urged in Report," February 1, 1962; "Outdoor Recreation Needs," February 2, 1962; Julius Duscha, "President Asks Park Taxes to Expand System," March 2, 1962; "ORRRC Survey Called 'Glittering Blunder'," March 30, 1962; Julius Duscha, "Old Rivalries Put Aside at Ceremony for New Outdoor Bureau's Director," April 3, 1962; "Sanction Sought for Outdoor Plan," May 13, 1962; Louis Cassels, "Most of our Recreation Land Is Where the People Aren't," August 1962.

36. Margaret Mead, "Outdoor Recreation in the Context of Emerging American Cultural Values: Background Considerations," ORRRC, July 15, 1961. George Siehl, "The Policy Path to the Great Outdoors: A History of the Outdoor Recreation Review Commissions," Resources for the Future, October 2008, p. 3. ORRRC produced 27 volumes of "study reports." George Siehl, "US Recreation Policies Since World War II," in William Gartner and David Lime, eds., *Trends in Outdoor Recreation, Leisure, and Tourism* (Cambridge: CABI Publishing, 2000), pp. 92–96.

37. The Wild and Scenic Rivers Act (P.L. 90–542) and the National Trails Act (P.L. 90–543) were both enacted in 1968. Chief, Office of Legislation to Director, "Drafting Service for Congressman Widnall," October 9, 1963. NPS PHP Files.

38. S. Herbert Evison, *The National Park Service: Conservator of America's Scenic and Historic Heritage* (unpublished and unpaginated manuscript, 1964), "Conrad Wirth as Director." Evison estimated that 1963 funding was more than $140 million.

39. "Bills to Promote the Coordination and Development of Effective Federal and State Programs Relating to Outdoor Recreation and to Provide Financial Assistance to the States for Outdoor Recreation Planning," Hearing before the House Committee on Interior and Insular Affairs, 87th Congress, Second Session, July 9–10; "Policies, Programs, and Activities of the Department of the Interior," Hearing before the House Committee on Interior and Insular Affairs, 88th Congress, First Session, January 31 –February 11, 1963; "A Bill to Promote the Coordination and Development of Effective Federal and State Programs Relating to Outdoor Recreation," Hearing before the Senate Committee on Interior and Insular Affairs, 88th Congress, First Session, February 5, 1963; "Supplemental Appropriation Bill, 1963," Hearings before the House Committee on Appropriations, 88th Congress, First Session, March 19–27, 1963.

40. Roderick Nash, "The American Invention of National Parks," *American Quarterly*, Vol. 22, No. 3 (Autumn 1970), pp. 726–735. See also: Roderick Nash, *Wilderness and the American Mind* (New Haven, CT: Yale University Press, 1967; revised 1973); NPS, "The Wilderness Act at 40," *Common Ground* (Fall 2004).

41. For more on the wilderness movement, see Paul Sutter, *Driven Wild: How the Fight Against Automobiles Launched the Modern Wilderness Movement* (Seattle: University of Washington Press, 2002); David Louter, *Windshield Wilderness: Cars, Roads, and Nature in Washington's National Parks* (Seattle and London: University of Washington Press, 2006). James Morton Turner, *The Promise of Wilderness: American Environmental Politics Since 1964* (Seattle: University of Washington Press, 2012); William Cronon, "The Trouble with Wilderness: or, Getting Back to the Wrong Nature," in William Cronon, ed., *Uncommon Ground: Rethinking the Human Place in Nature* (New York: W. W. Norton & Co., 1995), pp. 69–90.

42. Ronald Lee, Public Use of the National Park System, 1872–2000 (Washington, DC: NPS, 1968), p. 5. Ethan Carr, *Mission 66: Modernism and the National Park Dilemma* (Amherst: University of Massachusetts Press, 2007), pp. 28 and 268–275; Howard Stanger, *The National Park Wilderness* (Washington, DC: GPO, 1957).

43. The Wilderness Society, The Wilderness Act Handbook (Washington, DC: The Wilderness Society, 2004).Sara Dant, "LBJ, Wilderness and the Land and Water Conservation Fund," *Forest History Today* (Spring/Fall 2014), pp. 16–21.

44. Richard Sellars, *Preserving Nature in the National Parks: A History* (New Haven: Yale University Press, 1997), p. 193.

45. Prior to the creation of BOR, the URA supported local and statewide recreational planning as part of the Housing and Home Finance Agency (HHFA)'s Section 701 program. HHFA to Federal Inter-Agency Committee on Recreation, 12 Feb 1960. HHFA, "The Federal Urban Planning Assistance Program as an Aid to the Planning of Public Recreation Facilities," March 7, 1960. RG 368 HCRS Chronological Files, 1961–1963.

46. "Policies, Programs, and Activities of the Department of the Interior, Hearings before the Committee on Interior and Insular Affairs," House of Representatives, 88th Congress, First Session, Government Printing Office, Washington, February 7, 1963, pp. 207–221.Summary Minutes, Recreation Advisory Council, July 12, 1962. RG 368 HCRS General Correspondence, 1962–1971, Box 1.

47. Recreation Advisory Council, "Federal Executive Branch Policy Governing the Selection, Establishment, and Administration of National Recreation Areas," March 10, 1963; "Guidelines for the Selection of National Outdoor Recreation Areas," November 7, 1962. RG 263 HCRS General Correspondence 1962–1971, Box 1.

48. Conrad Wirth to Edward Crafts, "Proposed Policy Circular No. 1, Federal Executive Branch Policy, Governing the Selection, Establishment, and Administration of National Recreation Areas," February 7, 1963. RG 368 HCRS General

Correspondence 1962–1971, Box 1. Predicting that 10,000-acre NRA parcels would be impossible to identify close to urban centers, HHFA proposed that smaller discontinuous tracts might be administratively linked to meet recreational needs.

49. NPSAB, 48th Meeting Minutes, 1963, p. 24.
50. Thomas Smith, "John Kennedy, Stewart Udall, and New Frontier Conservation," *Pacific Historical Review*, Vol. 64, No. 3 (August 1995), pp. 329–362. Still working in a New Deal tradition, Smith argues (p. 329) that the administration "groped slowly and ambivalently" toward new approaches to conservation. Howard Brown, *Brief Legislative Analysis of the Land and Water Conservation Fund* (Washington, DC: Congressional Research Service, 1972); George Siehl, *The Land and Water Conservation Fund: Origin and Congressional Intent* (Washington, DC: Congressional Research Service, 1981).
51. Remarks by Heaton Underhill, Assistant Director, Bureau of Outdoor Recreation, Department of the Interior, at the Annual Meeting of the National Audubon Society, Tucson, Arizona, November 9, 1964. DOI Press Release, NPS PHP LWCF.
52. BOR, "Status of Land and Water Conservation Fund," 1965. RG368 HCRS BOR LWCF 68–69, Box 2. The report listed more than $4 million from "other" undefined sources that raised the total LWCF in 1965 to $50,134, 285. "The Crisis in the Land and Water Conservation Fund," Congressional Record, H11982-H111987, September 18, 1967. The Granville Corporation, *Study of Land and Water Conservation Fund Financial Assistance Alternatives* (Washington, DC: Heritage Conservation and Recreation Service, 1981), p. 8. In 1980 the LCWF received more than 30 percent of the total revenues from outer continental shelf mineral leases.
53. Joint HHFA Interior Study: Long-Range Program and Policy for Open Space & Orderly Development in Urban Area, 1961.
54. Executive Order 11237, Prescribing Regulations for Coordinating Planning and the Acquisition of Land under the Outdoor Recreation Program of the Department of the Interior and the Open Space Program of the Housing and Home Finance Agency, July 27, 1965.
55. NPS adopted this land classification system for its recreational properties. Ronald Lee, *Public Use of the National Park System, 1872–2000* (Washington, DC: NPS, 1968), p. 73. Charles Zinser, *Outdoor Recreation: United States National Parks, Forests, and Public Lands* (New York: Wiley, 1995), pp. 18–20. "Recreation Advisory Council Policy Circular No. 2: Declaration of National Outdoor Recreation Policy," May 24, 1963. RG 368 HCRS General Correspondence 1962–1971, Box 1. "Outdoor Recreation Grants-in-Aid Manual," Bureau of Outdoor Recreation, 1965. Summary of Land Acquisition Program (L&WCF) by Federal Agencies F.Y. 1967 according to BOR Land Classifications, October 25, 1965. RG 368 HCRS BOR LWCF 68–69 Box 2. NPS accounted for only 18.4 percent of federal acquisitions using LWCF support.
56. Nationwide Outdoor Recreation Plan: Work Group J Report, Federal Recreation Management Criteria and Organization, Preliminary Draft, for Review Only, January 3, 1973. In time, three national plans were produced: *The Recreation Imperative* (completed 1970 but released in 1974); *Outdoor Recreation: A Legacy for America* (1973); and, *The Third Nationwide Outdoor Recreation Plan* (1979).
57. "Outdoor Recreation Grants-in-Aid Manual," BOR, 1965.
58. "Special Conference on Historic Preservation," NPS Northeast Region, Philadelphia, PA, November 16–19, 1964. NPS WASO PHP Subject Files. Robert Rettig, *Conserving the Man-Made Environment: Planning for the Protection of Historic and Cultural Resources in the United States* (Washington, DC: NPS, September 1, 1975), p. 50.
59. Lawrence Stevens, Acting Director, BOR, "Memorandum 64–2: BOR Participation in Studies Relating to History and Archeology," July 18, 1963. NPS Park History Subject Files. John Littleton to Assistant Director, Resource Studies, "Clarification of Technical Advice and Assistance to Landmark Owners," February 8, 1966. NPS WASO PHP Subject Files.

60. Charles Peterson to Robert Gaede, May 20, 1963. Robert Gaede (AIA Committee on Preservation of Historic Buildings) to Ed Crafts, BOR, May 20, 1963. UMCP CEP Box 4.
61. "Meeting Monday (1/17) at 1:00 p.m., Mr. Utley's Office, Room 2224 on Inclusion of National Historic and Natural Landmarks in the Statewide Recreation Plans." NPS PHP LWCF. Robert Utley, "An Aid Program to Non-Federal Historic Preservationists," November 4, 1964; "Statement of Robert M. Utley, Chief, Division of History Studies, National Park Service, to Historic Sites Committee, Organization of American Historians, Kansas City, Missouri, April 22, 1965." NPS NHL AB CC. Director, NPS to Director, BOR, "Inclusion of National Historic and Natural Landmarks in the Statewide Recreation Plans," November 22, 1965. V. Flickeinger, Chief, Division of Federal Agency and State Assistance, to Assistant Director, Cooperative Activities, "Review of BOR Statewide Outdoor Recreation Plans," December 21, 1965. NPS PHP LWCF. Clark Stratton, AD NPS, to Rep. John Saylor, May 27, 1965, NPS PHP LCWF. "Remarks by Lawrence Stevens, Associate Director, Bureau of Outdoor Recreation," ACHP, September 27–28, 1967. RG200 NTHP ACHP Box 4. Even so, in 1971 NPS Director George Hartzog expressed concern about the "lack of emphasis" that preservation received at the expense of recreation use within his own agency's policy statements. Director, NPS to Director, Office of Program Analysis, "1973 Recreation Use and Preservation Program Memorandum," March 1, 1973. RG 79, General Records, Appendix 4 Index Files 1949–1971, Box 61.
62. *American Association for State and Local History, Committee on Federal Programs in History, First Annual Meeting* (Washington, DC: NPS, 1968), p. 81.
63. Coordination of the LWCF program (Bureau of Outdoor Recreation) and the Historic Preservation Grant program (NPS). *American Association for State and Local History, Committee on Federal Programs in History, First Annual Meeting* (Washington, DC: NPS, 1968), pp. 74–75.
64. "Outdoor Recreation Bureau Makes Preservation Grants," *Preservation News*, Vol. 9, No. 5, May 1, 1969.
65. Bureau of Outdoor Recreation, *Five Years of Progress: The Land and Water Conservation Fund, January 1965 to January 1970* (Washington, DC: Bureau of Outdoor Recreation, 1971).
66. NPSAB CC Minutes, March 11–12, 1964. NPSAB CC Files.
67. NPSAB 48th Meeting Minutes, 1963, pp. 30–35.
68. Ronald Lee, Family Tree of the National Park System, (Washington, DC: National Park Service, 1972).
69. Deputy Assistant Secretary of the Interior Robert M. Mangan to Representative William Cahill, June 18, 1964. NPS WASO PHP Subject Files.
70. *American Association for State and Local History, Committee on Federal Programs in History, First Annual Meeting* (Washington, DC: NPS, 1968), pp. 76–78.
71. First authorized in 1977, the HPF grew to about $40 million per year in 1998. This expanded to more than $81 million in 1999 mostly through the creation of the Save America's Treasures program (funded at $35 million), which operated until 2011, and a $10 million fund targeted for historically black colleges and universities, or HBCUs.
72. BOR, *Expanding America's Outdoor Recreation Estate: The Land Water Conservation Fund's First Three Years* (Washington, DC: GPO, 1968).
73. Still, even six percent of $344 million was substantial funding for historic preservation projects during the Johnson administration. Howard Brown, *Brief Legislative Analysis of the Land and Water Conservation Fund* (Washington, DC: Congressional Research Service, 1972); George Siehl, *The Land and Water Conservation Fund: Origin and Congressional Intent* (Washington, DC: Congressional Research Service, 1981).
74. Section 6(f)(3) of the Land and Water Conservation Act:

> No property acquired or developed with assistance under this section shall, without the approval of the Secretary, be converted to other than public

outdoor recreation uses. The Secretary shall approve such conversion only if he finds it to be in accord with the then existing comprehensive statewide outdoor recreation plan and only upon such conditions as he deems necessary to assure the substitution of other recreation properties of at least equal fair market value and of reasonably equivalent usefulness and location.

75. NPS, *Record of Decision for the Conversion of 207.0 Acres of Creve Coeur Lake Memorial Park, St. Louis, Missouri under Section 6(f)(3) of the Land and Water Conservation Act of 1965, as Amended*, April 1995.
76. The Granville Corporation, *Study of Land and Water Conservation Fund Financial Assistance Alternatives* (Washington, DC: HCRS, 1981), p. 10.
77. *America's Heritage: Proceedings of a Symposium on the 25th Anniversary of the Land and Water Conservation Fund, National Recreation and Park Association and the National Park Service, 1990.*
78. *America's Heritage: Proceedings of a Symposium on the 25th Anniversary of the Land and Water Conservation Fund, National Recreation and Park Association and the National Park Service, 1990*, pp. 14–16. Henry Diamond, "Lessons Learned for Today," *The Environmental Forum*, Vol. 33. No. 2 (March/April 2016), pp. 44–47.
79. *The Compact Edition of the Oxford English Dictionary, Volume II, P–Z* (New York: Oxford University Press, 1988), pp. 274–275 and 522–523.

6   A Crisis of Need, Time, and Money

For William Whyte and others concerned with the progress of land conservation within the United States, 1961 was a "breakthrough year." The Urban Renewal Administration initiated an open space grant program (see Chapter 4); Whyte's own study, *Open Space Action* (Sidebar 6.1), was about to be published; and President John F. Kennedy signed bills authorizing the creation of two new types of protected areas: Massachusetts's Cape CodNational Seashore and Maryland's Piscataway Park (see Chapter 2). [1] Describing a collection of legislative and other changes, Whyte envisioned that federal and state governments had finally recognized that "good conservation was good politics."[2] A principal component for this conservation optimism was the revitalization of administrative interest in the utility of easements as a mechanism to protect the values of landscape that were seen as being so vital in Cold War America. According to historian Thomas Wellock, "the open space crusade also expanded the constituency for the environmental movement and set environmentalism against those who sought to expand suburban development."[3] Conservation easements had the potential to:

- permanently protect the scenic, historic, and cultural values found at individual properties or within large landscapes;
- provide an increased level of protection for those historic properties thought worthy of national recognition by the federal government; and, perhaps most importantly;
- address the problem of rapidly escalating land values across the United States that threatened the success of the wider conservation movement.

Conservation Easements

Within the United States fee-simple ownership of land comes with certain provisions for the use of a private property: each parcel contains a bundle of rights held by an owner, some of which, such as mineral rights, that can be sold or transferred to other parties. Easements, as a less-than-fee acquisition of limited property rights, are legal instruments that "are most easily described in terms of the purposes they serve."[4] A power company may seek a right-of-way easement from a landowner in order to run an electrical transmission line across a parcel, and such an agreement often would be recorded in the land records housed at local courthouses and attached to the property's deed. As opposed to many right-of-way or similar easements, which permit access to a property for a specific use, conservation easements are often classified as "negative" instruments in that they restrict a property owner from certain activities. According to Fritz Gutheim (see Sidebar 2.1), the first conservation easement was prepared for a Massachusetts property in 1887, while others cite the authority given to the Boston Metropolitan Park Commission in 1893. Alfred Runte traces the concern for landscape aesthetics to late 19th century efforts—using easements—to preserve New York's Niagara Falls and its unique environment. Thus, during the early 20th century, establishing scenic easements for conservation purposes was a relatively new concept within property law (with multiple monikers) that included land use rights that were less-than-fee simple established through a formal agreement.[5]

By the mid-20th century the less-than-fee ownership agreement was viewed with great potential as one component of a package of land-use planning tools for the protection of historic properties. With the Historic Sites Act of 1935— as the federal government got into the business of identifying, evaluating and designating nationally significant historic sites—NPS leadership became concerned that official recognition required some increased level of protection.

> On the same plane with the scenic areas are areas or structures of historic, prehistoric, or scientific significance. There is need for continued and energetic effort on the part of public agencies to assure preservation of America's heritage of historic and archeological sites and structures for the enlightenment and inspiration of her people. As is recognized by the Historic Sites Act of 1935, such action does not necessarily involve immediate or even eventual public ownership, but may be accomplished in many cases without disturbing private or semipublic owners.[6]

National Historic Site designation, a new form of official recognition created via the Historic Sites Act, served as an early model for partial stewardship responsibility. During the 1930s, NPS historians quickly recognized that not only were there many more nationally significant historic sites than could ever be added to the federal portfolio, but also that several prominent sites, such as Mount Vernon, were already protected by private entities. The owners of privately held properties considered for National Historic Site declaration were invited to enter into cooperative agreements with the Secretary of the Interior that detailed mutual stewardship responsibilities. In practice, however, these agreements had little impact.[7]

Prior to World War II, easements were commonly used to support the development of scenic roadways. Following legislative mandates from the 1930s, the NPS used scenic easements as land protection devices during the development of various parkways, such as along the Blue Ridge Parkway and the Natchez Trace.[8] Scenic easements along highways and other linear resources were generally designed to protect views from rights-of-way, such as at Appomattox Courthouse, Virginia (see Sidebar 6.4); they worked well as long as landowners and easement holders concurred about the kinds of land uses permitted within the protected areas. An unspecified "sad experience" along the Blue Ridge Parkway demonstrated that the protection promised by "ineffective and quarrel-provoking" scenic easements was a "snare and a delusion."[9] Confused about their access to the right-of-way, farmers with land holdings adjacent to the parkway resented the federal government's management style and became distrustful of easements. Scenic easements along the Blue Ridge Parkway had become so contentious that their use was mostly abandoned by the 1940s. By the late 1940s, according to Whyte, easements were almost forgotten because most park acquisition programs were destined for rural areas that had yet to experience the land speculation that would accompany post–World War II metropolitan growth.[10]

Sidebar 6.1   The Man Who Loved Cities

William Hollingsworth "Holly" Whyte (1917–1999) was an American author and journalist whose vision for open spaces within urban communities influenced the conservation and historic preservation movements. A successful author—his 1956 book, *The Organization Man*, sold more than 2million copies—Whyte substantially contributed to the popularization and recognition of conservation easements as effective tools in the protection of open space.[11]

Whyte's gospel of protecting open space through conservation easements developed in the last years of the 1950s while he was still on staff at *Fortune* magazine. Properly identified and protected, open space had multiple positive public benefits. The inability of federal, state, and local governments to finance the acquisition of sufficient landscapes prevented progress in ensuring sound land-use planning. Whyte connected open space with forestry, wildlife management, and flood control as valid reasons for public ownership (if only partial ownership)—especially where there was a combination of public purposes that justified preservation of the parcel. His ideas, while not entirely new, expanded the conservation movement's constituency beyond traditional boundaries of wilderness to include the suburban landscape. Easements were a "complementary type of conservation" that had the potential to protect parcels in urban, rural, and wilderness settings.[12]

Frederick Gutheim credited Whyte with popularizing the concept of scenic easements. Whyte was "well able to launch a new major idea upon the world of conservation" that had "just commenced to deal with the massive problems of metropolitanization and its spread into the surrounding countryside." While in the decade after Whyte's ORRRC open space report easements appeared to have lost some of their "original character as a cure-all," they still represented a "durable tool in the steadily growing kit of public powers" to secure and preserve open space.[13]

In Whyte's testimony before Congress on the quality of urban life in 1969, he recounted how he came to focus on open space easements as a solution to suburban development. By the mid-1950s,

> The question that was facing us was, all right, we know that growth is going to take place. What can we do to accommodate this growth and at the same time channel it and save the really key parts of the landscape? Now it was obvious that no government could buy up enough land.[14]

The solution for Whyte was the pragmatic application of easements to protect certain features of the landscape, such as floodplains, or other relatively narrow linear features (disused railroads or canals) that could connect larger parcels of protected open spaces like parks. Government guidance and leverage was necessary, with a dose of administrative flexibility, but so was local imagination and creativity—the kind that Jane Jacobs brought to her observations of the characteristics of urban life.

An admirer of Jacobs's work, Whyte was creatively analytical in his own appreciation for urban spaces: in his introduction to a re-publication of the 1939 *WPA Guide to New York City,* he took the opportunity to compare the distribution of homes associated with members of the city's social elites to illustrate change (or lack thereof) through time, while at the same time using amendments to the city's zoning ordinances to characterize its post–World War II architectural history.[15] This passion for data-driven analysis was illustrated in his 1980 book and film *The Social Life of Small Urban Spaces.*

Throughout the 1960s, Whyte maintained his optimism that the United States could save enough open space "if good people would get to it." This "can-do" approach echoed the sentiments of Representative Francis Bolton espoused as part of Mount Vernon's Operation Overview.[16] Both proponents recognized that public ownership of protected lands would never address the rapidly growing need for open space within an increasingly suburban society. "The less of our landscape there is to save," Whyte prophetically argued in *The Last Landscape,* "the better our chance of saving it."[17]

States had greater success in the implementation of easement programs. During the 1950s, more than 17,000 acres were protected as part of the creation of Wisconsin's Great River Road. This project was frequently cited by proponents of conservation easements as a successful model—one that illustrated the benefits of less-than-fee ownership.[18] Other states experimented with easements during the 1950s. In 1956 Massachusetts authorized the use of restrictive easements to protect land of scenic or historical interest surrounding Boston in order to establish a tourist route known as "The Bay Circuit." Without dedicated funding this proposal made little progress in creating this greenbelt of interconnected historic properties.[19] Two years later Pennsylvania granted forest owners tax credits for conservation of particularly scenic timber stands. On the other side of the country, development pressures in Monterey County, California, led the state legislature to adopt the Scenic Easement Deed Act of 1959, the first statewide effort to encourage the preservation of large parcels in light of suburban and urban expansion.[20] Maryland addressed pressures on rural areas caused by the rapid suburbanization of the Baltimore and Washington, DC, metropolitan areas, where efforts to offer preferential tax assessments for farmlands began in 1956 (see Sidebar 6.3). Weathering constitutional challenges, legislation passed in 1960 permitted localities to help preserve Maryland farmlands.[21] Begun in

Figure 6.1 The Little House in the Big Woods, Pepin, Wisconsin. This three-acre property
        is one of the many historic sites located at waysides along the Great River Road
        in Wisconsin that was popular among automobile tourists. It is a reconstruction
        of the cabin where the popular children's author Laura Ingalls Wilder was born
        in 1867.

Source: LOC Prints and Photographs Division, Carol M. Highsmith Collection, LC-HS503–1172.

the mid-1950s, Maryland's Piscataway Park (see Chapter 2) was another successful application of scenic easements. As with Mount Vernon's Operation Overview, local organizations often were at the forefront of easement activities. Local preservation organizations began accepting easements on historic places in Charleston, South Carolina (1959); Savannah, Georgia (1959); and Annapolis, Maryland (1963).[22] Sometimes threats to individual properties, such as at the Merrywood estate (see Sidebar 6.2) across the Potomac River from Washington, DC, were precedent setting. In theory, the main advantage for pursuing conservation easements was reduced acquisition costs, while the main disadvantage was the potential for conflict between the landowner and the easement holder.

Sidebar 6.2   Merrywood

In mid-November 1963, "scenic easement history was made" when a federal court imposed restrictions on development rights at Merrywood, thus protecting the scenic integrity of the picturesque palisades of the Potomac River.[23] Built in 1919 in the colonial revival style and seated within a 46-acre parcel in Fairfax County, Virginia, Merrywood after 1942 was the girlhood home of Jaqueline Kennedy and later served as a campaign and social headquarters during her husband's 1960 presidential campaign. After President Kennedy's inauguration, the estate was offered for sale. The new owners proposed a complex of 17-story apartment buildings for the site, which local planning and zoning regulations were unable to prevent. The expansive project had "callously ignored the vehement and widespread protests" of both local officials and the neighboring community, resulting in a "chaotic situation" along the Potomac River.[24] Due to the influential families concerned, the federal government stepped in to stop the development, a week before the president's fateful trip to Dallas, Texas. Lacking a legitimate legislative mandate to acquire the property—the tract met none of the NPS criteria for parklands—a federal court imposed a scenic easement on the property that limited new construction to single-family homes on one-acre lots. Four months after Kennedy's assassination, it was left to Secretary of the Interior Stewart Udall to negotiate the value of the scenic easement, which he called a "very difficult decision." The valuation of the Merrywood scenic easement set important precedents for the future utility of this conservation tool.[25]

The estate's setting exacerbated plans for its protection: the entire Potomac River Valley was a case study for the new conservation espoused by President Kennedy and later adopted by the Johnson administration. Expanding the scope of the undertaking, by early March 1965, the

Department of the Interior had obtained agreements with more than 50 property owners within the Merrywood neighborhood. Local residents took advantage of the potential for federal tax deductions for their charitable donations. The architect and planner Carl Feiss was hopeful that Merrywood would become a precedent because, at that time, successful examples of using scenic easements to constrain develop could be "counted on the fingers of one hand."[26] This tax policy was indeed applied by an Internal Revenue Service ruling to all such similar conservation easement donations across the county. Merrywood provided an important threshold for the valuation of scenic easements, cementing the idea that a donor is entitled to a deduction for the fair market value of the restrictive covenant. That fair market value was established by the amount that the federal government paid for the easement.[27]

The Merrywood easement was quickly followed, in December 1966, by the acceptance of a unique easement on Tudor Place, a classically inspired estate designed by William Thornton in 1816 that overlooked the Georgetown section of Washington, DC. The easement limited changes to the 18-room mansion's exterior; prohibited most new construction within the approximately 5.5-acre grounds and gardens; limited public access during the lifetime of its owner, Armistead Peter, III; and restricted its subsequent use as either a residence or a museum. Designated a National Historic Landmark in 1960, Tudor Place was the first property protected via an easement using the authority of the Historic Sites Act of 1935, the legislation that served as the footing for Ronald Lee's creation of the National Historic Landmark Program in 1960. Donation of this easement and its acceptance by the Department of the Interior, soon after enactment of the National Historic Preservation Act of 1966, laid the cornerstone for similar conveyances.[28]

In 1966, at the same time it created the Virginia Outdoors Foundation, the Commonwealth of Virginia also established a historic preservation easement program. The first property, Old Mansion, near Bowling Green, was accepted in 1969. The program grew to include 400 properties in 40 years, including 23 National Historic Landmarks. In 1968, David Finley (former chairman of the NTHP) and his family donated an easement on the 250-acre core for Oatlands, a country estate near Leesburg, Virginia. Soon after, the NTHP began its own program of accepting conservation easements as a viable way to ensure stewardship on a wider range of historic properties.[29]

During the mid-1960s Secretary Udall grew increasingly troubled by the conflict among various federal agencies with regard to environmental planning, land conservation, and historic preservations. He wanted to "see to it that no future Merrywoods happen[ed]."[30] Coincidentally, at the same time the secretary was deeply involved in the relocation of the Pope-Leighy House, a Frank Lloyd Wright Usonian home that was threatened with demolition as part of the construction of Interstate 66, a new highway that ran westward from Washington, DC, through the Virginia suburbs. These episodes showed the "absurdity of having to solve problems which involved environmental values between two federal agencies at the last minute in the arena of political compromise."[31] The solution was the creation of an administrative procedure by which federal agencies could identify, evaluate, and resolve such conflicts on most undertakings without involving the highest levels of the executive branch, a process that was incorporated as Section 106 of the National Historic Preservation Act of 1966.

Conservation easements, noted Whyte, were the "middle way" along a continuum of potential land-use controls—with fee-simple purchase at one end and local zoning controls on the other (see Sidebar 6.5). Planners in the 1950s recognized open space was "essential to a well-ordered urban environment." Such provisions, though, sometimes ran afoul of Cold War sentiments. Land-use planner Morton Lustig asserted that "public control of open space" was not "directly descended from the Communist Manifesto."[32] "Time and again," Whyte noted, "you could hear people bemoan the desecration of the countryside," but "short of socialism" the problem was thought unstoppable.[33] In this context, any form of increased federal land-use regulation was viewed as contrary to constitutionally protected rights of private property. Although not untried as instruments of land control, easements were, in the early 1960s, a less well understood approach, with a bad reputation among some land management agencies. Despite Whyte's advocacy for the potential contribution of conservation easements, none of his 13 recommendations for state and federal government open space programs focused on this technique. A few years after *Open Space Action* was published, Whyte's prescription for land-use conservation was "now proving effective.[34] But not everyone thought that easements were the best cure for expanding protected areas in the United States. Resources for the Future economist Marion Clawson predicted liability and fiscal problems, and Norman Williams's ORRRC report on recreational land acquisition recommended fee-simple acquisition over conservation easements. By the late 1960s, many of the legal issues regarding conservation or scenic easements were still under legal review. Twenty years after their first application to open space conservation, such instruments were still considered untested and unreliable.[35]

Federal Land Acquisition

In 1966 the federal government held more than 764 million acres of land within the United States—of which the Department of the Interior oversaw more than 70 percent, principally though the appropriately named Bureau of Land Management (BLM).[36] The problem from a conservation and recreational perspective—perhaps even more so than with historic sites—was that places suitable for public enjoyment were not conveniently located to the growing metropolitan areas across the country. For nearly half a century, new units of the NPS had come from either existing federal lands or the donation of private property. In 1961, this pattern was dramatically changed with the congressional authorization to use appropriated funds to acquire lands at the proposed Cape Cod National Seashore in Massachusetts.[37] As another new type of park unit, National Recreational Areas (as distinct from the Recreational Demonstration Areas developed in the 1930s), held locally important values and resources, much to the chagrin of the NPS, whose mandate focused on nationally important areas (see Sidebar 5.1).[38] With the new conservation of the 1960s, especially after the establishment of the Land and Water Conservation Fund (LWCF), the federal government embarked on an aggressive program of land acquisition. For example, from 1961 to 1967 the NPS acquired 683,000 acres of land at 34 new park units, for a total cost of more than $118 million. In 1967 federal agencies combined to plan for the purchase of 261,000 acres of recreational lands with a total value of more than $48 million—the limit of funds available from the LWCF. The proposed properties ranged from 35,000 acres (valued at $3.4 million) in Missouri to only 12 acres (for $17,500) in North Dakota.[39] There was "very little, if any, coordination" of federal acquisition activities with those of state and local governments or private institutions, primarily because nationally significant resources at natural or historical parks were solely the responsibility of the NPS.[40]

After Congress authorized federal agencies to acquire new parks, reserves, and recreational areas, it also had to appropriate the necessary funds. The Bureau of Outdoor Recreation (BOR) was given oversight of NPS land acquisition proposals, which exacerbated inter-agency rivalries.[41] At Fort Necessity—the rural site of a French and Indian War battle in Pennsylvania that involved a young George Washington—the NPS estimated that land values were increasing at 7 percent per year during the 1960s, thus forcing the agency to reprogram funds to meet a higher sales price.[42] Congress was especially wary when agencies asked for increases in the amounts authorized for real estate purchases, while bureaucrats and local proponents were frustrated by the length of time involved in completing federal land transactions.

Quickly recognizing that the funding levels established by Congress for the LWCF were not adequate to address land acquisition needs at all levels of government, in 1965 the president's Recreation Advisory Council established guidelines and priorities for allocating the appropriated funds. First among the criteria was to:

> Acquire areas in greatest danger of being lost for public recreation or preservation, or greatest escalation in cost of acquisition—this consideration includes unique natural, historic, or scientific sites as well as open space for amenity purposes near, or within urban areas.[43]

As delays in federal acquisition contributed to escalating costs, Congress urged agencies to quickly acquire properties within recently authorized areas, while putting a lower priority on substantially improved properties and "those having mainly archeological or historic values as distinct from recreation values."[44] Historic properties were consistently undervalued in federal land acquisition programs.

A Crisis of Need, Time, and Money

In 1967, the Accokeek Foundation (the group established by Representative Frances Bolton in the late 1950s to oversee Operation Overview) completed an analysis of the problems associated with preserving recreational and open space lands:

> There is a fast growing realization that we must take positive action to preserve our environment if this Nation is to continue to be a fit place to live. The great needs for open space, the rising costs of securing that space have brought a crisis of need, time, and money.[45]

As noted in the study, the concept of scenic easements—and their potential utility—was a relatively new tool in the conservationist and planners tool kits, with the primary operational challenges centered on acquisition and appraisal of such instruments. By the late 1960s the jury was still out regarding best practices to follow in the creation and administration of scenic easements: there were simply too few case studies with enough time depth with which to conduct any quantitative analysis of their relative benefit and costs.

Congress was quite concerned with the unabated escalation of land prices in areas scheduled for new parks or recreational areas. Across the country, land prices were rising from 5 to 10 percent per year: at Flaming Gorge Dam in Utah, parcels that were $39 per acre in 1956 had risen to $429 per acre a decade later. In 1966 President Lyndon Johnson noted the spiraling cost of land acquisition, with inflationary increases in property values naturally following after a declaration of federal interest in a particular area. The BOR concluded appropriated funding was $2.3 billion short of what was needed to meet the country's needs at the end of the 1960s. The problem was so significant that metropolitan planners suggested enhancing public transportation networks to give city dwellers easy access more distant outdoor recreation facilities where land costs were cheaper. The commitment to provide substantial outdoor recreation opportunities using federal funds characterized park and recreational planning during the 1960s where congressional authorizations "leapt ahead of funding." Many conservationists saw the upcoming Bicentennial of the Declaration of Independence as an opportunity to complete system of parks and protected areas.[46]

Perhaps not surprisingly, conservation easements represented one solution to the dual issues of rising land costs and increasing need for protected landscapes. In 1966, the Senate appropriations committee "evidenced considerable interest" in consideration of less-than-fee-simple acquisition and directed the Department of the Interior to make every effort to use such mechanisms. However, only 4 percent of lands (6,346 acres) proposed for federal purchase in 1967 used this technique.[47]

> Acquisition planning should first consider whether the recreation objectives might be met though cooperative agreements or by zoning practices or other means without acquisition, and secondly, whether acquisition short of fee, such as an easement, will satisfy recreation requirements.[48]

During the 1960s there were several federal experiments that tried to address these issues.[49] In 1964, after years of debate over the appropriate management strategy for a seemingly unique recreational resource, the NPS was authorized to establish the Ozark National Scenic Riverways (OSNR)—another new type of federal designation. At the ONSR, NPS planners anticipated an adverse reaction toward easements among local landowners and recommended only fee-simple purchases as the best alternative.[50] Perhaps because it was commonly used by its bureaucratic rival, the U.S. Forest Service, for land acquisition, the NPS consistently derided scenic easements claiming that such instruments

> Caused misunderstandings (especially during subsequent title transfers), created administrative difficulties, were hard to enforce, cost almost as much as fee simple acquisition, and contradicted the tradition of American land ownership.[51]

Despite this opinion, the agency was willing to use the promise of scenic easements as a bargaining chip in political negotiations regarding the creation of new park units. Despite substantial administrative hesitancy, the use of scenic easements became the most successful "phenomenon" developed during land acquisition at ONSR. Afterwards, scenic easements reportedly became a common alternative to purchase in new national lakeshores and riverway additions to the national park system.[52]

Sidebar 6.3   Appomattox Courthouse

Few historic sites hold the symbolic importance of the "surrender grounds" at Appomattox Courthouse, Virginia, where Robert E. Lee capitulated to Ulysses S. Grant on April 9, 1863, effectively ending the American Civil War. Nonetheless, its acquisition, development, and

Figure 6.2 Appomattox Courthouse, Virginia.
Source: LOC Prints and Photographs Division, HABS VA, 6-APPO, 6–5.

interpretation as a historic site illustrates changing attitudes toward the conservation of historic properties during the 20th century. Efforts to complete a comprehensive system of national parks often lead to controversies between the "inconsequent opportunism" of local park boosters and the long-range view of professional historians within the NPS.[53] Originally seated within a typical mid-19th century crossroads village, the McLean House, which hosted the actual surrender, was dismantled in the early 1890s with an eye to exhibiting it at the Worlds Columbian Exposition in Chicago and other venues. Initial proposals in the 1920s to mark the site with an appropriate memorial located on one acre adjacent to a state highway that cut through the village were soon cast aside over criticism regarding design issues—a statue had the potential to symbolically reflect issues of loyalty, patriotism, and disunion that were still controversial some six decades after the event.[54]

Local concerns strongly backed plans to extensively reconstruct the historic scene, following the pattern set by the successful restoration of Colonial Williamsburg. Reconstruction would include the McLean house and would be based on a detailed set of architectural drawings, in an "attempt to fix forever a static cross-section. . . as it existed at one given time interval."[55] However, reconstruction was contrary to the ascribed historic preservation policy of the NPS, which strongly discouraged the re-creation of historic landscape elements. At Appomattox—despite consistent opposition from NPS historians—local opinions, backed by extensive political power within the Congress, held sway and vanished elements of the community's build environment and landscape were recreated after an extensive program of interdisciplinary historical, architectural, and archaeological research.[56]

In 1938, as the NPS developed plans for the development of the historic site, a local landowner donated a scenic easement for farmland in a ¾mile long, 300 foot wide, corridor along the state highway that passed through the village. This easement protected the site's environs for more than 30 years. Then, in 1971, a real estate developer proposed construction of a subdivision adjacent to the historical park with access roads that would have changed the rural character of the historic setting and perhaps compromised the park's integrity. This controversial proposal pushed the NPS to acquire full title to the easement parcel and surrounding lands in order to ensure their stewardship.[57]

Originally conceived of as a one-acre lot suitable for the location of a commemorative statue, the park has grown to encompass more than 1,700 acres. In addition, its interpretive mission has expanded to include not only the McLean House and the mostly reconstructed core of the mid-19th century village, but also the outlying headquarters camps of the opposing generals. Living history and interpretive media at the park have broadened its scope to provide a "more comprehensive visitor experience" and a "more complete version of the history" of this rural Virginia community, including the restoration of its agricultural landscape. Moreover, based on a national policy and responsibility to "protect all resources within regardless of the impetus behind a park's establishment," the park's environmental program has grown since 2000 to include numerous studies that document existing conditions within the unit. This beyond-the-borders vision for the park is reflective of a continuing 20th-century paradigm wherein protected areas provide much-needed comfort and solace for an increasingly urban population.[58]

Easements were a substantial part of NPS land acquisition at several parks during the 1960s and into the 1970s, having been used in the Guadalupe Mountains, Texas; Dinosaur National Monument, Utah; Nez Perce National Monument, Idaho; and Acadia National Park, Maine. The agency used easements to control land use adjacent at its battlefield parks at Sharpsburg, Maryland; Manassas, Virginia; and Vicksburg, Mississippi. Recognized for its vast natural landscape located between Cleveland and Akron, Ohio, the creation of the 15,000-acre Cuyahoga Valley National Park illustrated some of the issues with mixed land acquisition as part of President Nixon's campaign to bring parks to the people. In 1972 Ohio Congressman John Seiberling and his wife donated an easement on their substantial home and 18-acre grounds, Stan Hywet Hall, to the Akron Metropolitan Park District. Two years later, the NPS began acquiring property—with an emphasis on fee simple parcels in the core of the 18-mile long, 4-mile wide valley. The agency planned to negotiate 350 easements and purchase 1,000 tracts, including Stan Hywet Hall.[59]

Easements were also part of the LWCF tool kit—but it was unclear how much emphasis the BOR placed on this form of acquisition. Congress periodically debated the utility of open space easements for improving urban environments across the country.[60] By the late 1960s the situation was seen as dire: "It is manifestly clear that unless imaginative and bold measures are taken within the next few years, conservation will simply be 'priced out of business.'" Reduced LWCF appropriations and the nationwide escalation of land costs "foreshadow[ed] a virtual stalemate" in meeting the country's forecasted outdoor recreational needs. Private philanthropy, once a common source for the establishment of parks and other protected areas, had limited application to the growing problem. While nearly one third of the 16,000 acres now in federal ownership at Cape Cod National Seashore were donated and, to a large degree, Maryland's Piscataway Park was made up of donated easements, this approach required closer relations between the NPS and conservation organizations.[61]

By the late 1960s, it was clear to most within the broader conservation movement that the national acquisition effort of protected areas had been outpaced by development.[62] Land values, fueled by suburban speculation, had skyrocketed; local citizen-led experiments with cluster zoning (see Sidebar 6.5) and voluntary conservation easements were of limited success. In order to work, easements required some form of tax abatement, like those initiated at Piscataway Park as part of Operation Overview, as well as increased oversight and regulation.

After a decade of increased federal involvement, in the early 1970s land conservationists gathered to take stock of the progress in securing sufficient acreage to meet open space goals. Their conclusions echoed many of concerns coming out the late 1950s, but with an increased sense of urgency. One continuing issue, in the era before geographical information systems (GIS), was that individual communities did not know how much open space was being lost, nor had they prioritized the parcels deserving of permanent protection. A decade of renewed active federal involvement in land conservation reiterated the conclusion that "too often" conservationists looked "for answers in Washington" that were more appropriately found in state houses and local courthouses. Envisioning a shared effort to identify and preserve unique assets—and recommending an increase in LWCF funding to $1 billion annually—the "current thrust" for the 1970s was to seek a "rounding out of the federal land estate." The challenges, suggested the land-use lawyer Joseph Brenneman, were not only a conservation issue, but a social issue as well. A senior Department of the Interior official, Douglas Wheeler, concluded: "Just as surely as the Federal government cannot afford to buy the open space that adds so much to the quality of life for an increasingly urban population, we cannot afford to lose it by default."[63]

National Historic Landmark Easements

Since the late 1960s the NPS has explored the possibility of using easements as an additional protective measure for properties designated as National Historic Landmarks. Speaking before the National Park System Advisory Board (NPSAB) in 1969, Ernest Connally, the director of the Office of Archaeology and Historic Preservation (OAHP), reported that:

> To further the Landmark Program by more adequate preservation of historic sites and structures it has been suggested that the National Park Service perfect a system for holding easements on landmark properties. This would provide an intermediate measure of control short of the Federal Government having to assume ownership of a property, thus giving the necessary insurance for the preservation of historic properties of national significance that remain in private ownership.[64]

This approach harkened back to early National Historic Site designation orders that included the proscription that: "Warning is expressly given to all unauthorized persons not to appropriate, injure, destroy, deface, or remove any feature of this historic site."[65] It seems clear that because of the deliberative and lengthy process leading to the designation of a National Historic Site or National Historic Landmark, this included a considerable investment of prestige by the Secretary's office and there was a desire to enhance the protection of these properties. In creating the National Historic Landmark program in 1960, Ronald Lee envisioned that other federal agencies would recognize the National Historic Landmark plaque as an outward and visible sign of a building's national significance and the inherent protection afforded by the Interior Department.[66] While both National Historic Site declaration and National Historic Landmark designation came with a certain expectation of federal guidance and technical assistance, the fundamental problem remained one of fostering resource protection without complete ownership.

During the early 1970s, the upcoming Bicentennial of the Declaration of Independence provided a backdrop for a far-reaching proposal that would have added to the federal government's responsibility for the stewardship of National Historic Landmarks. During 1973 the OAHP drafted guidance to govern NPS selection of easements and surveyed the owners of existing NHLs regarding attitudes toward such protective measures.[67] As a result, in 1974 the NPS commissioned land-use lawyer Russell Brenneman to evaluate the issues and implications of appending federal easements on certain existing and newly designated National Historic Landmarks.[68] In his three-volume study, Brenneman concluded that National Historic Landmarks were "shielded to a degree from certain kinds of federal activities," but less-than-fee interests would provide more permanent legal protections.[69] At that time, with more than 1,100 National Historic Landmarks designated since 1960, implementing this proposal would have had serious legal and administrative implications for the NPS, especially within historic districts with multiple property owners. On the whole, the agency was reticent about the proposal because its previous experience with scenic easements had not been encouraging. Perpetual easements often led to questions of enforcement in later years. Despite these concerns, Lady Bird Johnson, a former First Lady who served on the NPSAB, recommended that the agency move forward anticipating that within a short time the study would become "somewhat of the Bible on the use of easements—their values and their pitfalls."[70]

Presented to the NPSAB in April 1975, Brenneman's National Historic Landmark easement study concluded that the administrative burden to the NPS was worth the stewardship benefits to these nationally significant historic properties. A conservation easement placed on Tudor Place in 1966 had set a precedent for federal acceptance of easements at National Historic Landmarks.[71] By the mid-1970s, about 10 percent of existing National Historic Landmarks were already protected by some form of easement held by other parties. The study suggested that the agency should require easements as a condition of grants-in-aid projects funded via the National Historic Preservation Act, and that National Historic Landmarks should receive a higher percentage of federal matching funds for preservation and restoration. Although initial estimates placed the cost of the new administrative duties at more than $860,000 annually, as with land conservation programs in general, less-than-fee ownership was considered a viable preservation tool for the protection of historic properties. In December 1976, during the lame duck period of the Ford administration, NPS Director Gary Everhardt announced the creation of the NHL preservation easement program.[72] While the initial focus was on historic districts within urban settings, considerable groundwork had been laid by the agency's experience in accepting easements associated with the Green Springs Historic District in the Louisa County, Virginia, countryside.[73]

Green Springs Historic District

In April 1974 the NPSAB recommended that the Secretary of the Interior designate the Green Springs Historic District as an National Historic Landmark and accept easements on more than 7,000 acres of rural farmland from land conservation advocates in Louisa County, Virginia. Limited by the conditions of the Historic Sites Act, the secretary could accept easements only on nationally significant properties, as such an authority was not included in the National Historic Preservation Act. Thus, local conservationists had to pursue not only National Register listing, but also National Historic Landmark designation by the Secretary of the Interior.[74]

The initial threat to Green Springs was a 1970 proposal to locate a state correctional institution within the area. Opponents were successful in forcing the Department of Justice—a source of partial funding for the project—to

Figure 6.3 Green Springs, Louisa County, VA. This 18th century residence represents the
domestic landscape that was the focus of the Green Springs Historic District.

Source: Historic American Buildings Survey.

implement provisions of the newly enacted National Environmental Policy
Act (NEPA), a step that delayed the project while the agency completed an
Environmental Impact Statement. At one point the state considered aban-
doning the use of federal funds in an attempt to avoid compliance with
both NEPA and the National Historic Preservation Act. In 1972, Virginia
Governor Linwood Holton apparently capitulated and announced that the
proposed 200-acre state prison facility would not be seated within the Green
Springs community.[75] The governor called for local landowners to demonstrate their commitment to the area by establishing conservation easements
that would protect its qualities in perpetuity. Hiram (Rae) Ely, a proponent
of the historic landscape, called this action a "victory of major proportions."
It was ironic, thought Ely, that the governor's preferred means to protect the
area, conservation easements, had been previously rejected by the Commonwealth during the late 1960s. Led by Ely, local constituents nominated and
listed a 14,000-acre tract on the National Register of Historic Places—at that
time "by far the largest unit on the Register." Historic Green Springs Incorporated (HGSI) received a planning grant from the National Endowment for
the Arts in 1973 to support its efforts to obtain historic recognition.[76]

   While the controversy received nationwide press coverage with articles in
both *Time Magazine* and the *Readers Digest*, and despite the local proponents

having secured a checkerboard pattern of conservation easements on nearly 7,000 acres, Holton changed his mind a year later and again proposed placing the prison in the district. In a precedent-setting conservation action, President Richard Nixon's newly created Council on Environmental Quality (CEQ) mobilized a united federal opposition to this undertaking, calling for an effort to relocate the proposed prison and preserve the landscape via a network of conservation easements. It was Governor Holton's successor, Mills Godwin, who finally killed the prison project on June 13, 1974.[77]

The "Green Springs controversy," as it was called, was the foundation for the Department of the Interior's evaluation of a preservation easement program during the 1970s. Establishing criteria for which National Historic Landmarks were easement eligible, the Interior Department adopted a traditional approach: a property had to have a high potential for inclusion in the national park system if private ownership ever proved incapable of meeting the preservation restrictions of the easement.[78] In 1974 the NPSAB and its National Historic Landmark Committee reviewed a National Historic Landmark nomination for the Green Springs Historic District. The rural landscape was characterized as a:

> unique assemblage of rural architecture and a rare phenomenon of fine to outstanding examples of architecture preserved in their original context. . . . While only several of the historic buildings might qualify as exceptional, the ensemble amounts to a product much larger than the sum of its parts.[79]

The NPS's reluctance regarding recognition of the property and its conservation easements tempered its support for the National Historic Landmark designation. Philip Stewart, the agency's chief of land acquisition, summarized the agency's 40 years of scenic easement experience by noting that there was a general disillusionment with these instruments and a firm belief that the Green Springs easements would be problematic in the future. Landscape conservation through easements was labor intensive, not only in the acquisition phase, but also in their continual maintenance, as Stewart noted was the case at Maryland's Piscataway Park. In contrast, Bruce Blanchard, a senior Department of the Interior environmental regulator, enthusiastically supported the easement approach, despite some uncertainty regarding reduced taxation associated with less-than-perpetual easements.[80]

Just as the threat of the prison waxed and waned, the W. R. Grace Company announced plans to mine vermiculite on some 1,500 acres within the rural landscape. During the Bicentennial, the Secretary of the Interior appealed to the company's patriotic sentiment, arguing that the corporation had other vermiculite holdings that it could mine without damage to the country's only rural national historic district. Here again, the fundamental issue was whether the historic designation and easements could stop the proposed strip mining, a controversy that was termed "Virginia's Cat Litter War."[81]

Conservation easements and national historic designation were not enough to prevent mining on certain parcels within the landscape; Green Springs was frequently listed as being an endangered National Historic Landmark. Even the area's 1973 listing on the National Register of Historic Places and its 1974 designation as a National Historic Landmark were challenged due to inadequate public notice for this official federal recognition.[82] After a series of public hearings regarding the historic designation and the potential impacts from the proposed vermiculite mining, Secretary of the Interior Cecil Andrus announced the acceptance of donated conservation easements covering nearly one half of the 14,000-acre Green Springs historic district in December 1977.[83] With the creation of the Heritage Conservation and Recreation Services (HCRS) bureau by the Carter administration in 1978, the NPS was soon assigned the job of managing the easements. The conservation of the Green Springs Historic District influenced the 1980 amendments to the National Historic Preservation Act and has since continued to present a variety of challenges to historic preservation advocates.[84]

Sidebar 6.4   Farmland Preservation

In the summer of 1966, Grandma Clara Enger wrote from Clayton, Missouri to Secretary of the Interior Stewart Udall with the query: "What can we women of America do to help save some of the farm land in our beautiful country?" She was concerned that good agricultural fields in her community were being "'sliced' as thin as baloney sandwich cold cuts for subdivisions."[85] As witnessed in Maryland, Pennsylvania, and other states, the agricultural landscape found on the periphery of most metropolitan areas was most at risk during the rapid suburbanization of the post–World War II period when, between 1950 and 1970, more than 35 million people moved to the suburbs.[86] Urban and suburban concerns for open space and outdoor recreation eventually led to the recognition of increasing threats to rural historic and traditional landscapes.

Following the BOR's lead, the Department of Agriculture tried to promote land conservation on privately owned farmlands through the growth of recreational operations. On-farm recreation—like camping, fishing, and hunting—had the dual impact of meeting increasing outdoor needs of urban and suburban citizens and providing additional income for economically challenged small family farms. Certain federal farm programs helped local farmers to develop recreational facilities on former croplands, issuing $3.6 million in loans to 564 farmers during 1966. The Farmers Home Administration provided $33.2 million in loans to 280 nonprofit organizations in support of large-scale community recreation projects, many of which appeared to be similar in scope to projects supported by the LWCF.[87]

This approach to multiple-use land conservation helped to promote a particular vision of the small family farm that was in tune with American traditions of economic independence and the picturesque qualities of rural life seated within a diversified landscape of farmhouses, barns, and silos surrounded by fields, streams, and woodlands. Historic sites, along with swimming holes and fishing ponds, were some of the attributes that agricultural vacationers found attractive. At least one 1960s commentator believed that the "museum quality and recreational value of rural areas" would continue to grow as this idealized agricultural landscape became increasingly rare.[88]

By the end of the 1960s it was clear that recreational farmlands could not address the growing crisis as suburban and exurban development rapidly consumed prime farmland. The Department of Agriculture estimated that the country lost 3 million acres of farmland annually from 1967 to 1975.[89] One Lancaster County, Pennsylvania farmer, Amos Funk, noted that two thirds of the farms in his community were owned by land speculators. By 1980, Douglas Wheeler, the director of the newly established American Farmland Trust, could cite that Americans were still losing irreplaceable agricultural farmland at the seemingly horrific rate of 320 acres per hour! Seeking to escape a system of resource-based stovepipes, the NTHP launched its own efforts to "bridge the gap between open space protection and farmland preservation as two separate issues."[90] This early stage of the rural preservation movement was supported by the newly created (and short lived) Heritage, Conservation, and Recreation Service (HCRS), which combined the activities of the BOR with the non-park programs of the NPS. Multiple strategies were proposed by federal agencies to combat the loss of prime farmlands: many states gave agricultural lands preferential tax assessments, while some created programs to purchase development rights[91]

As documented by Tim Lehman, the concern for farmland preservation grew out of and was incorporated into other aspects of the environmental movement during the early 1970s. Farmland became a scarce and critical resource to be enumerated as part of Senator Henry Jackson's proposed federal land-use planning legislation.[92] From a planning perspective, the concern for farmland preservation was intertwined with urban revitalization, which was seen as the best antidote to combat what seemed to be an unstoppable suburban sprawl. Advocates sought to improve the practice of local land-use planning as part of President Richard Nixon's overall environmental agenda, which faltered in the aftermath of the Watergate scandal.[93] Agricultural land protection would not successfully reappear on the federal agenda until the early 1980s with the Farmland Protection and Policy Act, after which prime farmland joined wetlands and threatened and endangered species as non-renewable resources enumerated during the planning review mandated by the National Environmental Policy Act.

Figure 6.4 Burnley Farm, Gordonsville, Orange County, VA, 1984. More typical of the farms within the Green Springs Historic District, this property, while not individually significant, contributed to the unique assemblage of rural architectural styles within the cultural landscape.

Source: Historic American Buildings Survey

A New Role for Easements

Administrative distrust of the overall utility of conservation easements continued through the 1970s. As experience with the programs grew, it appeared that easements did not work well in situations where public access was required, such as for recreational purposes. NPS planners agreed that on the surface less-than-fee acquisition appeared to be more economical and prudent—yet, their preference was for full purchase because, over the long run, easements were more expensive and less effective because of the perpetual costs of management.[94] Absent some level of benefit/cost analysis on the costs of long-term management, there were both tangible and intangible problems with easements that were difficult to address in the field. For example, along the Lower St. Croix River in Minnesota, 32 tracks (1,150 acres) were purchased in fee, while easements were placed on only 18 parcels (94 acres). It was apparent that as easement costs approached that of fee simple, the likelihood of full acquisition increased.[95]

By the early 1980s rising land costs had created a crisis. In 15 years the LWCF had funded the acquisition of more than 2.7 million acres at the cost of some $2.3 billion, and yet, the backlog of congressionally authorized land acquisition was estimated at another $2.3 billion. With the advent of the Reagan administration, land conservation funding was reduced to the extent that it significantly impaired the ability of federal agencies to adequately finance outdoor recreation acquisition programs.[96] Clearly alternatives to fee-simple ownership were vital to extend and expand land conservation gains.

> For example, rising real estate costs have significantly eroded purchasing power and rendered the costs of public ownership prohibitive in many situations. The price per acre of farm real estate, to cite one instance, has increased in excess of two hundred percent over the last ten year period (1970 to 1980). The rising value of all types of real property has justifiably made local jurisdictions increasingly reluctant to remove real estate from tax rolls through public acquisition, because of the implied negative impact on their tax base. Generally high real estate costs have greatly contributed to the increasing emphasis throughout the recreation/conservation community on alternatives to fee-simple acquisition of lands.[97]

In 1982 the LWCF adopted a new approach for federal land acquisition programs: agencies were directed to "use to the maximum extent practical cost effective alternatives" to fee-simple purchases. By 1984 the national park system held easements on 69,000 acres within 86 individual parks. Outside of Alaska the system included more 1 million acres of privately held inholdings (parcels of private property contained within park boundaries). Plans for the decade called for protecting more than one third of these parcels (358,000 acres) through easements. States had used LWCF funds to acquire only 53 less-than-fee interests in recreational lands, primarily because of the limitations on public use usually dictated by such conservation agreements.[98]

Still, the most common reservations regarding the use of less-than-fee acquisition included their relative expense and the long-term costs of their management. Along the Appalachian Trail (a 2,200-mile mixed-use recreational path with a patchwork of owners), scenic easements averaged 70 percent of the full fee value. Recognizing this conflict, conservation groups frequently sought to study the benefit/costs of easement management versus full ownership. Despite its official reluctance to use easements as part of its own land acquisition programs, the NPS supported historic preservation easements that would be maintained by other institutions.[99] For its part the National Trust for Historic Preservation (NTHP) offered guidance on creating easement programs, especially in light of changes in tax policy, after 1980, that expanded the definition of what qualified as a deductible conservation contribution. As a result the NTHP also revised its policies regarding easements, such that donated protective easements had to be endowed with sufficient funds to cover the costs of annual administration.[100]

Sidebar 6.5   Cluster Development and Zoning

Conservation easements were included in a bundle of land-use planning tools that proponents thought would address the complications of
an increasingly suburban landscape that was itself created by a variety
of factors, not the least of which was "white flight" from urban centers in the aftermath of the *Brown v. Topeka Board of Education* Supreme
Court decision in 1954.

Cluster Developments

The suburban expansion of portions of American society in the postwar period was facilitated by the greater efficiency and impact of
earthmoving equipment and the assumption that sprawling subdivisions laid down within the mass-produced crabgrass frontier would not
require public spaces previously set aside for recreation or other park
uses. Cluster planning focused development on suitable areas, avoided
parcels with special attributes, reduced infrastructure requirements,
and increased commonly held open spaces protected by easements.
In California, one community assigned credits to landowners who
preserved scenic open space along the coastline, allowing for greater-
density developments along inland parcels. Cluster developments were
contrary to traditional models of suburban residential development;
they required not only community support, but also imaginative planning at the earliest stage of a project. During the 1950s and 1960s, as
noted by historian Adam Rome, new values were assigned to protected
lands—conservation, aesthetic, and recreational—each contributing
something to address social challenges presented by suburbanization.[101]
Cluster developments, like the widespread application of conservation
easements, were never broadly accepted by either suburban developers
or their customers.

Zoning

President Johnson's Recreation Advisory Council considered the
use of zoning as a valuable "management tool" for the "control of
scenic values."[102] Zoning is a police power exercised by local governments that constrains the uses permitted within defined areas in
a jurisdiction. Within the historic preservation movement, zoning
was first used in Charleston, South Carolina, beginning in 1931 and
was adopted by numerous urban communities in the aftermath of
urban renewal programs during the 1950s and 1960s. Recognizing
its value as a preservation tool, the NPS conducted a national survey

of preservation zoning laws as part of its recreational planning efforts during the 1930s. At its 1967 annual meeting the NTHP debated the utility of easements versus zoning.[103] As a locally based land-use planning tool, zoning had the potential to augment federal land conservation programs. Viewing new federal parks and protected areas as beneficial ("without exception") to local communities, Congress urged the federal bureaucracy to work with local governments to implement zoning measures in order to prevent unwarranted increases in land prices. It urged greater use of zoning to protect the perimeters of national parks and monuments.[104] However, few states or local governments had the authority to use their zoning authorities to regulate land uses in areas with historical, natural, or recreational values; most controls were concerned with restricting development along floodplains. Since the 1960s there have been consistent and regular—albeit ultimately unsuccessful—calls for federal agencies to develop alternatives to fee-simple ownership, known as "alternative protection strategies." One 1967 study concluded that the inadequacies of zoning as a land control device to achieve conservation objectives had been demonstrated.[105]

Established at the request of President Kennedy in 1961, land acquisition at the Cape Cod National Seashore offered a means by which local zoning could reduce the need for further purchases, but "zoning was never intended as a substitute for acquisition." Recognizing its unique role in the changing climate surrounding federal land acquisition activities, the NPS revised its approaches in 1979.[106] Due to the political nature of most local land-use decisions, zoning, unlike easements or other deed restrictions, was fundamentally an impermanent approach to land conservation.

A Perpetual Alternative

Conservation easements are most effective when public goals are consistent with the existing private uses—where, for example, farmland retains its agricultural land use, and where there is little need for access by the general public. They work best when employed in concert with a clear public purpose, such as the creation of parklands of highways, where the public value of easements enhance the commitment of public funding for the enhancement of a community's total environment. The primary quality is that they are both voluntary and efficient, thus avoiding the pitfalls of takings and eminent domain. Despite these advantages, conservation planners generally saw limited utility for conservation easements. Such devices were highly favorable when applied in rural areas characterized by a relatively static land-use pattern, while their use in urban or suburban areas often resulted in problems of serious proportions.[107] The pattern of NPS acquisition of more than 4,100 conservation easements over nearly nine decades (1929–2017) is illustrated in Figure 6.5.[108] The mid-1970s was the high-water mark for less-than-fee agreements, with more than one third of all easements executed (1,532 out of 4,119). In 2017, the National Conservation Easement Database contained records for more than 25,000 federally held easements.[109]

In the mid-1960s, the NPS saw fee-simple ownership to be the preferred option for its acquisition programs in natural and historical areas, although it acknowledged cases where it would be "advantageous to encourage eclectic action involving alternative land control devices" as an exception to a rigid policy of fee-simple ownership.[110] Easements were considered most appropriate for parcels where the historic use was agricultural and the agency's goal was to continue such practices in order to preserve the historic scene. Less-than-fee ownership appeared ideally structured for newly established federally sponsored recreation areas, where planners envisioned a series of concentric rings of land use surrounding a central recreational attraction. Here again, the goal was to maintain appropriate traditional land uses such as farming, ranching, or forestry. The 1960s were a decade of recreation, with ever-increasing pressure on outdoor recreation that transformed the role of the federal government as it established realistic priorities and criteria to balance recreation versus other land values and uses.[111]

Adapting to the growth of the environmental movement at the beginning of the new decade, the NTHP saw easements as a way to protect historic properties within the total environment. At the first Earth Day celebrations, the NTHP argued that "those despoilers of the environment" were "the same insensitive individuals and organizations that for years had been the

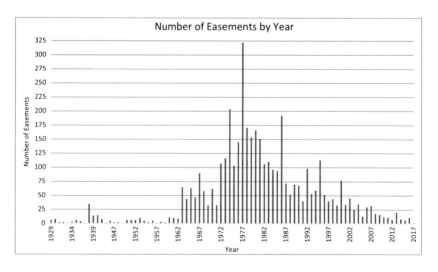

Figure 6.5 Conservation easements held by the National Park Service.

destroyers of our nation's cultural landmarks." While certain civic-minded individuals (such as Supreme Court Justice Hugo Black) could be expected to donate easements on their privately held historic properties, the "most sensitive persons have not only discovered indoor spaces but outdoor spaces, and not just open spaces, but spaces created by streets and buildings."[112]

During the mid-1970s, easements were still considered a significant part of the conservation tool kit. Jess Phelps contends that: "other property programs, such as those involving preservation restrictions or easements, offer a promising alternative with greater potential benefits for an equivalent investment." Conservation easements were perpetually viewed, with some enthusiasm, as an alternative to fee-simple ownership. Characteristically, as the initial easement donors transitioned to a new generation of landowners, difficulties ensued as the relationship between grantee and grantor changed. Easements, then, were in many ways short-term fiscal solutions that came with long-term management responsibilities that were not unlike those found with total ownership. Regarding conventional wisdom on the use of conservation easements, Russell Brenneman concluded: "It is unsafe, for example, to make the generalization that [easements] are always significantly less expensive than the fee and equally unwise to content that they impose no significant management responsibilities on the holder."[113]

Conservation easements played a significant role in the land-use debates of the third quarter of the 20th century, but they were not—as had been predicted in the early 1960s—the solution to rising land values. The realities of perpetual management, especially the need for frequent and meaningful interaction with grantor landowners, were often unanticipated or neglected by easement-holding institutions. That said, conservation easements presented advantages over the protections provided through federal land acquisition programs because their restrictions were permanently attached to official land records. Unlike LWCF parcels, which retained options for land-use conversion by local communities, or HUD–funded open space acquisitions where the conversion procedures were removed after the early 1980s, the restraints established with easements were much harder to alter. The protective capacity for easements was adapted by the historic preservation community in order to ensure investments made through Historic Preservation Fund that restored or rehabilitated historic properties, a practice that continued through subsequent grant programs such as Save America's Treasures. Conservation easements, at least in theory, demonstrated a community's commitment to perpetual protection for significant parcels that enhanced the qualities of the local environment.

Notes

1. For a discussion of the development of coastal parklands see: Jacqueline Alyse Mirandola Mullen, *Coastal Parks for a Metropolitan Nation: How Postwar Politics and Urban Growth Shaped America's Shores*, Ph.D. Dissertation, State University of New York at Albany, 2015

2. William Hollingsworth Whyte, *Open Space Action,* ORRRC Study Report 15 (Washington, DC: Outdoor Recreation Resources Review Commission, 1962), p. 3.
3. Thomas R. Wellock, *Preserving the Nation: The Conservation and Environmental Movements, 1870–2000* (Wheeling, IL: Harlan Davidson, Inc., 2007), pp. 168–169.
4. Fee simple is a permanent and absolute tenure of an estate in land with freedom to dispose of it at will. Rutherford Platt, *Land Use and Society: Geography, Law and Public Policy* (Washington, DC: Island Press, 2014), pp. 160–164.
5. The Accokeek Foundation, *A Study Analysis of the Problems of Preserving Recreational and Open Space Lands,* Prepared for the Bureau of Outdoor Recreation, October 1967, p. 14; Russell Brenneman, *Should 'Easements' be Used to Protect National Historic Landmarks?* (Washington, DC: NPS, 1975), p. 10. Alfred Runte, "How Niagara Falls Was Saved: The Beginning of Esthetic Conservation in the United States," *Conservationist* (April–May 1972); "Beyond the Spectacular: The Niagara Falls Preservation Campaign," *New York Historical Society Quarterly*, Vol. 30 (1973); Henry Fagin and Robert Weinberg, eds., *Planning and Community Appearance* (New York: Regional Planning Association, 1958). Will Sarvis, "Old Eminent Domain and New Scenic Easements: Land Acquisition for the Ozark National Scenic Riverway," *Western Legal History*, Vol. 13, No. 1 (Winter/Spring 2000), p. 15.
6. NPS, *A Study of Park and Recreation Problem of the United States* (Washington, DC: NPS, 1941), p. 125.
7. John H. Sprinkle, *Crafting Preservation Criteria: The National Register of Historic Places and American Historic Preservation* (New York: Routledge, 2014), pp. 134–138 for a discussion of the lack of federal assistance at St. Paul's Eastchester Church, a National Historic Site in Mount Vernon, New York.
8. William Whyte, *The Last Landscape* (Garden City, NY: Doubleday, 1968), p. 84.
9. S. Herbert Evison, *The National Park Service: Conservator of America's Scenic and Historic Heritage* (unpublished manuscript, 1964), pp. 469–490.
10. Gary Day, "An Environmental Approach to Land-Use Planning for Rural Counties," in *Blue Ridqe Parkway and the National Park Service: Planning Frontiers in Rural America: Papers and Proceedings of the Boone Conference, Boone, North Carolina, March 16–18, 1975,* pp. 207–208. Prepared for the Subcommittee on Rural Development of the Committee on Agriculture and Forestry, United States Senate, February 17, 1976. Anne Whisnant, *Super-Scenic Motorway: A Blue Ridge Parkway History* (Chapel Hill: University of North Carolina Press, 2006), p. 117. William Whyte, *The Last Landscape* (Garden City, NY: Doubleday, 1968), p. 84.
11. Norman Glazer, "The Man Who Loved Cities," *The Wilson Quarterly*, Vol. 23, No. 2 (Spring 1999), pp. 27–34. Rutherford Platt, "Holly Whyte: Visionary for a Humane Metropolis," *LandLines*, Vol. 15, No. 1 (January 2003). William Whyte, *The Organization Man* (Garden City, NY: Doubleday, 1956). Adam Rome, "William Whyte, Open Space and Environmental Activism," *Geographical Review*, Vol. 88, No. 2, Historical Geography and Environmental History (April 1998), pp. 259–274; Carol O'Connor, "Sorting out the Suburbs: Patterns of Land Use, Class, and Culture," *American Quarterly*, Vol. 37, No. 3 (1985), pp. 382–294.
12. Alexander Bergstrom, Review of William Whyte, Securing Open Space for Urban American: Conservation Easements, Technical Bulletin 36 (Washington, DC: Urban Land Institute, December 1959); Bird Banding, Vol. 31, No. 3 (July 1960), pp. 169–170. Will Sarvis, "Old Eminent Domain and New Scenic Easements: Land Acquisition for the Ozark National Scenic Riverway," *Western Legal History*, Vol. 13, No. 1 (Winter/Spring 2000), p. 15.
13. William H. White, "A Plan to Save Vanishing U.S. Countryside," *Life Magazine*, August 17, 1959, pp. 88–90, condensed in "Let's Save our Vanishing Countryside," *Readers Digest*, November 1959, pp. 198–204; "How to Save Open Spaces While

There Are Still Some Left to Save," *House and Home* (February 1958), pp. 102–106, 202.

14. Hearings before the Ad Hoc Subcommittee on Urban Growth of the Committee on Banking and Currency, House of Representatives, 91st Congress, First and Second Sessions, on the Quality of Urban Life, Part 2, 1969–1970, p. 379.

15. William H. Whyte, "Introduction," in *The WPA Guide to New York City* (New York: The New Press, 1992).

16. Adam Rome, "William Whyte, Open Space and Environmental Activism," *Geographical Review*, Vol. 88, No. 2, Historical Geography and Environmental History (April 1998), p. 272.

17. William Whyte, *The Last Landscape* (Garden City, NY: Doubleday, 1968), p. 15.

18. Russell Brenneman, *Should 'Easements' be Used to Protect National Historic Landmarks?* (Washington, DC: NPS, 1975), p. 40.

19. Massachusetts Acts, 1956, Chapter 631: An Act Providing for the Establishment and Development of the Massachusetts Bay Circuit.

20. Morton Lustig, "Early Reservation of Open Land," Land Economics, Vol. 35, No. 4 (November 1959), pp. 313–318. Thomas Barrett and Putnam Livermore, *The Conservation Easement in California* (Covelo, California: Island Press, 1983), pp. 9–27.

21. Whyte, *Open Space Action*, p. 3.

22. Russell Brenneman, *Should 'Easements' be Used to Protect National Historic Landmarks?* (Washington, DC: NPS, 1975), pp. 43–45.

23. Donald Lee, "Scenic Easements in the National Park Services Program," *Trends in Parks and Recreation*, Vol. 2, No. 3 (July 1965), pp. 15–17; "U. S. Court Halts Work at Merrywood Estate," *The New York Times*, November 17, 1963.

24. "Cooperation Withheld," *The Washington Post*, July 28, 1962.

25. Department of the Interior and Related Agencies Appropriation Bill, 1965, 88 Congress, Second Session, House of Representatives Report No. 1237, March 13, 1964, pp. 44–45. New construction was limited to a 40-foot height. The easement was later modified to allow for clusters of homes on one acre lots, thus ensuring the preservation of larger areas of open space. Udall estimated that the easement would be valued at $500,000. The actual value was more than $700,000, a sum that was close to amount paid by the developers for fee-simple ownership in the early 1960s. Donald Lee, "Scenic Easements in the National Park Services Program," *Trends in Parks and Recreation*, Vol. 2, No. 3 (July 1965), pp. 15–17.

26. "Udall Tours Scenic Potomac," *The Washington Post*, March 3, 1965. Clark Feiss, "Development Standards, Systems and Regulations Used for Their Implementation in Urbanizing America," Submitted as an Appendix to: Hearings before the Ad Hoc Subcommittee on Urban Growth of the Committee on Banking and Currency, House of Representatives, 91st Congress, First and Second Sessions, on the Quality of Urban Life, Part 2, 1969–1970, p. 625.

27. "Tax Break on Scenic Help Urged," *The Washington Post*, June 10, 1964. Carolyn Agger to Robert Straus, "The Accokeek Foundation, Inc.," May 3, 1965. *Report of the Land Acquisition Policy Task Force* (Washington, DC: NPS, September 1965), p. 16.

28. Edward Weinberg, Deputy Solicitor, Department of the Interior, to Secretary of the Interior, "Authority to Accept Scenic Easements: Historic Sites Act," November 23, 1966. Mark Hudson, "'For the Inspiration of the People of the United States . . .' Tudor Place's Scenic Easement at 50," *Tudor Place* (Spring 2006), pp. 1–2; "Scenic Easement in Georgetown," *Preservation News*, February 1, 1967.

29. Calder Loth, "Forty Years of Preservation: Virginia's Easement Program," *Notes on Virginia* (2005), pp. 49–54; "Easement Protects Virginia Mansion," *Preservation News*, May 1, 1969. "Scenic Easements Protect Oatlands Setting," *Preservation News*, August 1, 1968. "Easements and the Trust," *Preservation News*, January 1, 1973.

30. "Department of the Interior and Related Agencies Appropriation Bill," 1965, 88 Congress, Second Session, House of Representatives Report No. 1237, March 13, 1964, pp. 44–45.

31. "Pope-Leighey House in Preservation History," *Preservation News*, March 1, 1968.

32. Morton Lustig, "Early Reservation of Open Land," *Land Economics*, Vol. 35, No. 4 (November 1959), pp. 313–318.

33. William Whyte, "Research and the Open Space Problem," *The American Journal of Economics and Sociology*, Vol. 21, No. 4 (October 1962), pp. 405–406.

34. Roy Wolfe, "Perspective on Outdoor Recreation: A Bibliographical Survey," *Geographical Review*, Vol. 54, No. 2 (April 1964), pp. 203–238.

35. Will Sarvis, "Old Eminent Domain and New Scenic Easements: Land Acquisition for the Ozark National Scenic Riverway," *Western Legal History*, Vol. 13, No. 1 (Winter/Spring 2000), pp. 16–17. Dumbar Holmes, "Legal Problems of Conservation Easements," *Real Property, Probate and Trust Journal*, Vol. 2 (1967), pp. 352–354 & 360–361. Ronald H. Rosenberg and Pamela G. Jacobstein, "Historic Preservation Easements: A Proposal for Ohio," *University of Dayton Law Review*, Vol. 7, No. 2 (Spring 1982), pp. 313–349.

36. "Resume of Departmental Land Holdings and Their Status." RG368 HCRS Councils and Committees, Box 6.

37. Jacqueline Alyse Mirandola Mullen, *Coastal Parks for a Metropolitan Nation: How Postwar Politics and Urban Growth Shaped America's Shores*, Ph.D. Dissertation, State University of New York at Albany, 2015.

38. In the 24th NPDAB meeting the NPS and its advisory board declared that "there is no such thing as a recreation area of national significance," but with the rise of the outdoor recreation movement, this strict view was modified to new federal mandates. Howard Stagner, "Boards, Committees and Commissions," NPSAB Papers, 60th Meeting, April 21–24, 1969. NPS WASO PHP.

39. Authorized Expenditures for Acquisition and Development of Additions to the National Park System Since July 1961 (revised October 19, 1966). RG 368 HCRS BOR LWCF 68–69 Box 2. BOR, "State Summary of Proposed Federal Land Acquisitions, Land and Water Conservation Fund, F.Y. 1967," October 21,1965. RG 368 HCRS BOR LWCF 68–69, Box 2.

40. NPS, "A Long-Range Federal Outdoor Land Acquisition Program 1967–71 as of September 6, 1965." RG368 HCRS BOR LWCF 68–69, Box 1.

41. BOR, "Appropriations Committee Directions Relating to the Land and Water Conservation Fund," 1969. RG368 HCRS BOR LWCF 68–69, Box 2.

42. BOR, "Reprograming Actions Approved During the Quarter Ending June 30, 1965." RG368 HCRS BOR LWCF 68–69, Box 2. The Secretary of the Interior had to approve any reprograming of acquisition funds when the actual costs rose more than 10 percent above agency estimates.

43. Recreation Advisory Council, "Guides for Federal Outdoor Recreation Investment," July 8, 1965. RG 368 HCRS BOR General Correspondence 62–71, Box 2. In 1964 the Bureau of the Budget had asked BOR to develop criteria for allocating federal funding.

44. Senate Report No. 233, 90th Congress, Second Session, FY 1968, p. 9.

45. The Accokeek Foundation, *A Study Analysis of the Problems of Preserving Recreational and Open Space Lands,* Prepared for the BOR, October 1967, p. 5

46. Edward Crafts to Secretary of Commerce John Connor, May 17, 1966. RG368 HCRS BOR General Correspondence 62–71, Box 1. House Report No. 206, 90th Congress, First Session, FY1968, p. 5. Lawrence Stevens, Associate Director, BOR to Lois Fisher, "New Programs on Recreation and Natural Beauty," September 25, 1965. Fisher was a part of the White House staff. RG368 HCRS BOR General Correspondence 62–71, Box 2. By 1971, NPS estimated that acquisition of its

authorized boundaries and inholdings would cost $302 million to acquire 432,000 acres. Conservation Foundation, *National Parks for the Future: Task Force Reports* (Washington, DC: Conservation Foundation, March 1972), pp. 37–40. The Conservation Foundation was established in 1948 by Henry Fairfield Osborn, retired director of American Museum of Natural History, and received substantial funding from Laurence Rockefeller. Mark Dowie, *Losing Ground: American Environmentalism at the Close of the Twentieth Century* (Cambridge: The MIT Press, 1995), p. 90.

47. BOR, "A Review of Proposed Outdoor Recreation Land Acquisitions by the National Park Service, Forest Service, and Bureau of Sport Fisheries and Wildlife under the Land and Water Conservation Fund Act, 1965, with Recommendations for Fiscal Year 1967 Action," October 1965. RG368 HCRS BOR LWCF 68–69.

48. BOR, "Criteria for Federal Acquisition: Land and Water Conservation Fund," June 14, 1966. RG368 HCRS BOR LWCF 68–69, Box 2.

49. Samuel Hays notes the experimental nature of land conservation efforts in *A History of Environmental Politics Since 1945* (Pittsburgh: University of Pittsburg Press, 2000), pp. 44, 70–71.

50. Will Sarvis, "A Difficult Legacy: Creation of the Ozark National Scenic Riverways," *The Public Historian*, Vol. 24, No. 1 (Winter 2002), pp. 31–52; Donald Stevens, "Ozark National Scenic Riverways: Another Perspective," *The Public Historian*, Vol. 24, No. 2 (Spring 2002), pp. 83–88.

51. Will Sarvis, "Old Eminent Domain and New Scenic Easements: Land Acquisition for the Ozark National Scenic Riverway," *Western Legal History*, Vol. 13, No. 1 (Winter/Spring 2000), p. 17.

52. R. Christopher Anderson, "Some Green for Some Green in West Virginia an Overview of the West Virginia Conservation and Preservation Easements Act," West Virginia Law Review, Vol. 99 (Spring 1997), pp. 617–637; James Boyd, et al., "The Law and Economics of Habitat Conservation: Lessons from an Analysis of Easement Acquisitions," Stanford Environmental Law Journal, Vol. 91 (January 2000), pp. 209–256. Donald Stevens, "Ozark National Scenic Riverways: Another Perspective," *The Public Historian*, Vol. 24, No. 2 (Spring 2002), p. 86.

53. Fiske Kimball Papers, Box 159, "Historic Monuments." MS, n.d. Philadelphia Museum of Art Archives. An accomplished architect and museum curator, in private, Kimball was critical of the non-professional members of the NPSAB.

54. Caroline Janney, "War over a Shrine of Peace: The Appomattox Peace Monument and Retreat from Reconciliation," *The Journal of Southern History*, Vol. 77, No. 1 (February 2011), pp. 91–120.

55. Preston Holder, "Archeological Excavations at the McLean Site, Appomattox Court House National Historical Monument, Virginia, 1941."

56. Ralph Happel, "The McLean (or Surrender) House at the Village of Old Appomattox CH, VA: A Study for the Reconstruction Thereof," NPS, 1940.

57. NPS, "Scenic Easements," Appendix B, in Russell Brenneman, ed., *Should 'Easements' be Used to Protect National Historic Landmarks?* (Washington, DC: NPS, 1975), pp. 11–12.

58. National Parks Conservation Association, "Appomattox Court House National Historical Park: A Resource Assessment," 2008.

59. Russell Brenneman, Should 'Easements' be Used to Protect National Historic Landmarks? (Washington, DC: NPS, 1975), pp. 35–37. "Cuyahoga Park Bills Introduced," Preservation News, June 1, 1974.Comptroller of the United States to Representative John Seiberling, "Allegations That Congressman Seiberling Received Preferential Treatment Regarding Land Transactions in the Cuyahoga Valley National Recreation Area," August 27, 1980.

60. "Outdoor Recreation Grants-in-Aid Manual," Bureau of Outdoor Recreation, 1965. "Hearings before the Ad Hoc Subcommittee on Urban Growth of the

Committee on Banking and Currency," House of Representatives, 91st Congress, First and Second Sessions, on the Quality of Urban Life, Part 2, 1969–1970, pp. 373–398.

61. Chairman, NPSAB to SOI, "Land Acquisition," April 24, 1969.

62. Adam Rome, "William Whyte, Open Space and Environmental Activism," *Geographical Review*, Vol. 88, No. 2, Historical Geography and Environmental History (April 1998), p. 265.

63. Emily Jane Stover, ed., *Protecting Nature's Estate: Techniques for Saving Land* (Washington, DC: BOR, December 1975). This volume presented the results of a two-day conference, "The Land Protection Battle: Some Sparring Techniques," held at the Institute on Man and Science, Rensselaerville, New York, May 1974.

64. Ernest A. Connally, "Historic Preservation," in *Advisory Board on National Parks, Historic Sites, Buildings and Monuments*, pp. 49–54. Papers, 60th Meeting, April 21–24, 1969, pp. 52–53, NPS PHP.

65. NPS, *National Historic Site Designation Orders* (Washington, DC: U.S. Department of the Interior, October 24, 1944).

66. Ronald Lee to Ada Louise Huxtable, October 11, 1963. NPS PHP.

67. Ernest Connally to Douglas Wheeler, "Program of Easements for Historic Properties," December 28, 1973. NPS PHP NHL. Connally was concerned with the implications of having to enforce easement provisions in the future.

68. 71st NPSAB Meeting, October 7–10, 1974. Attachment No. 10. Cornelius Heine, Chief, Historical and Architectural Studies Division, "Transmittal of Study on 'Easements'," April 25, 1975. UMCP Murtagh V8.

69. 72nd NPSAB Meeting, April 21–23, 1975. Attachment No. 10.

70. October 8, 1974: NPSAB HAC Minutes and October 31, 1974. NPSAB Recommendations. Director, HCRS to Assistant Secretary for Fish and Wildlife and Parks, "Easements on the Properties within the Green Springs National Historic Landmark District," January 15, 1979. The study cost $26,000.

71. Russell Brenneman, *Should 'Easements' be Used to Protect National Historic Landmarks?* (Washington, DC: NPS, 1975), p. 121.

72. April 23, 1975 NPSAB to SOI. April 23, 1975 HAC Chair to NPSAB. June 9, 1975: NPS Director to NPSAB. July 10–11, 1975: NPS NHL Regional Coordinators Meeting, DC. October 1975: NPSAB HAC. Gary Everhardt, Director, NPS to Assistant Secretary for Fish and Wildlife and Parks, "Preservation Easement Program," December 21, 1976. The NHL easement policy was adopted in late 1975, with an estimated annual cost of $1 million to support the work of 18 new staff. This additional funding was not apprpriated the program was set aside.

73. OAHP, "Conservation of the Urban Environment: A Report to the Secretary of the Interior," October 1977, p. 25. NPS estimated that monitoring individual National Historic Landmark easements would cost $4,350 per year. Gary Everhardt, Director, NPS to Assistant Secretary for Fish and Wildlife and Parks, "Preservation Easement Program," December 21, 1976.

74. NPSAB Chair to SOI, April 24, 1974. This proposal was affirmed at the subsequent NPSAB History Areas Committee (HAC) meeting in October 1974. The district contained a "unique assemblage of architecture" and a large number of surviving outbuildings at 30 major plantation homes. Acting Associate Solicitor, Conservation and Wildlife to Assistant Secretary for Fish and Wildlife and Parks, "Legal Considerations Concerning the Adoption of a Policy of Accepting Easements over Real Properties on the National Register of Historic Places," October 10, 1973, Appendix B. Russell Brenneman, *Should 'Easements' be Used to Protect National Historic Landmarks?* (Washington, DC: NPS, 1975).

75. The proposed prison received extensive coverage in the Washington Post: Helen Dewar, "Virginia Prison Plan Scored," August 26, 1972; "State Criticism Clouds

Virginia Prison Project," September 27, 1972; "Holton Acts to Dump Va. Prison Site," October 11, 1972; "Holton Proposal for Prison At Green Springs Criticized," February 4, 1973. "Va. Is Told to Comply on Jail Site," The Washington Post, May 9, 1974.Helen Dewar, "Despite Local Objections: Virginia Prison Site Decided," *The Washington Post*, March 31, 1972.

76. Carleton Knight, III, "State Moves Prison from Green Springs," Preservation News, November 1, 1972.Bill Matuszeski to Chairman, Council on Environmental Quality, "Green Springs Virginia Historic Preservation Efforts," April 6, 1973. RG 429, CEQ, Executive Director, 1970–1976, Box 8, Historic Preservation File.*Revitalization by Design, FY 66–77* (Washington, DC: National Endowment for the Arts, 1978).

77. Carleton Knight, III, "Who Is Linwood Holton and Why Is He Doing These Terrible Things to Us?" Preservation News, May 1, 1973; Helen Dewar, "Morton Asks Change in Site for Green Springs Prison," The Washington Post, August 21, 1973. Bill Matuszeski to Chairman, Council on Environmental Quality, "Green Springs Virginia Historic Preservation Efforts," April 6, 1973. RG 429, CEQ, Executive Director, 1970–1976, Box 8, Historic Preservation File. CEQ Chairman Russell Train to Governor Holton, April 19, 1973. Helen Dewar, "Prison Site Chosen as Historic District," *The Washington Post*, May 14, 1974; "Victory in Green Springs," *The Washington Post*, June 21, 1974; "W.R. Grace Reassesses Green Spring Mining," *Preservation News*, May 1, 1976.

78. Earnest Connally to Assistant Secretary of the Interior for Fish and Wildlife and Parks, "Green Springs Easements," August 31, 1973. NPS PHP Green Springs File.

79. Benjamin Levy and Katherine Cole, Report on Green Springs Historic District for the Secretary of the Interior's Advisory Board on National Parks, Historic Sites, Buildings, and Monuments at Its Meeting April 1974. NPS, OAHP, 1974.

80. Despite these concerns, the Secretary of the Interior designated the Green Springs NHL historic district soon after the NPSAB's recommendation of April 24, 1974. "Green Springs District, VA., Declared a National Historic Landmark," DOI New Release, May 16, 1974. Philip Steward to Assistant Chief, Administration, Division of Land Acquisition, "Restrictive (Development) Easements over National Historic Landmarks," October 9, 1974. NPS PHP Green Springs File.

81. Carleton Knight, III, "State Moves Prison from Green Springs," Preservation News, November 1, 1972; "N.Y. Firm Studies Open-Pit Mining in Historic Va. County," The Washington Post, December 31, 1972. "W.R. Grace Reassesses Green Spring Mining," Preservation News, May 1, 1976. Megan Rosenfeld, "Historic Area Strip Mining Triggers Fight in Louisa," *The Washington Post*, September 5, 1974; Gordon Chapman, "Virginia's Kitty Litter War," *The Washington Post*, October 3, 1976.

82. "Developments & Varied Problems Threaten 117 National Landmarks," National Parks and Conservation Magazine, Vol. 53, No. 3 (March 1979), pp. 20–28. "Green Springs Action Is Ruled Improper," *The Washington Post*, May 3, 1975; Assistant Secretary, Fish and Wildlife, and Parks to Secretary of the Interior, "Recommendation to Re-Designate and Relist Green Springs Historic District and to Accept Certain Preservation Easements on Lands within the Historic District," NPS draft, n.d. NPS PHP Green Springs File.

83. Robert Herbst, Assistant Secretary for Fish and Wildlife and Parks to Secretary of the Interior Cecil Andrus, "Green Springs Historic District, Louis County, Virginia," December 2, 1977; "Andrus to Accept Easements for Green Springs Historic District," DOI Press Release, December 15, 1977; "U.S. to Accept Easements on Historic Area," *The Washington Post*, January 22, 1977; "Update: Green Springs," *Preservation News*, February 1, 1978. This action was vacated by federal court order August 11, 1980. Ben Franklin, "Appeal Weighed as Judge Voids U.S. 'Landmark'," *The New York Times*, August 13, 1980; "Landmark Designations are Upheld by New Law," *The New York Times*, December 14, 1981,

84. Robert Herbst to Director, NPS, "Green Springs National Historic Landmark District," April 10, 1979. Director, NPS to Assistant Secretary for Fish and Wildlife and Parks, "Easements on the Properties within the Green Springs NHL District," March 15, 1979; Director, HCRS to Assistant Secretary for Fish and Wildlife and Parks, "Easements on the properties within the Green Springs National Historic Landmark District," January 15, 1979. Privately, NPS estimated that development of an easement management plan would cost $300,000 over two years, but afterward oversight activities would be minimal. NPS PHP Green Springs File. Ben Levy to Ross Holland, "Green Springs," May 27, 1980. Levy equated the "heavy responsibility" for managing the easements to that of units of the national park system. NPS PHP Green Springs File.

85. Grandma Clara to Stewart Udall, July 6, 1966 and Stewart Udall to Mrs. Morris Enger, July 27, 1966.

86. Tim Lehman, "Public Values, Private Lands: Origins and Ironies of Farmland Preservation in Congress," *Agricultural History*, Vol. 66, No. 2, History of Agriculture and the Environment (Spring 1992), pp. 257–272.

87. Laura Kolar, "'Selling the Farm': New Frontier Conservation and the USDA Farm Recreation Policies of the 1960s," *Agricultural History*, Vol. 86, No. 1 (Winter 2012), pp. 55–77.

88. Ronald Bird and Buis Inman, *Income Opportunities for Rural Families from Outdoor Recreation Enterprises*, United States Department of Agriculture (Washington, DC: GPO, 1965). Roy Buck, "An Interpretation of Rural Values," in *A Place to Live: The 1963 Yearbook of Agriculture* (Washington, DC: GPO, 1963), p. 11.

89. Neal Pierce, "Rural Dilemmas," *Preservation News*, Vol. 20, No. 11, October 1980.

90. Douglas Wheeler, "Rural Efforts," Preservation News, Vol. 20, No. 13, December 1980. Neal Peirce, "Rural Dilemmas," Preservation News, Vol. 20, No. 11, October 1980. "Can Rural America be Saved?" *Preservation News*, Vol. 19, No. 2, February 1979. Annapolis, Maryland, hosted a regional rural preservation conference in April 1979.

91. Maryland was the first state to offer farmers reduced tax burdens. Michael Burns, "Disappearing Farms," *The Washington Post*, May 19, 1974. Loudon County, Virginia authorized a special tax rate for farmlands. "Land Planning," *Preservation News*, Vol. 12, No. 11, November 1972. Suffolk County, New York established a program to purchase development rights from farm owners. "Trust in Land," *Preservation News*, Vol. 18, No. 1, January 1978.

92. Tim Lehman, "Public Values, Private Lands: Origins and Ironies of Farmland Preservation in Congress," Agricultural History, Vol. 66, No. 2, History of Agriculture and the Environment (Spring 1992), pp. 257–272. "Land Use or Abuse?" *Preservation News*, Vol. 12, No. 10, October 1972; Jayne E. Daly, "A Glimpse of the Past: A Vision for the Future: Senator Henry M. Jackson and National Land Use Legislation," *The Urban Lawyer*, Vol. 28, No. 1 (Winter 1996), pp. 7–39; Robert Kaufman, *Henry M. Jackson: A Life in Politics* (Seattle: University of Washington Press, 2000), pp. 201–208.

93. Douglas Wheeler, "Rural Efforts," Preservation News, Vol. 20, No. 13, December 1980. Russell Train, "Environment," *Preservation News*, Vol. 13, No. 5, May 1973; "President Calls for Environmental Laws," *Preservation News*, Vol. 12, No. 4, April 1973; Marquis Childs, "Burying the Land Use Bill," *Preservation News*, Vol. 14, No. 5, May 1974, reprinted from *The Washington Post*, March 24, 1974.

94. Robert Coughlin and Thomas Plaut, "Less-Than-Fee Acquisition for the Preservation of Open Space: Does It Work?" American Institute of Planners Journal, Vol. 44, No. 4 (October 1978), pp. 452–262. Charles Rinaldi, Chief, Land Acquisition Division to Mike Lambe, Chief, Legislative Division, "Request for Drafting Service on Acquisition of Fee versus Scenic Easements," January 17, 1978, NPS Park Planning and Special Studies Subject Files.

95. More that 84 percent of fee-simple parcels were voluntarily purchased, with only 46 percent easement parcels. Land Acquisition Officer to John Wright, Chief, Division of Lands, Midwest Regional Office, "Scenic Easements in the Lower St. Croix National Scenic Riverway," November 17, 1976. NPS Park Planning and Special Studies Subject Files.

96. Department of the Interior, New Tools for Land Protection: An Introductory Handbook (Washington, DC: Office of the Assistant Secretary for Fish and Wildlife and Parks, July 1982).The Granville Corporation, *Study of Land and Water Conservation Fund Financial Assistance Alternatives* (Washington, DC: Heritage Conservation and Recreation Service, 1981), p. 5.

97. The Granville Corporation, *Study of Land and Water Conservation Fund Financial Assistance Alternatives* (Washington, DC: Heritage Conservation and Recreation Service, 1981), pp. 5–6.

98. NPS, "NPS-2: Planning Process Guidelines, Chapter VIII: Easements," 1986.Acting Deputy Director to Regional Directors, "Land and Water Conservation Fund: Acquisition of Scenic or Conservation Easements," October 11, 1984. NPS Park Planning and Special Studies Subject Files.

99. American Land Forum, Alternatives for Land Protection: A Review of Case Studies in Eight National Parks (Washington, DC: NPS, 1982). Charles Fisher, William Macrostie, and Christopher Sowick, *Directory of Historic Preservation Easement Organizations* (Washington, DC: NPS, September 1981).

100. A. Elizabeth Watson, "Establishing an Easement Program to Protect Historic, Scenic and Natural Resources," Information Sheet No. 25, NTHP, 1980; Emma Jane Saxe, "How to Qualify Historic Properties under the New Federal Law Affecting Easements," NPS, National Register Division, Summer 1981.The endowment was set at 20 times the anticipated cost of annual administration. NTHP, "Easement Endowment Guidelines," April 19, 1983. UMCP Murtagh Series V, Box 21.

101. Adam Rome, "William Whyte, Open Space and Environmental Activism," *Geographical Review*, Vol. 88, No. 2, Historical Geography and Environmental History (April 1998), pp. 259–274.

102. Recreational Advisory Council, "Notes on Meeting of Recreational Advisory Council Staff, July 21, 1964," July 24, 1964. RG 368 HCRS BOR General Correspondence 62–71 Box 1.

103. Branch Spaulding, "Memorandum for the Director,"October 12, 1936. NPS NHL History Files. NTHP 21st Annual Meeting Agenda, St. Louis, Missouri, October 19–22, 1967.

104. House Report No 1405, 89th Congress, Second Session, FY 1967, p. 5; BOR, "Appropriations Committee Directions Relating to the Land and Water Conservation Fund," 1969. RG368 HCRS BOR LWCF 68–69, Box 2. House Letter of February 7, 1967 in response to a NPS reprogramming request #67–12 quoted in BOR, "Appropriations Committee Directions Relating to the Land and Water Conservation Fund," 1969. RG368 HCRS BOR LWCF 68–69, Box 2. At certain Civil War sites, Congress restricted acquisition unless local governments had adopted zoning regulations to restrict adjacent commercial development. Conference Report, House Report No. 797, 87th Congress, First Session, FY 1962; Conference Report, House Report No. 1446, 87th Congress, Second Session, FY 1963.

105. The Accokeek Foundation, *A Study Analysis of the Problems of Preserving Recreational and Open Space Lands,* Prepared for the BOR, October 1967, p. 12.

106. General Accounting Office, *The Federal Drive to Acquire Private Lands Should be Reassessed* (Washington, DC: Government Printing Office, December 14, 1979), pp. 66–69.

107. Timothy Fox, Land Conservation and Preservation Techniques (Washington, DC: Heritage Conservation and Recreation Service, 1979), pp. 14–15. James

Boyd, Kathryn Caballero, and R. David Simpson, "The Law and Economics of Habitat Conservation: Lessons from an Analysis of Easement Acquisitions," Stanford Environmental Law Review, Vol. 19 (2000), pp. 209–255. NPS, *Report of the Land Acquisition Policy Task Force* (Washington, DC: NPS, September 1965), pp. 14–15.

108. There are 4,119 easements held by the NPS, as recorded by the NPS Land Resources Division.

109. While the entire database includes information on 130,000 easements, only 761 of the 25,000 federal easements were listed with a historic preservation purpose (http://conservationeasement.us/).

110. NPS, *Report of the Land Acquisition Policy Task Force* (Washington, DC: NPS, September 1965), pp. 56–57.

111. NPS, Report of the Land Acquisition Policy Task Force (Washington, DC: NPS, September 1965), pp. 58–59. Panel Discussion: Forecast, NPSAB 60th Meeting Papers, April 21–24, 1969, p. 19. NPS PHP.

112. Easements and zoning were two primary topics at the NTHP conference "Preservation Law, 1971," May 1–2, 1971, Washington, DC. "Are Landmarks Part of the Environment?" *Preservation News*, March 1, 1970.

113. Russell Brenneman, *Should 'Easements' Be Used to Protect National Historic Landmarks?* (Washington, DC: NPS, 1975), p. 12. See Jess Phelps, "Preserving Preservation Easement? Preservation Easements in an Uncertain Regulatory Future," Nebraska Law Review, Vol. 91, No. 1 (2012), pp. 121–256; "Preserving Perpetuity? Exploring the Challenges of Perpetual Preservation in an Ever-Changing World," Environmental Law, Vol. 43, No. 4 (2013), pp. 941–988; "Moving Beyond Preservation Paralysis? Evaluating Post-Regulatory Alternatives for Twenty-First Century Preservation," Vermont Law Review, Vol. 37, No. 1 (Fall 2012), pp. 113–156; "'Scarcely a Vestige of Antiquity Remains': Evaluating the Role of Preservation Easements in Protecting Historic Religious Architecture," Environmental Law Reporter, Vol. 44, No. 9 (2014), pp. 10808–10831; "Preserving National Historic Landmarks?" New York University Environmental Law Journal, Vol. 24 (2016), pp. 137–200.

7 Preservation and Enhancement of the Cultural Environment

Old buildings, open spaces, and easements made for ungainly partners in the conservation of non-renewable resources in the third quarter of the 20th century. Linked at times by the concept of beauty, historic buildings were both symbols of architectural achievement and continuity with the past, while scenic vistas presented an idealized landscape of a natural world, seemingly untouched by human activity. Both nature and history had utility: they provided multiple potential recreational opportunities and served to refresh the increasingly hectic souls of post–World War II Americans. Yet, as noted by Roderick Nash, the concept of protecting a landscape's intangible values was complicated by the "perplexing subjective dimension" of defining how these places led to happiness for individuals and communities.[1] Led by several federal agencies (the primary sources of funding for land acquisition), the identification, evaluation, and designation of protected areas, whether historic or scenic, was shaped by the administrative stovepipes of bureaucratic regulation and policy that constrained any potential collaboration or integration. Beginning in the 1960s, the environmental movement slowly erased some of the boundaries between land conservation and historic preservation as both sides began to recognize the limitations of their fundamental precepts.[2] In a world full of seemingly constant change, preservation and conservation were two sides of the same coin, much as sustainability and resiliency have become in today's world of a changing climate. By the 1970s, the phrase "cultural environment" began to integrate consideration of what was, at the same time, a landscape of nature and culture.

Over the years, the intersection of the wider land conservation bureaucracy with the historic preservation movement was in many ways one of semantics, as expressed in the definition of the keywords "conservation" and "preservation." Many European and some American preservationists used the phrase "historic conservation," but in the United States most advocates adopted "preservation" to distinguish the practice from more traditional uses of "conservation" that tended to focus on the stewardship of natural resources.[3] In North America, "conservation"—adapted from the fine arts field—had been adopted by natural resource advocates long before Fiske Kimball's 1941 announcement of the preservation movement.[4] For many in the postwar period, conservation retained its close relationship to the land, as in the protection of agricultural soil from erosion. Yet senior NPS architects like Thomas Vint could remark in the 1950s: "Our business isn't laying out lawns; we are in the conservation business."[5]

Harkening back to the value concepts put forward by Alois Riegl at the beginning of the 20th century, in 2003 Miles Glendinning described the European conservation movement for the protection of historic properties as a "cult of the modern age." The preservation of historic sites, or by extension the official recognition of any property, parcel, or landscape, was one of the 20th century's "most powerful and alluring substitutes for religious mystery and eternity."[6] Yet, just as the preservation movement had to accept at a fundamental level that it could not save every historic place, its practitioners had to acknowledge the thermodynamic principle that all physical evidence of the past, both cultural and natural, is destined to change. Can we accept, asked Glendinning, "the concept that all buildings, like nations, are ephemeral social constructions, and that the built environment is a testament to change rather than something of enduring materiality"?[7] Rooted in the American experience and its many post–World War II transformations, the land conservation and historic preservation movements share the conflict of permanence and transience.[8]

The transitory essence of protected spaces and places is somewhat countered by the relative permanence of private property rights within the American system. Zoning overlays that constrain (or rather shape) changes to the architectural fabric within locally designated historic districts are only as fixed as the will of the local city or town council of elected officials. Easements, which are tied to the deed that legitimizes and documents ownership of a particular parcel, are instruments of land-use control that maintain at least stronger illusion of permanency.

At first, historic preservation's principal conventions were seated in stewardship and resistance to physical change. In the third quarter of the 20th century, the preservation movement expanded in scope and complexity, moving from a focus on the educational and inspirational values of individual historic properties to one that centered on managing change through adaptive use found in historic districts, cultural landscapes, and the total environment.

Both historic preservation and land conservation were significantly impacted by the nationwide rise of the environmental movement during the 1960s. The cultural and political change fostered by Rachel Carson's *Silent Spring* (1962) was supplemented by the response to Steward Udall's *Quiet Crisis* (1963), which called for a reassessment of the American relationship with wilderness, open space, and landscape from an ecological perspective.[9] Increasing concern for the quality of the natural environment not only recognized the constancy of change, but also acknowledged the need for comprehensive land-use planning at all levels of government.

Despite the growing influence of government through programs like the Urban Renewal Administration (URA) open space grants or the Land and

Water Conservation Fund (LWCF), individuals still played important roles in the movements: the faithful in both groups shared similar attributes. Among the various gentry that supported conservation, there was "at least one white-haired lady," noted William Whyte, "of vast energy, not the kind who wears tennis shoes," but who were "bridge sharks and winners of battles."[10] In rural communities many of the fiercest protectors of the countryside were "come heres," or recent transplants from suburbia and the cities:

> They are also keenly interested in its history and usually know more about it that the longtime residents. If there is an old building threatened by a highway, they are the ones who will discover that its 1910 façade masks an old structure of great architectural and historical significance, and they will organize the drive for its preservation, with the white-haired lady at the lead.[11]

Many activists belied the characterization of "white-haired old ladies." Take for example Pittsburgh, Pennsylvania, native and Bryn Mawr graduate Barbara Hoffstot, who began her tenure as a trustee for the National Trust for Historic Preservation (NTHP) in 1964 (at age 45) by hosting a party to generate support for the association and kick-start the Pittsburgh Historic Landmarks Foundation. To illustrate preservation's dire situation, she noted the continuing failure of federal efforts to fully fund the acquisition of properties included within George Washington's Mount Vernon Potomac River overlook. She helped lead the fight to save her city's Old North Side Post Office, which had been transferred via an urban renewal authority to a private company for redevelopment as the Allegheny Center.[12] Consulting with her fellow NTHP trustee Austin Leland, who was engaged in his own campaign to save the Old Post Office and Custom House in St. Louis, Missouri, she questioned how the surplus property actions of the General Services Administration (GSA) fit into President Lyndon Johnson's "fine talk on saving the beauty of America."[13] While the Old North Side Post Office was salvaged and eventually rehabilitated as a city museum in 1972, Hoffstot complained about the GSA's removal of various pieces of interior ornamentation and woodwork, including five eagle-shaped plaques from another surplus property, the Fourth Avenue Post Office. From her perspective, after a 75-year presence in the city, the building—and its contents—had become a locally significant resource and was properly the property of local citizens, despite its federal ownership.[14]

The dedication of Hoffstot, Leland, and other activists was augmented by the appearance of an emerging class of preservation and conservation professionals: individuals like Fritz Gutheim, William Whyte, and Russell Brenneman. The old-school bureaucrats, like Conrad Wirth, Ronald Lee, and Charles Peterson, were replaced in the 1960s by a new generation of practitioners, including Robert Utley, William Murtagh, and Ernest Connally. Robert Garvey, another leading administrator of the "new preservation," agreed with Hoffstot's justifiable frustration with historic preservation practice. Overlapping layers of bureaucracy were "core of our many problems" within the federal stovepiped approach to both conservation and preservation, as was the influence of the real estate market on the value of land.[15]

During the post–World War II generation, property values fast outpaced the historic, scenic, and natural values that the majority of individual citizens could bring to bear in adapting to a rapidly changing urban and suburban landscape. Cassandra-like predictions from the postwar period were seemingly confirmed as the nation was unable to marshal the funds necessary to ensure the conservation of valued spaces.

> Recent years have witnessed the neglect, destruction, and loss of a rapidly growing number of the important historic sites and buildings of America. Some of these are historic houses on the outskirts of expanding cities where modern industrial or real estate developments engulf them. Other places, associated with great men and event happen to be in the way of highway, turnpike, or bridge construction.[16]

Areas of National Concern

The challenges facing those individuals interested in the conservation of the natural and historic environment during the third quarter of the 20th century were substantial, and the bureaucratic responses were equally significant.[17] The Bicentennial of the Declaration of Independence in 1976 presented an opportunity to address many of the land protection issues that confronted the land conservation and historic preservation movements. Preservationists made significant gains, including:

•   creation of the Historic Preservation Fund (HPF), which placed the source of potential federal historic preservation appropriations within the same outer continental shelf revenues that supported the LWCF;
•   establishment of the historic rehabilitation tax credit program, which fostered the adaptive use of income producing properties; and,
•   separation of the Advisory Council on Historic Preservation (ACHP) from the Department of the Interior, which increased its independence and avoided conflicts of interests with the National Park Service (NPS).

At the same time, President Gerald Ford, the only chief executive to have served as an NPS employee, proposed, while on a visit to Yellowstone National Park, the Bicentennial Land Heritage Act, which would have created a $1.5 billion program to support land acquisition within the national park system, as well as support grants to cities and towns to improve local and regional park infrastructure. This proposal enhanced the Bureau of Outdoor Recreation (BOR) Legacy of Parks program, which transferred surplus federal lands and waters to state and local governments at no cost.Some viewed the Bicentennial Land

Heritage Act as a partisan political ploy, one designed to soften criticism of the Ford administration's conservation policies during the ongoing presidential election campaign. The legislation never reached the president's desk.[18]

During the subsequent administration of President Jimmy Carter, land-use planners put forward the concept of "areas of national concern" (ANC) during the late 1970s as a means to transfer the wider engagement with the conservation of the cultural and natural environment from the federal government to the states, thereby increasing their role in local planning decisions. Some states followed suit in trying to identify critically important parcels that were environmentally fragile, historically important, or with substantial scenic or recreational values.[19] For its part, the Department of the Interior wanted to "deal in an equal and consistent way with a wide variety of proposals for the conservation of large and complex natural, cultural, and recreational landscape."[20] The ANC approach also addressed continuing restrictions on the funds available to purchase—not to mention develop and maintain—protected lands. As communities became more unwilling to use local tax revenues to acquire open spaces, they came to increasingly rely on federal programs such as the LWCF.

During this period, as was seen at Virginia's Green Springs community, localities that sought to retain their rural character found that state governments were not always supportive of historically based aesthetic concerns as a basis for broad land-use regulation, whereas the protection of environmentally critical areas such as wetlands was often considered legitimate. The environmental movement helped to integrate the concerns of the conservation and preservation movements through a growing appreciation for both the natural and cultural landscape.[21] By the late 1970s, however, some planners thought that

> The time may now be ripe for public acceptance of using the wide variety of regulations, taxation, and less-than-fee acquisition tools to conserve special places—conservation strategies that get more at less cost to the taxpayer, not only now but in the future.[22]

The ANC system proposal, a product of the ill-fated administrative experiment that had been the Heritage Conservation and Recreation Service, was designed to achieve national goals for the protection of unique landscapes and resources—especially those that local governments were unwilling to protect and that did not meet national standards for historical significance or ecological uniqueness. In some ways its goals paralleled those of the "expanded" National Register of Historic Places after 1966, which comprised an official list of those properties thought to be worthy of conservation at the state and local level.[23] It represented a partial commitment on the part of the national government, a partnership that required state and local jurisdictions to take active and substantial planning and land-use measures to identify and protect areas with unique natural, cultural, and recreational resources.

The inauguration of the Reagan administration in 1981 signaled a reevaluation of the country's land conservation and historic preservation policies. "Debates over public lands and environmental politics thus played a supporting role," according to James Morton Turner, "in a central transition in postwar American politics: the decline of liberalism and the rise of modern conservatism."[24] Six months after being sworn in as the 43rd Secretary of the Interior, the former director of the BOR, James Watt, participated in a Senate-sponsored workshop on public land acquisition. Senator Malcolm Wallop introduced the session by reflecting on the history of land conservation within the United States, stating that the country had a "heavy moral obligation" to care for its protected lands "of rare quality" and it was time to "husband—not necessarily to own—our heritage." Acknowledging another period of rapidly increasing land values, Senator Dale Bumpers countered that exploring less-than-fee ownership was a viable alternative only if the significant values contained within the areas were adequately protected. Thus the ongoing debate over the nature of land conservation and historic preservation entered another chapter.[25]

Preservation and Enhancement of the Cultural Environment

There was considerable overlap between participants in the recreation and the environmental movements during the postwar period, primarily because of their shared concern for the conservation of natural landscapes and open spaces. There was also a growing awareness of recreation as a "social movement with major economic and social significance."[26] Riding this wave of emerging environmental concern, preservationists tried to acquire supplemental support for saving historic places. Soon after joining the leadership of the NTHP, Gordon Gray spoke to the Garden Club of America in New York City. Admitting that his topic, "Conservation by Preservation of Our Heritage" (see Appendix 7.1), was "less than crystal clear," Gray opined that "conservation in its broadest and most patriotic sense cannot ignore historic preservation." He stressed the idea that conservation and preservation were not static, "dust-covered anachronisms," but rather were dedicated to safeguarding things that were "important, meaningful, and beautiful." Viewing historic communities from an increasingly environmental perspective became trendy during the 1960s.[27]

Before he left the NTHP to join the newly created Advisory Council on Historic Preservation, Robert Garvey reflected that "the act of preservation and the product preserved are a part of a meaningful life and a meaningful total environment." Across the country, the concentration on single buildings or sites had led to the neglect of the total environment and increased hazards on individual properties.[28] As with so many other advances in saving spaces during the period, the total-environment concept grew out of planning issues found in urban areas. Would the NPS have expanded its historic site criteria in 1965 to include historic districts as a property type without the extensive and significant impact of urban renewal programs of a diverse assemblage of historic resources? William Murtagh, the first keeper of the National Register of Historic Places, traced trace the history of the preservation movement as flowing from house museums to "total environment projects seen in historic district preservation."[29] During the early years of the National Register, Murtagh "energetically preached" the environmental values of the Johnson administration's new preservation. This approach and terminology even found its way into the official policies of the NPS.[30]

By 1968 the NTHP had embraced the new paradigm: "Today we prize the total [historic] development of the country and the total environment of cultural and natural resources." In fact, the organization adopted "Preservation and the Total Environment" as the theme for its annual meeting held in Savannah, Georgia, during October 1968.[31] Not surprisingly, the editorial staff of *Preservation News* pushed the concept:

> History and preservation must be related to the needs of the total community, the total environment. Its importance to the ghetto life as well to the suburbs, to the fabric of the close city spaces as well as to the order of the still, open rural landscape, must be dramatized to its true urgency.[32]

In 1968, then-presidential candidate Richard Nixon congratulated the leadership of the NTHP for its annual conference theme. During Nixon's first term the phrase "total environment" was augmented by the mantra expressed in Executive Order No. 11593: the "preservation and enhancement of the cultural environment."[33] By the 10th anniversary of the National Historic Preservation Act in 1976, many people had begun to see that disfiguration of urban areas impaired the total environment just as much as water pollution and wildlife degradation.[34] It also appeared that, just as preservationists were becoming more aware of the natural environment, conservationists had become aware of the contribution made to daily life by the human-built environment.[35] Adopting a landscape perspective forced both the conservation and historic preservation movements to become less isolated and to see themselves as facets of the broader environmental movement.[36]

Valuing Vision

The consortium of individuals and organizations that banded together as part of Operation Overview to preserve the viewshed from the piazza of George Washington's Mount Vernon estate was consistently surprised by the difficulties in obtaining the necessary legislative and financial support for its objective. It was patently obvious, at least to Frances Bolton, Rosamund Beirne, Robert Straus, and Charles Wall, that the remarkably pristine view of fields and forests was indeed worthy of permanent protection as a national treasure. Reluctantly accepting the necessity of relying on governmental rather than private intervention, this consortium was quite creative in its core and

Figure 7.1 Secretary of the Interior Stewart Udall, Lady Bird Johnson, and Laurance
Rockefeller looking at an architectural model of the Washington DC Mall area
during a White House luncheon on beautification in April 1967.

Source: LBJ Library photo by Robert Knudsen

periphery model of fee-simple and less-than-fee landscape stewardship, as well as the creation of tax adjustments for donated easements. Despite any misgivings the NPS might have had regarding the creation of a new park with hybrid ownership, the agency included information on the Piscataway Park easement program (and its taxation advantages) as background for creation of the National Historic Preservation Act.[37]

In the spring of 1965, with the strong support of the First Lady, the Johnson administration sponsored the White House Conference on Natural Beauty. President Johnson chose Laurance Rockefeller to shepherd an ambitious agenda that included a wide range of land conservation issues facing the country, especially full funding for BOR's and HUD's grant programs.[38] Recognizing the necessity for government intervention in the protection of historical and natural resources and reflection on her experience with Operation Overview, Ohio Representative Frances Bolton concluded that there would "never be enough money in the public treasury to do all that is necessary for preservation and conservation."[39] This position was echoed a decade later by the Carter administration: "There simply are not enough dollars in the Federal treasury to buy everything we might want to buy."[40] Adequate funding, or the lack thereof, was an issue shared by the many participants in the broader conservation movement. This fact perpetuated the desire for a less-expensive solution, one seen in the acquisition of less-than-fee easements. This pattern would continue throughout the 20th century.

In contrast to concerns across the country about the relative lack of protected open spaces, the problem with surplus federal property was that there were simply too many old forts and seemingly obsolete federal buildings (courthouses, post offices, and custom houses). Many of these structures were simply too large for local communities to absorb only as historic monuments. Transferring former military installations and other lands to local communities addressed some open space and recreational needs in situations where the lands were conveniently seated, readily accessible, and adaptable to their new purpose. However, although recycling older buildings seemed a natural fit, continuing the contribution of a substantial federal real estate investment within urban settings ran counter to the inclinations and policy directives of the renewalists and their approach to urban infrastructure. After 1972, as a result of complicated and long-drawn-out battles over the fate of the Old San Francisco Mint and other great white elephant buildings, GSA allowed local communities to use surplus historic properties for profit-generating activities. The result has been an increased number of historic properties being productively reused by states and localities, while maintaining their historic characteristics and community vitality.[41]

Urban affairs dominated much of the domestic and land-use policy in the third quarter of the 20th century as the impact of Supreme Court rulings (*Berman v. Parker* and *Brown v. Board of Education*), the interstate highway system, and the 30-year residential mortgage enabled the exodus of many middle-class white communities from metropolitan centers to the crabgrass frontier. Cities had not planned for the conservation of open spaces within their central business districts, so the well-considered plans of the renewalists provided the opportunity—with federal financial assistance—to lay waste to and reshape urban communities across the country. Because urban open spaces were so easily vulnerable to compromise and outright destruction, the planner Lawrence Halprin thought that these parcels should be "considered inviolate."[42] The national application of the URA's open space program clearly illustrated the unmet need that local communities had for the acquisition of places to play, relax, and recreate. Its bureaucratic success was mimicked and magnified by the creation of the LWCF in 1965.

"Our brave front of optimism," announced Udall, "has been warranted" as the LWCF augmented the process and fulfilled the mission begun with the Outdoor Recreation Resources Review Commission in the late 1950s.[43] Late in his NPS career, Charles Peterson was initially enthusiastic about the new Bureau of Outdoor Recreation, but found that the agency was generally unable to incorporate them into its land conservation mission.[44] When the LWCF was proposed by the Kennedy administration, it was controversial, not only because it represented a new guarantee of federal assistance for land acquisition, but also because it endorsed the practice of entrance and user fees at national parks and other protected lands. This change was equal to that authorized just a few years before that allowed federal agencies to purchase shorelines, parkland, and other protected spaces (as opposed to accepting donations). In the same way, the National Historic Preservation Act of 1966 was an expansion of the federal role in historic preservation that had been established with the Historic Sites Act of 1935. Initial optimism espoused by Udall and others that the LWCF would be fiscally self-supporting proved inaccurate: land price escalation across the country easily outpaced the funding generated by user fees, marine fuel taxes, and conservation stickers on automobiles. Since the 1970s, land conservation has relied on non-tax source of funding through receipts from outer continental shelf resource extraction.[45] Statewide outdoor recreation and historic preservation planning shared certain attributes, chief among them the desire for federal assistance to guide the standards used in the identification and classification of resources. Confronting the fiscal limitation of the period, both open space and historic preservation advocates sought to develop creative land-use tools that could protect significant resources without the need for direct ownership and management.

Following the doctrine preached by William Whyte and others, Robert Garvey, while still at the National Trust, argued that the use of easements to maintain open space and the environment of historic properties was a significant endeavor. "Freezing the surround" of Georgetown's Tudor Place and the arboreal setting at Merrywood via easements during the 1960s solved both urban conservation and preservation problems.[46] As easements proved their worth in urban and suburban areas, some historic preservation advocates sought to measure their possible impact in rural areas as well.[47] In mid-1970s, after facilitating more than a quarter century of conservation use, easements were still touted as being usually less costly than outright acquisition while continuing a historic property in private ownership. For the Department of the Interior, executing easements on federally designated National Historic Landmarks was seen as an expeditious way to protect the gravitas and honor of the Secretary of the Interior's authority to recognize certain distinctive historic properties. However, expectations by some preservation advocates that the Secretary would continue expand use of the authority granted by the Historic Sites Act to acquire easements of nationally significant properties were ultimately disappointed.[48] That said, easements still protect federal investments in historic preservation as a mandatory component of many grant programs.

The New Conservation

The visionaries who crafted the administrative structures that supported the transformation of the land conservation and historic preservation movements during the third quarter of the 20th century were confident that their efforts would address many of the challenges facing American society.[49] Urban communities in crisis could find rejuvenation and recreation in the open spaces, parks, and historic properties that were found on the periphery of most metropolitan areas. Wrapped in a cloak of Cold War ideology, the historic preservation movement viewed itself as the antidote for the transformation of American homes and neighborhoods. The Johnson administration's adoption of the idea of natural beauty—broadly defined—as worthy of federal consideration enhancement was embraced by a wide range of activists and others as the "New Conservation."

> Yesterday's conservation battles were for superlative scenery, for wilderness, for wildlife. Today's conservation battles are for beautiful cities, for clean water and air, for tasteful architecture, for the preservation of open space. To meet today's challenges; conservationists must project themselves into the main stream of American Life.[50]

The pragmatic theme struck by the new conservationists was one of balance. The challenge in building a quality society, in managing the change that was to come, was not just to preserve the equilibrium between the wants and needs of the population and its institutions, but also to "improve the heritage" handed down to the next generation.[51] The identification and stewardship of wilderness and other protected areas presented a continuing challenge to ensure that all Americans had permanent access to some form of outdoor heritage.[52] For the new historical conservation the goals were equally lofty, filled with references—provided by Edward Everett, one of the principals who advocated for the preservation of Mount Vernon during the mid-19th century—as to how the "spirit of a free people" was to be "formed and animated and cheered," from the "storehouse of its historical recollections."[53]

In 1924 the Metropolitan Museum of Art opened its American wing, which housed a permanent exhibit containing the decorative bones of architectural gems from across the country. At that time the creation of period rooms from threatened buildings was considered one form of historic preservation. Fifty years later, a 14,000-acre historic district within Piedmont Virginia was listed on the National Register of Historic Places for its constellation of historic resources seated within a rural cultural landscape. The expanded vision for the identification and protection of significant spaces both large and small that had been established in the mid-1950s continued to grow, despite the machinations of the political process. This vision was expanded via the total environment conventions of the 1970s to foster consideration of cultural and natural resources as part of a greater whole. By the mid-1980s the concept of cultural landscapes as valued resources was foremost in the minds of preservationists and their allied disciplines.[54] More than a decade later, advocates were still seeking an assessment of the collective impact of historic preservation and land conservation movements, with an eye toward identifying a "working connection" between historic recognition programs and the proliferation of land trusts created since the early 1980s.[55] In the new century, acceptance of an integrated landscape approach to natural and cultural resources continues to thrive (See Sidebar 7.1).[56]

The historic preservation movement operated on the periphery of the great land conservation programs of the third quarter of the 20th century. It goals were never the focus of urban renewal programs, land and water conservation funding, or surplus property planning. This reflected the constant reality of inadequate funding among all conservation endeavors. By the late 1970s Ernest Connally concluded that the $35 million appropriated in 1977 through the newly established HPF was, in fact, equal to less than 10 percent of the $400 million that his office had estimated as the actual need of the various state preservation programs. In 1977 there were some 13,000 listings on the National Register, of which perhaps 10 percent were historic districts containing about 450,000 individual buildings. Even if the HPF were to be fully funded, its grants-in-aid program could never reach the majority of properties listed on the National Register.[57] Despite their bureaucratic reluctance to broadly support historic preservation activities, the HUD, BOR, and GSA—with their substantially enhanced federal appropriations and policy control—had a far greater potential to impact many more historic neighborhoods than did the Department of the Interior.[58]

During the Great Depression, as Steinbeck's Oklahoma tenant farmer families selected which of their belongings to preserve, the fathers were "ruthless because the past had been spoiled" while the mothers knew "how the past would cry to them" as they journeyed to California. Together they questioned: how would it be "not to know what land's outside the door?"[59] Even as they abandoned a failed environment and watched the remains of their material heritage burn in the distance, these Okies retained some seed of faith in the land and its heritage. For conservationists active in the third quarter of the 20th century, the post–World War II transformation of the American landscape meant similar hard choices: which properties to protect and which to let go? There simply was never enough money, political will, or administrative techniques to preserve all that was worthy for recognition and stewardship. Federal programs and funding established in the 1960s empowered the conservationists, and yet ironically, as Samuel Hays noted, proponents were often more optimistic regarding the movement's potential, while bureaucrats were "consistently the bearers of bad news."[60]

Sidebar 7.1   Acquiring Alexandria's Brigadoon

It looked as if it were frozen in time—or as the architectural historian Carolyn Pitts might have said, "even the dust was ancient." Located at 517 Prince Street within the Alexandria, Virginia, National Historic Landmark District, the Murray-Dick-Fawcett House comprised a relatively unaltered remnant of the city's 18th century landscape. Seated on a one-third of an acre lot, the property contains a 244-year-old timber frame-and-brick dwelling with multiple additions, and a small adjacent garden. Local historians have recognized the home as a "fascinating microcosm of the complete single family dwelling, containing in

Figure 7.2 Murray-Dick-Fawcett Home, Alexandria, Virginia. In 2017 this property was acquired by the City of Alexandria using grants from two organizations designed to protect open space.

Source: Office of Historic Alexandria

addition to the usual living, dining and bedrooms, a kitchen, a necessary, rooms for slaves or servants and storage rooms, all under one roof."[61]

At the time of its construction in early 1770s, the one-and-a half-story dwelling was seated far outside the original 1749 town limits, which had expanded to include the site during the 1790s. The home was built by Patrick Murray, a local blacksmith, who had also constructed a livery stable on the property. From the early 1790s to 1816 the parcel had successive owners, settling into the tenure of John Douglas Brown, whose descendants held the property for the next 184 years. Few changes were made to the structure during that long period of ownership, resulting in the property's remarkable physical integrity and strong historical associations. The property was documented by the Historic American Buildings Survey in 1936.

In 2017, after a complicated series of negotiations, the City of Alexandria acquired this unique property, ensuring its long-term contribution to a historic community. Grants from the Virginia Land Conservation Foundation ($900,000) and the Virginia Outdoors Foundation ($350,000), along with a substantial equity donation by the home's last private steward (Joseph Reeder), were used to secure the site.[62] The grants were awarded because, despite its small size, the parcel represented one of the largest open space or garden areas within Old Town Alexandria and its preservation enhanced the city's important heritage tourism enterprise by providing public access to an urban green space in a downtown neighborhood. Using funding from two distinct conservation organizations, this acquisition demonstrated the continuing necessity of creative approaches to the conservation of historic resources. Its success harkened back to the hard work of the Alexandria Historical Restoration and Preservation Commission in the late 1960s to secure Housing and Urban Development open space funding to purchase the Lloyd House (see Sidebar 4.2) and its adjoining garden spaces.

The historic preservation movement has always been adaptable to new sources of support for its particular mission, relying on creative or experimental approaches among both the private sector and official bureaucracy to secure and enhance the conservation of the built environment. With its cultural, educational, aesthetic, inspirational, economic, and energy benefits (as outlined in the preamble to the National Historic Preservation Act), it was often seen, at least by advocates, as just the right prescription for what was currently ailing the country. Whatever the present crisis, the United States continued to need a sense of orientation, spirit, and direction found in viable communities that embraced a living historic heritage.

Five decades on, the great conservation programs of the 1960s continue to shape how Americans interact on a daily basis with urban, suburban, and rural landscapes. LWCF parklands, HUD open spaces, and National Register historic districts populate our cities, towns, and neighborhoods, although the sponsorship and designation of these parcels and parks is often unnoticed (and unappreciated) by their users. Over the last quarter century, the political and economic calculus that informed the goals and aspirations of conservation movements has changed—and yet the essential dilemma of saving spaces remains the same. How much of the American landscape and American heritage is worthy of perpetual stewardship for the common good?

Notes

1. Roderick Nash, "Conservation as Quality of the Environment," in Roderick Nash, ed., *The American Environment: Readings in the History of Conservation* (Reading, MA: Addison-Wesley Publishing Co., 1968), pp. 155–156.
2. See Adam Rome, *Bulldozer in the Countryside: Suburban Sprawl and the Rise of American Environmentalism* (Cambridge and New York: Cambridge University Press, 2001); Samuel P. Hays, *Beauty, Health, and Permanence: Environmental Politics in the United States, 1955–1985* (Studies in Environment and History) (Cambridge: Cambridge University Press, 1987); Robert Gottlieb, *Forcing the Spring: The Transformation Of The American Environmental Movement* (Washington, Covelo, and London: Island Press, 1993); Hal K. Rothman, *The Greening of a Nation? Environmentalism in the United States Since 1945* (Fort Worth, Texas: Harcourt Brace College Publishers, 1998); Neil Maher, *Nature's New Deal: The Civilian Conservation Corps and the Roots of the American Environmental Movement* (Oxford: Oxford University Press, 2008).
3. Nicholas Cooper, "Englishman Observes American Preservation," Preservation News, October 1, 1968. For Europeans the term "conservation" generally includes consideration of historic resources, while in archaeology and art, conservation is a technical specialization referring to the preservation of objects and artifacts. Early on, those in the historic preservation community often referred to "historical conservation"; e.g., Herbert Kahler, "Ten Years of Historical Conservation under the Historic Sites Act," *Planning and Civic Comment* (January 1946), pp. 20–24.
4. The terminology was even more complex in that within the conservation movement itself there was "preservationist" or "protectionist" camps, such as individuals who supported wilderness designations. Thomas R. Wellock, *Preserving the Nation: The Conservation and Environmental Movements, 1870–2000* (Wheeling, Illinois: Harlan Davidson, Inc., 2007), pp. 143–151. Robert Gotlieb, *Forcing the Spring: The Transformation of the American Environmental Movement* (Washington, DC: Island Press, 2005), p. 82. Paul Sutter, *Driven Wild: How the Fight against Automobiles Launched the Modern Wilderness Movement* (Seattle: University of Washington Press, 2002), pp. 15–20.
5. Charles Hardin, "A Rounded Land Conservation Program," The Annals of the American Academy of Political and Social Science, Vol. 281, The Future of Our Natural Resources (May 1952), pp. 146–154. Charles Peterson related Vint's quote. Constance Greiff, "Interview with Charles Peterson, 8 January 1981," p. 31. UMCP CEP Box 136.
6. Miles Glendinning, "The Conservation Movement: A Cult of the Modern Age," *Transactions of the Royal Historical Society*, Vol. 13 (2003), pp. 259-376, quote is from p. 375.
7. Miles Glendinning, "The Conservation Movement: A Cult of the Modern Age," *Transactions of the Royal Historical Society*, Vol. 13 (2003), p. 374.
8. Mitchell Schwarzer, "Myths of Permanence and Transience in the Discourse on Historic Preservation in the United States," *Journal of Architectural Education*, Vol. 48, No. 1 (September 1984).

9. Stewart Udall, *The Quiet Crisis* (New York: Holt, Rinehart and Winston, 1963).

10. William Whyte, *The Last Landscape* (Garden City, New York: Doubleday, 1968), p. 22.

11. Ibid.

12. Barbara Drew Hoffstot (1919–1994) was an architectural and community preservationist. "To the Pittsburgh Area Members of the National Trust and the Society of Architectural Historians," May 15, 1964. Hoffstot to Gordon Gray, May 17, 1964. RG 421 NTHP. She was also instrumental in creating the Preservation Foundation of Palm Beach. In 1974 she wrote "Landmark Architecture of Palm Beach," *Preservation News*, December 1994.

13. Hoffstot to Austin Leland, August 20, 1965. RG 421 NTHP.

14. James Van Trump, "Doomed Dome? Pittsburg Battles to Save North Side Post Office," Preservation News, Vol. 4, November 1964. The post office was built in 1897. The Pittsburgh Historic Landmarks Foundation was established in 1964 to address threats posed by urban renewal. Diane Maddex, "A Modern Fable: The Tale of Three Post Offices," *Preservation News*, Vol. 12, No. 2 (February 1972).

15. Robert Garvey to Mrs. Henry P. Hoffstot, Jr., March 8, 1966. For the GSA perspective see: Lawson Knott to Gordon Gray, March 24, 1966. RG421 NTHP.

16. "Furthering the Policy Enunciated in the Historic Sites Act," House of Representatives Report No. 855, June 20, 1949. This report supported the creation of the NTHP in order to supplement the work of the NPS.

17. Samuel Hays, *A History of Environmental Politics Since 1945* (Pittsburgh: University of Pittsburg Press, 2000), pp. 70–71 and 76–78.

18. Gerald Ford, "Special Message to the Congress Transmitting Proposed Bicentennial Land Heritage Legislation," August 31, 1976. Public Law 91–485. Enacted in 1970 under President Nixon, the program transferred 639 federal parcels totaling more than 80,000 acres valued at $240 million to state and local governments.Senate Subcommittee on Parks and Recreation of the Committee on Interior and Insular Affairs, 94th Congress, Second Session, "Oversight Hearing on the President's Bicentennial Land Heritage Land Program," September 1, 1976. See: George H. Siehl, "The Bicentennial Land Heritage Program," Congressional Research Service, November 16, 1976.

19. "Areas of National Concern, Implementation Options," June 28, 1978. HCRS; Chief, Division of Federal Lands Planning to HCRS Deputy Director for Planning, "Outline of ANC Work Plan," May 21, 1979. NPS PHP Files.James Spencer, "Rural Development: An Activity in Search of a Direction," in *Planning Frontiers in Rural America: Papers and Proceedings of the Boone Conference, Boone, North Carolina, March 16–18, 1975.* Prepared for the Subcommittee on Rural Development of the Committee on Agriculture and Forestry, United States Senate, February 17, 1976, p. 26.

20. "Areas of National Concern: Implementation Options," HCRS, June 28, 1978, p. 2.

21. Dallas Miner, Urban Land Institute, "Visual Environmental Aesthetics: A Response," pp. 218–219. Planning Frontiers in Rural America: Papers and Proceedings of the Boone Conference, Boone, North Carolina, March 16–18, 1975. Prepared for the Subcommittee on Rural Development of the Committee on Agriculture and Forestry, United States Senate, February 17, 1976.

22. "Areas of National Concern: Implementation Options," Heritage Conservation and Recreation Service, June 28, 1978, p. 2.

23. The ANC System was tied to efforts to preserve the Channel Islands and Santa Monica Mountains in California. In 1978 the administration testified against the creation of this park unit and used congressional hearings to propose the ANC system as an alternative. "Statement of Robert Herbst, Assistant Secretary of the Interior for Fish and Wildlife and Parks, before the Senate Committee on Energy and Natural Resources on S. 1096," May 5, 1978.

24. James Morton Turner, *The Promise of Wilderness: American Environmental Politics since 1964* (Seattle: University of Washington Press, 2002), p. 11. See: Jacob Hamblin, "Ronald Reagan's Environmental Legacy," in Andrew Johns, ed., A Companion to

Ronald Reagan (New York: Wiley & Sons, 2015), pp. 257–274; Thomas R. Wellock, Preserving the Nation: The Conservation and Environmental Movements 1870–2000 (New York: Wiley-Blackwell, 2007); Adam Rome, "Give Earth a Chance: The Environmental Movement and the Sixties," Journal of American History, Vol. 90, No. 2 (September 2003), pp. 525–554; Michael Lacey, ed., Government and Environmental Politics: Essays on Historical Developments since World War Two (Baltimore: Johns Hopkins Press, 1989).

25. Senate Committee on Energy and Natural Resources, "Workshop on Public Land Acquisition and Alternatives," Publication No. 97–34, October 1981. The lasting environmental legacy of the Reagan administration was nuanced. Philip Shabecoff, "Reagan and Environment: To Many, a Stalemate," *The New York Times*, January 2, 1989.

26. Douglas Sessoms, Review of *NRPA Recreation and Park Perspective Collection* (30 vols., Washington, DC: McGrath Publishing, 1972); *American Journal of Sociology*, Vol. 79, No. 6 (May 1974), pp. 1594–1597. Ronald Faich and Richard Gale, "The Environmental Movement: From Recreation to Politics," The Pacific Sociological Review, Vol. 14, No. 3, Sociology of Leisure (July 1971), pp. 270–287.

27. Gordon Gray, "Conservation by Preservation of our Heritage," Garden Club of America, March 11, 1964. RG 421 NTHP Gordon Gray Speeches. The 1965 Pan American Symposium on the Preservation and Restoration of Historic Monuments placed a special emphasis upon total environment preservation problems at cities such as Cartagena, Columbia; Cuzco, Peru; Morelia, Mexico; and Antiqua, Guatemala. The host city (St. Augustine, Florida) was celebrating the 400th anniversary of its establishment. "Pan American Symposium on the Preservation and Restoration of Historic Monuments," *Preservation News*, June 1, 1965 and April 1, 1965. *Old Cities of the New World: Proceedings of the Pan American Symposium on the Preservation & Restoration of Historic Monuments* (St. Augustine, Florida, June 20–25, 1965).

28. Robert Garvey, "Look Back in Anger?" Preservation News, February 1, 1967. Nicholas Cooper, "Englishman Observes American Preservation," *Preservation News*, October 1, 1968.

29. Terry Morton, "National Park Service holds Second Preservation Conference," *Preservation News*, February 1, 1968.

30. James Glass, The Beginnings of a New National Historic Preservation Program, 1957–1969 (Nashville: AASLH, 1990), p. 59. NPS, *Administrative Policies for Historic Areas* (Washington, DC: NPS, 1968), "Quality of Environment: To achieve the purpose of a historical area, i.e., preservation and appropriate public use, planning and management should be related to the total environment in which the area is located."

31. "Conservation-Preservation," Preservation News, September 1, 1968. "22nd Annual Meeting," *Preservation News*, July 1, 1968.

32. "Where Is our Preservation Power?" *Preservation News*, May 1, 1968. The NTHP President James Biddle editorialized: "As a part of the community the property affords the means to sharpen the student's awareness of the role of preservation in the evolution of the total environment as we determine the future of our land and its structures." "President's Column," *Preservation News*, May 1, 1968.

33. John H. Sprinkle, Jr., *Crafting Preservation Criteria: The National Register of Historic Places and American Historic Preservation* (New York: Routledge, 2014), pp. 196–215.

34. ACHP, *The National Historic Preservation Program Today* (Washington, DC: GPO, January 1976), p. 8.

35. Ibid., p. 2.

36. Ibid.

37. NPS, "Preliminary Notes for Use of Special Committee on Historic Preservation," 1965. Included with this study was selections from Internal Revenue Service Bulletin No. 1964–30, July 2, 1964, on the valuation of donated easements; a "Proposed Letter to the donors of scenic easements—Piscataway;" and a letter from NPS National Capital Regional Director Jackson Price to Commissioner of Internal

Revenue Sheldon Cohen, April 28, 1965, regarding the donation of scenic easements to the federal government. RG 421 NTHP With Heritage So Rich.

38. Lyndon B. Johnson, "Special Message to the Congress on Conservation and Restoration of Natural Beauty," February 8, 1965. Online by Gerhard Peters and John T. Woolley, The American Presidency Project. www.presidency.ucsb.edu/ws/?pid=27285.

39. "Remarks of Honorable Frances P. Bolton at the White House Conference on Natural Beauty, Water and Waterfronts Panel." MVLA Overview, May 24, 1965.

40. "Areas of National Concern: Implementation Options," Heritage Conservation and Recreation Service, June 28, 1978, p. 2.

41. ACHP, *The National Historic Preservation Program Today* (Washington, DC: GPO, January 1976), p. 9.

42. Robert Garvey ("Look Back in Anger?" *Preservation News*, February 1967) quoted several passages from Halprin's forthcoming book, *Freeways*. Halprin had worked on the adaptive use of San Francisco's Ghirardelli Square featured in the HUD and NTHP film, *How Will They Know It's Us?*

43. Secretary of the Interior Stewart Udall, *Department of the Interior Press Release* (Chicago: Tribune New Service, June 4, 1964). MVLA Overview.

44. Charles Peterson to John Carver, April 4, 1964. UMCP CEP Box 15.

45. The limitations of the initial funding sources for the LWCF were quickly recognized. See: "The Crisis in the Land and Water Conservation Fund," Congressional Record, H11982-H111987, September 18, 1967.

46. Robert Garvey, "Look Back in Anger?" *Preservation News*, February 1, 1967.

47. NTHP, *Preservation: Toward an Ethic in the 1980s* (Washington, DC: The Preservation Press, 1980), pp. 205–207.

48. ACHP, *The National Historic Preservation Program Today* (Washington, DC: GPO, January 1976), p. 38.

49. Louis Heren, "America the Middle-Aged," *Harper's Magazine*, August 1965, p. 104. "Programs on Medicare, poverty, education, unemployment, beauty, conservation—they proliferate enough to scare the middle aged. But most of America does not seem scared."

50. NPS, "Quotes: Conservation, Parks, Natural Beauty," 1966, p. 8.

51. Department of the Interior, "Quest for Quality," quoted in "Quotes: Conservation, Parks, Natural Beauty," p. 9. See quotes by Thomas Jefferson, John Ruskin, Henry David Thoreau, and Walt Whitman. Nancy Germano, "Negotiating for the Environment: LBJ's Contributions to the Environmental Movement." Federal History: Journal of the Society for History in the Federal Government, Issue 9 (2017), pp. 48-68.

52. *Outdoor Recreation for America*, 1962, quoted in "Quotes: Conservation, Parks, Natural Beauty," p. 13.

53. *Quotes: Conservation, Parks, Natural Beauty* (Washington, DC: NPS, 1966), p. 25.

54. In 1986, Mary Washington College sponsored a conference on the 20th anniversary of the National Historic Preservation Act: *Remembering the Future: The Legacy of the Historic Preservation Act of 1966*. Papers included Dell Upton, "Whose Side are we on: The Cultural Landscape as a Preservation Frontier;" and Carroll Van West, "Viewing Survey and Comprehensive Planning through the Prisms of the Cultural Landscape."

55. Chip Dennerlein, Regional Director, National Parks Conservation Association, NPSAB Meeting, October 20, 1998. NPS PHP Files.

56. For example see: *Expanding Horizons: Highlights from the National Workshop on Large Landscape Conservation*, 2014 and the *Living Landscape Observer: Nature, Culture, and Community*. http://livinglandscapeobserver.net.

57. "An Adequate Loan Program for Historic Resources," Hearings before the Subcommittee on Historic Preservation and Coinage of the Committee on Banking, Finance, and Urban Affairs, House of Representatives, 95th Congress, First Session, May 24, June 29, and July 27, 1977, pp. 28, 38–39, 116.

58. "Preservation Programs of the Federal Government in the Area of Housing and Community Development," p. 6. HUD estimated that only 1 percent of its grants (approximately $15 million) went toward historic preservation.
59. Steinbeck, *The Grapes of Wrath*, pp. 91–92.
60. Samuel Hays, "Three Decades of Environmental Politics: The Historical Context," p. 64, in Michael Lacey, ed., *Government and Environmental Politics: Essays on Historical Developments since World War Two* (Baltimore: Johns Hopkins Press, 1989).
61. Office of Historic Alexandria, "A Gem of a House on Prince Street," *Alexandria Times*, July 20, 2017.
62. Reeder retained life tenancy in the home, with public access for special events provided several times per year. The house will join the Office of Historic Alexandria's system of city museums, focusing on local domestic life during the 18th and 19th centuries.

Appendices

Appendix 2.1

Frances Bolton's Remarks at the White House Conference on Natural Beauty, 1965

It is most heartening to have this Conference put emphasis upon new methods of procedure. Our world—yes, our whole concept of the Great Universe—has been changed in ways we could not have foreseen even a decade ago. We can no longer use the old ways when preservation of natural beauty was primarily in private hands.

As an example let us take the events as they have evolved concerning the most famous of our national shrines: Mount Vernon, the home of our first President, George Washington.

Something over a century ago a frail woman, Ann Pamela Cunningham, undertook the task and created the Mount Vernon Ladies' Association of the Union. This private group purchased and still preserves this national shrine.

In 1955 the Maryland shore opposite Mount Vernon was threatened with the wave of expansion from the District of Columbia. An oil tank farm was projected for the shoreline in the center of the view that thrills millions of visitors each year.

As Vice Regent from Ohio of the Mount Vernon Ladies' Association, I accepted Miss Cunningham's charge, and caused the Accokeek Foundation to be established for the purpose of acquiring the land and preserving the view.

Then an unthinking local agency, armed with the pose of eminent domain, determined to condemn the land we sought to preserve for use as a sewage treatment plant. No private entity could withstand that threat!

No help was available from local or state governments, but the Congress acted in 1961 delineating the area as a National Park. This was based on lands to be donated by the foundations along the river front, land to be acquired by the Federal Government, and donations by private owners of scenic easements on a much greater area.

In this day of big government and big corporations, it sometimes seems that the individual has become superfluous. But our project has created a place for the individual. I am proud to report that the owners of 120 parcels of land have voluntarily donated scenic easements on their own properties to make the project possible.

In recognition of the generosity of private landowners' contributions, the Federal Government is evolving a policy of income tax deduction for the donation of scenic easements. The State of Maryland has cooperated in pioneering tax reform legislation to encourage the donation of easements. To make this possible, it was necessary to amend the State Constitution, pass statewide policy legislation, and then to amend the State Tax Code. The ultimate change in the County Codes cannot be made until after June 1 when the State Law becomes effective. This model tax reform which brings local tax and natural beauty policies into harmony, is now well on its way to completion, for all to examine.

Out task is far from finished, but what we have done has opened up some exciting new ways of getting the job done. There are still basic studies in progress dealing with possible ways of preserving the land.

There will never be enough money in the public treasury to do all that is necessary for preservation and conservation of natural beauty. But there is no limit to what an imaginative program utilizing new approaches to public and private cooperation can do.

Because the Accokeek Foundation had a problem which could not be solved by existing methods and could not wait, we had to pioneer some of these new techniques of preservation. We have made a beginning, but we have done that.

The next step is clear. *It is hoped that this White House Conference will call for a major effort to develop the tremendous potential locked up in new types of public-private cooperation.* Through this effort, we can, and will, evolve new and better tools for preservation and conservation, on a much broader base.

We of the Accokeek Foundation are ready to help to the best of our ability. We look to you to do your part.

Source: "Remarks of Honorable Frances P. Bolton at the White House Conference on Natural Beauty, Water and Waterfronts Panel, Monday, May 24, 1965, 3:30 pm." MVLA Overview, Box 2.

Appendix 3.1

Criteria for Evaluation of Surplus Federal Historical Properties, 1948

Criteria to be used in determining what Surplus Federal Properties are Suitable and Desirable for State and Regional Historic Monument Purposes and should be granted to States, Political Subdivisions, and Municipalities for that Purpose:

1. *The prime requisite is historical significance.* The chief determining factor is that the area or structure must possess certain important historical associations which entitle it to a position of high rank in the history of the State or region requesting the property for historic monument purposes. This quality exists:

    a. In such historic properties or sites as are naturally the points or bases from which the broad political, military, social or cultural history of the State or region can best be presented, and from which the student of history, or visitor, can sketch or grasp the large patterns off the State or regional historical story. Such areas are significant because of the relationship to other areas, each contributing its part to the historical story that is to be told.

    b. In such properties or sites as are associated with the life of some key figure in State or regional history and which may not necessarily have any outstanding qualities other than that association.

    c. In such properties or historic sites as are associated with some sudden or dramatic incident in State or regional history, and which, though possessing no great intrinsic qualities, are unique and symbolical of some great idea or ideal.

    d. The above (a. b. c.) are the minimum requirements as to historical significance. State and regional agencies are to be encouraged to preserve historic lands or buildings which transcend state historical importance and are of national significance, i.e. having historical associations important to the people of the United States as a whole.

    e. Sites or properties of recent historical importance, relating to events and persons in the period after 1900, will, as a rule, not qualify under the heading of historical significance.

2.   *Suitability*, as measured by the following standards, will be an important consideration.

   a.   *Surviving historical remains.* While it will be possible in some instances to justify a State or regional historic monument project even though no historical remains or evidence of historic events have survived to modern times, the deciding factor in most cases will be the presence of important historic buildings, structures, or physical remains that should be preserved. A project calling for an elaborate restoration or reconstruction of historic buildings that have long been destroyed may be considered to be less meritorious than one requiring simple preservation and repairs.

   b.   *Other physical characteristics.* The extent to which civilization or industrialization presses in and around an historic site or property must be considered when these factors impair historical values or inhibit public use and appreciation.

   c.   *Accessibility and location* with respect to roads, streets, highways and public transportation, and adequacy of utilities and location with respect to population are factors to be considered.

   d.   *The adaptability* of the historic property to effective treatment in the interest of public use and enjoyment will be considered. *The cost of necessary treatment and development* must not be beyond the means of the State or municipality undertaking the project.

   e.   Closely allied to (d) is the question of reasonableness of the *cost of proper maintenance*, of the area and its developed features.

   f.   *The proposed boundaries* of the historic monument project should be adequate to insure property preservation of historic features and public appreciation of their historical significance. The reasons for requesting any lands in excess of such needs should be explained and justified.

   g.   It is desirable for the projects to have a *logical place in the State or regional plan* for the conservation of park and historical resources.

   h.   *The proposed use program* should be consistent with the proper and dignified preservation of the historic remains, or terrain, and the reasonable public access thereto. In studying the proposed use of the property in accordance with these criteria, sympathetic consideration will be given to the public use of historic structures and property for educational or similar social or cultural activities which are not inconsistent with the historical values of the property.

3.   Consideration will be given to the responsibility of the proposed administering agency as determined by (a) legal authority, (b) adequacy of financing, (c) experience in historical work, (d) adequacy of staff, and operational and administrative experience and similar problems or areas.

Source: Approved by the Advisory Board on National Parks, Historic Sites, Buildings and Monuments, April 28, 1948.

~ ~ ~ ~ ~

Additional Criteria for Evaluation of Surplus Federal Historic Properties

The Advisory Board at its 50th meeting in Washington, DC, April 13–16, 1964 resolved that, in light of National Park Service experience, the Criteria adopted April 28, 1948, by the Advisory Board for the evaluation of surplus Federal historical properties be brought up to date by including the following:

1. Structures or sites which are primarily of significance in the field of religion or to religious bodies but are not of national importance in other fields of the history of the United States, such as political, military or architectural history, will not be eligible for consideration.
2. Birthplaces, graves, burials, and cemeteries, as a general rule, are not eligible for consideration and recognition except in cases of historical figures of transcendent importance. Historic sites associated with the actual careers and contributions of outstanding historic personages are more important than their birthplaces and burial places.
3. Structure or sites associated with persons of historical importance whose major contributions occurred during the last 50 years, and historical events of the same period, as a rule will not be eligible for consideration.

~ ~ ~ ~ ~

[The following criteria were refined at the Advisory Board's 51st Meeting, October 5–14, 1964]

1. Structures that represent the characteristics of an architectural type specimen, important to a period style or method of construction in a particular state or region; or an important structure representing the work of a master builder, designer, or architect in a State or region.
2. Structures or sites which are primarily of significance in the fields of religion or to religious bodies but are not of importance in other fields of history of the State or region, such as, political, military, or architectural history, will not be eligible for consideration.
3. Historic birthplaces, burials, and cemeteries, as a general rule, are not eligible for consideration. Historic sites associated with the actual careers and contribution of historic personages important in the State or region are more important that their birthplaces or burial places.

Appendix 4.1

Criteria for Evaluating Historic Properties, 1961

Historic sites and buildings are considered to possess outstanding value in the history of the State, county, or municipality, local communities or instrumentalities thereof and, therefore, to be historic historically significant in the following instances:

1. Structures or sites at which occurred events that have made an outstanding contribution to, and are identified prominently with, or which best represent the broad cultural, political, economic, military, or social history of the state, county, or municipality and from which the visitor may grasp the larger patterns of state, county or municipal heritage.
2. Structures or sites associated importantly with the lives of key historic personages in the State, county, or municipality.
3. Structures or sites associated significantly with an important event which best represents some important idea or ideal of the people of the State, county, or municipality.
4. Structure which embody the distinguishing characteristics of an architectural type specimen, exceptionally valuable for a study of a period style or method of construction; or a notable work of a master builder, designer, or architect of note in the State, county, or municipality.
5. Archeological sites which have produced information of major scientific importance by revealing new cultures, or by shedding light on periods of occupation in the State, county or municipality. Such sites are those which have produced, or which may reasonably be expected to produce, data which have affected theories, concepts, and ideas to a major degree.
6. Every historic and archeological site and structure should have integrity—that, there should not be doubt as to whether it is the original site or structure, and in the case of a structure that it is on its original location. Intangible elements of feeling and association, although difficult to describe, may also be factors in weighing the integrity of a site or structure.
7. In appropriate instances, historically important, but clearly defined and limited, sections of States, counties or municipalities may be considered as entire historic districts or communities eligible for Federal grants under Title VII, Housing Act of 1961. The preservation and development of

such historic districts under the open space land program requires that the defined district fit into a comprehensive plan for the pertinent urban area of the State, county, or municipality, and that an active program of comprehensive planning be underway in that particular urban area.

Examples of such historic districts would be appropriate portions of Old Georgetown, District of Columbia, and the Vieux Carre of Old French Quarter, in New Orleans. The site involving a complex of structures or remains of structures significant in history or prehistory for cultural reasons (e.g. social, political, economic, religious) within specific boundaries. The historic district may have physical structures surviving from an earlier period and still utilized today, or encompass a deteriorated section of the city which has survived more or less intact. Interrelationships of the structures is important. Such interrelationship implies a degree of physical proximity of the individual components sufficient to have permitted social or cultural interaction on the part of former inhabitants.

8. Structures or sites of recent historical importance, relating to events or persons within 50 years, will not, as a rule, be eligible for consideration.

Source: Herbert Kahler to Chief, Branch of Recreational Surveys, "Statement on Historical Programs and Criteria Useful in the Planning Procedures under the 'Open Space' Legislation," October 17, 1961. RG 79 Administrative Files 49–71, Box 333.

Appendix 4.2

Historic Preservation within Urban Renewal Projects 1961–1965

Name	Location	Comments
Project No. Minn. 29	St. Paul, MN	General neighborhood plan includes "studies of old mansions which will be preserved."
701 Plan No. Ill. P-83	Galena, IL	"Preservation and restoration of this historic community is a principal element."
Crescent City Disaster Project, Calif. R-86	Crescent City, CA	Urban Renewal Project
Historic Preservation Restoration Project, Ore. R-13 and P-55	Jacksonville, OR	Urban Renewal Project and Urban Planning Assistance Project
Custom House Project, Calif. R-34 Calif. P-27	Monterey, CA	Urban Renewal Project and Urban Planning Assistance Project
Central Mall Riverfront, Calif. R-6	Sacramento, CA	Urban Renewal Project
Western Addition Extension, Calif. R-54	San Francisco, CA	Urban Renewal Project. Designed to preserve "the character and charm of older residential areas."
Pueblo Center Project, Ariz. R-8	Tucson, AZ	Urban Renewal Project
Calif. P-35	Placerville, CA	Urban Planning Assistance Project
Calif. P-79	San Buenaventura, CA	Urban Planning Assistance Project
Calif. P-89	Sonoma, CA	Urban Planning Assistance Project
Calif. OS-19	Fremont, CA	Open Space Project: "Vallejo Historical Park"
Calif. OS-50	Hayward, CA	Open Space Project: "Meeks Estate Historical Park"
Calif. OS-42	Marin County, CA	Open Space Project: "Old St. Hilary Church"
Calif. OS-35	Oakland, CA	Open Space Project
Calif. OS-10	Portland, OR	Open Space Project

Name	Location	Comments
Pa. R-97	York, PA	"Gates House Project"
Adams Urban Renewal Area Project No. PA. 148	Lancaster, PA	"Colonial Adamstown covers a two block area within the project boundaries and contains a variety of homes which were inhabited by the poorer classes of Lancaster in the eighteenth century."
Germantown Urban Renewal Area, Project Pa. R-229	Philadelphia, PA	"Project plans call for the rehabilitation of Market Square and a number of structures having historical significance. Germantown was the home of many social, financial and political leaders during the colonial era and was the scene of the Battle of Germantown (October 4, 1777) which stopped the advance of the Continental Army and allowed the British to occupy Philadelphia."
Mother's Day Shrine West Va. R-10	Grafton, WV	"This project is designed to redevelop the area surrounding the Andrews Methodist Church as a shrine in honor of motherhood. The first Mother's Day service was held here."
School-Museum Project, Pa. R-242	Altoona, PA	"One of the aims of this project is the conversion of the nation's largest roundhouse into a railroad museum housing antique locomotives and cars and other railroad memorabilia."
Old Hampton Urban Renewal Area, Va. R-41	Hampton, VA	"This project contains numerous structures of various types having architectural value which will be restored."
Northside, Va. R-22	Portsmouth, VA	"The Northside GNRP area contains many historical structures which are worthy of preservation; some will be included in the two rehabilitation projects which are planned."
Gadsby Commercial Project Va. R-32	Alexandria, VA	"While no provision was made in the URP for improvement to it, the Gadsby Tavern, located in the project area has been subject to preservation activity."
Mount Vernon Projects I and II, Md. R-15 and R-28	Baltimore, MD	"The Mount Vernon area contains many residential structures which have been certified by the Baltimore Historical and Architectural Commission and which have been designated for preservation by resolution of City Council."
Victorian Village, NJ No. R-133	Cape May, NJ	"This project provides for the rehabilitation and conservation of the largest assemblage of authentic Victorian architecture (over 200 structures) in the nation."
John Fitch Way Project, NJ No. R-74	Trenton, NJ	"Project Plans call for the development of a park area surrounding the Trent House, colonial home of William Trent, first Supreme Court Justice in the colony of New Jersey."

(Continued)

(Continued)

Name	Location	Comments
Mercer-Jackson Project, NJ No. R-142	Trenton, NJ	"A portion of this project will be developed as a public park on the site of the First and Second Battles of Trenton, turning points of the Revolutionary War. Also, the Stacy Mill will be the subject of preservation; Stacy was the founder of Trenton, which was named for William Trent. In addition, the Douglas House, Washington's headquarters during the Battles of Trenton and locate outside the project area will be relocated to the park site and restored."
Hollow Project NJ R-2	Morristown, NJ	"This project involved the relocation to a site outside the project boundaries of two examples of colonial architecture, the Major Moses Estey House and the Major Benoni Hathaway House. Majors Estey and Hataway were prominent figures during the Revolution."
Project No. Del. P-1	New Castle, DE	"This Urban Planning Assistance project includes plans for the preservation of the 'Commons' in New Castle."
Project Pa. P-25	Cumberland Township, PA	"One of the goals of this project is the preservation of Gettysburg National Park located in Pennsylvania's Adams County."
GNRP Old San Juan R-44	San Juan, PR	
VI CRP R-4 Water Gut VI R-2	Virgin Islands Christiansted, St. Croix, VI	
Barracks Yard VI R-1	Charlotte Amalie, St. Thomas, VI	
West End UR Area R-90	Atlanta, GA	"'The Wren's Nest' was built in 1841 and occupied by Joel Chandler Harris. It is here where Harris wrote the famous 'Uncle Remus Stories.'"
Troup Ward UR Area R-53	Savannah, GA	"'Troup Trust Building' has historical and architectural importance as an example of early row housing and the use of 'Savannah Handmade Brick.'"
East End UR Area R-31	Washington, NC	"'The Wynne House' also known locally as the 'The Cannonball House' because of the cannonball which remains lodged in its wall from a shelling during the Civil War, is of historical value and will be preserved as a point of interest."
Downtown Waterfront UR Area R-38	Washington, NC	"'The Warehouse' has only historical significance. It was used during the Civil War for storage of military supplies and for housing some prisoners of war. Its historical

Name	Location	Comments
		interest, structural soundness, waterfront location and accessibility to the CBD should, it is hoped, influence someone to develop it into an appropriate commercial facility."
P-7	Wilmington, NC	"The document 'Wilmington, North Carolina: Historic Area' identifies an area near the CBD of historic significance and recommends steps for its preservation. The area contains some thirty-five structures dating back to the American Revolutionary period. See Page 26 of 'Historic Preservation through Urban Renewal.'"
Ybor City Project R-13	Ybor City, FL	"The Ybor City Area is the Latin community whose booming commercial and social life in the 1880s supplied the impetus for Tampa's economic development."
North Frankfort Area R-4	Frankfort, KY	"The Land Development Plan, pp. 76–78, identifies the Corner of Celebrities area as having historic significance and recommends actions for its preservation. The area contains, primarily, the homes of some of Kentucky's greatest leaders of both state and national stature."
Old Louisville Restoration Area R-34 and R-59	Louisville, KY	"These two projects represent the fashionable and aristocratic sections of early Louisville history. There are no particular buildings of historic significance; however, there are many doorways, balconies, leaded windows and wrought iron work that will be preserved when clearance is done."
Golden Gateway UR Area R-10	Chattanooga, TN	"Cameron Hill will contain a Civil War Memorial Park and War cannon and other relics will serve as a grim reminder of our hard earned heritage."
Beale Street UR Area R-77	Memphis, TN	"The lively past of Beale Street was made up of varied and many characters. They ran the gamut from notorious to heroic. The enclosed brochure 'Beale Street USA' is descriptive of the historical importance of this area."
Riverfront-Willow St. Area 3–2	Knoxville, TN	"By Section 311 of the Housing Act of 1961 the Knoxville Housing Authority was authorized to donate a specified parcel of project land to an association for the relocation, restoration and preservation of an historic log house."
Court Avenue #3 UR Area R-49	Memphis, TN	Six (6) antebellum houses of the 1850s having architectural and historical significance are in this area. The most important ones were owned by famous riverboat captains and carried their name. They are: the Lee House, the Fontaine House, the Mallory House."

(Continued)

Name	Location	Comments
Capitol Hill Area	Nashville, TN	"The 'State Capitol' has great historical and architectural significance; it was modernized and restored at a cost of more than one million dollars. This clearance project eliminated all blighting influences, acquired land for public use and redevelopment."
P-4	Natchez, MS	"The document 'Master Plan' for the City of Natchez presents on pp. 30–31, an architectural plan for the Natchez Historic District. The district contains the antebellum structures of the most significance in the city."
Handy Heights UR Area 5–1	Florence, Al	"'The W.C. Handy Cabin' birthplace of the man who made Memphis and its Beale Street famous as the place where blues began. The area is total clearance; however, the cabin was dismantled and stored for restoration later."
Big Spring UR Area R-32	Huntsville, AL	"'The Big Spring' was and is the oasis that gave birth to Huntsville and has nurtured it from its beginning to a thriving and ever expanding city."
East Church Street Area R-33	Mobile, AL	"In addition to the valuable historical and architectural structures shown on page 10 of 'Historic Preservation through Urban Renewal' there are many other examples throughout the city."
R-57 GN (R-69)	Montgomery, AL	"'The Square' has considerable historical significance and provides Montgomery with a spacious and beautiful open area for the heart of the CBD."
Resources Development Plan	New Mexico	"As part of the New Mexico State Planning Program, the Museum will provide the state with specific knowledge concerning historic sites of major interest and importance to the state, the nation and the world, provide data on lesser sites for use in possible future development, recommend planning measures for the present and future preservation and development of this vital resource."
La. R-6(CR)	New Orleans, LA	"In addition to the Vieux Carre Demonstration Grant in New Orleans, this Community Renewal Program will make a study of the existing structures of historical value that might be worthy of restoration."
Open Space Land Program Mo. OS-8	Kansas City, MO	"This OS land application from the Board of Park Commissioners, Kansas City, Missouri, is presently being processed. The proposed acquisition of land covered by this application included approximately one-half mile of the original Santa Fe Trail. The Park Department proposes to preserve and enhance this strip of the trail which has not yet been obliterated by progress."

Name	Location	Comments
Central Project Ark. R-12	Little Rock, AR	". . . has extensive historic preservation; however, the work is being done by private interest with the cooperation of the Little Rock Housing Authority."
Central West No. 1, R-39;	San Antonio, TX	"contains areas, monuments, etc. of historical value that have been incorporated into the Urban Renewal Plan due not to the Plan's main objectives but to their historical value."
Rosa Verde R-78	San Antonio, TX	"contains areas, monuments, etc. of historical value that have been incorporated into the Urban Renewal Plan due not to the Plan's main objectives but to their historical value."
Del Alamo, R-82	San Antonio, TX	"contains areas, monuments, etc. of historical value that have been incorporated into the Urban Renewal Plan due not to the Plan's main objectives but to their historical value."
Civic Center, R-83	San Antonio, TX	"contains areas, monuments, etc. of historical value that have been incorporated into the Urban Renewal Plan due not to the Plan's main objectives but to their historical value."
Wooster Square R-1	New Haven, CT	
Savin Rock No. 2	West Haven, CT	
Government Center Mass. R-35	Boston, MA	
Charlestown, Mass. R-55	Boston, MA	
Waterfront, Mass., R-77	Boston, MA	
South Cove, Mass., R-92	Boston, MA	
Waterfront Project, R-33	Gloucester, MA	
Central Business Mass. R-80	Newburyport, MA	
Summer and High Sts. Mass. R-26	Plymouth, MA	"Plymouth's project plans for the preservation of a few remaining historic structures and emphasizes the clearance of blighted areas which are having a depressing effect on historic sites adjacent to the project areas."
Winnepesaukee Ren. Project R-12	Laconia, NH	
Marcy-Washington Project, R-1	Portsmouth, NH	a.k.a. Strawberry Banke
Upton Ren. Project R-121	Kingston, NY	
Third Ward Project R-144	Rochester, NY	
Liberty Pole Green R-158	Rochester, NY	
Fort Stanwix, R-173	Rome, NY	

(Continued)

(Continued)

Name	Location	Comments
Thames St. GNRP R-6	Newport, RI	
Long Warf-Market Square R-12	Newport, RI	
Slater Project, R-11	Pawtucket, RI	
East Side Project, R-4	Providence, RI	
Weybossett Hill R-7	Providence, RI	
Conn. R-49	Guilford, CT	
Conn. R-36	Tolland, CT	
Conn. R-33	Wethersfield, CT	
Me. P-16	Kennebunkport, ME	
Mass. P-4	Bedford, MA	
Mass. P-7	Concord, MA	
Mass. P-26	Groton, MA	
Mass. P-27	Salem, MA	
Mass. P-21	Sudbury, MA	
Mass. P-47	Sturbridge, MA	
Monocacy Creek	Bethlehem, PA	Historic Bethlehem will acquire nine acres of the project area to restore a group of early Moravian buildings as ". . . an outdoor history museum and an easily accessible recreational and educational facility for the entire community."

Source: Mary Carrol to John Willmont, August 27, 1962. Sen. Henry Jackson to William Slayton, May 28, 1965. William Slayton to All Regional Administrators, "Information on Historic Preservation in Urban Renewal Projects." June 7, 1965. William Slayton to Sen. Henry Jackson, June 16, 1965. William Slayton to Sen. Henry Jackson, July 20, 1965. RG 207 HUD URA Box 736.

Appendix 4.3

Urban Renewal for Historic Areas: Some Suggestions toward Getting Good Results, 1962

    I. Urban Renewal Manual: work into the master Manual the precept that historic landmarks should be preserved

    II. Definition of Policy: establish clear understandable written policy to guide planners in each area. (The usual effort along these lines ends in a sematic sump.)

    III. Study of individual Buildings: Require the identification of every building and its evaluation as to architectural worth and human association. (This needs the direction of specially qualified people who would be paid in each case as pro to the contribution of the local government.)

    IV. Design of Street Elevations: Predict the architectural effect of new buildings planted among the old by drawing up street elevations. (Ground plans do not give the picture; artists' sketches and very small scale models often avoid the issues and sometimes they deceive.)

    V. Protection of Buildings: For safety during the awkward—and sometimes protracted—period of title transfer set up well in advance a really effective protection against vandalism, weather and other hazards. (Charge it against the local contribution.)

    VI. Sample Restorations: As examples for private emulation—and to give the local redevelopment staff some experience—require each authority to execute a couple of good demonstration restorations earl in each program.

    VII. Selection of Developers: Plan so you can get redevelopers who will approach your problems sympathetically. Rebuilding an historical neighborhood involves many questions with which the big scale builders do not wish to be bothered.

    VIII. Tax Lenience: Offer tax relief. Historic restorations may be enjoyed and appreciated from the street and in more than one sense the public has an interest in each example. In San Juan the expense to the owner of authentically restoring a building is somewhat offset by special real estate tax benefits. This legislative innovation should be studied and emulated elsewhere if possible.

Source: Charles Peterson, June 23, 1962. UMCP CEP Box 307.

Appendix 4.4

The Historic Community, 1959

A. Definition of a Historic Community: The Historic Community or District may be defined as a complex of structures or remains of structures significant in history or prehistory for cultural reasons (social, political, economic, religious). The Community may be represented by physical structures surviving from an earlier period and still utilized today, or it may be an extinct Community (such as a ghost town or prehistoric ruin) which has survived more or less intact. Interrelationships of the structures is important. Such interrelationship implies a degree of physical proximity of the individual components sufficient to have permitted social or cultural interaction on the part of former inhabitants.

> A group of closely related aboriginal sites may be classified under this category if the smaller aggregates are culturally related in such a way as to indicate that they would have thought of themselves as parts of a larger interacting whole and the Community as a whole is of exceptional value.

B. Criteria for Evaluation of Historic or Prehistoric Communities: To qualify for classification as being of exceptional value, the Community or District should be measured against the following standards:

1. It must be associated with events, personages, or movements that affected in a significant way the course of U.S. history, or be representative of, and reflect the flowering or, a culture or way of life that existed for an appreciable period of time.

2. Sufficient physical remains of the period represented must have survived to illustrate effectively without major distortion the architecture and cultural characteristics of the period. The physical remains should predominate over interjacent [sic] buildings to such a degree as to convey to the visitor a strong sense of the historical scene involved. On this point there can be no hard and fast rule of percentages or portions of the whole that once existed that will determine whether the physical remains of the Community have integrity.

Rather it will in each instance be a matter of judgment on the effect the surviving remains will have in representing a picture of a past historic period. In general, these remains should be extensive rather than minor.

Source: NPSAB Consulting Committee, 16 September 1959.

Appendix 5.1

An $11 Billion Memo, 1962

January 23, 1962

Memorandum

To: Secretary of the Interior
From: Director, National Park Service
Subject: Financing the President's Program on Conservation

Financing a nationwide land conservation and recreation program for the acquisition of open space, recreation areas and scenic areas have been the subject of considerable discussion. Many proposals have been advanced as to sources of additional revenue to fund the program. Of all the proposals that have come to my attention none, in my opinion, have hit the mark. All have the same common fault—another tax on commodities or in some instances an additional tax on items already taxed for other purposes. All of the proposals lack the most essential ingredient—*personal appeal.*

   The kind and scope of programs we are all interested in has as its end purpose the conservation of human resources, such being achieved through the conservation of land for human use and enjoyment. It is a program the of tremendous human and humane appeal affecting as it does the lives of every individual. It promotes in an enjoyable way a better understanding of the finer things of life. The selfless desire to enhance the social and cultural values of human existence is the motivating force for all our actions. That is the spirit that prompted conception of the program and only that kind of spirit will bring it to fruition.

   As a Bureau we are the agents of the people, we can only propose while they dispose. If this program is to be for the whole people, then all the people must want it, all must be able to partake of its benefits and all must want to invest in a legacy that benefits them and theirs.

   In short, the program that is presented must be capable off appealing to all segments of the population and all parts of the country. Consequently, in must be of sufficient scope to span the entire country and the full range of human interests. It should embrace the full scale of human experience from

the realm of the individual's normal daily environment to the once in a lifetime experience. Every American should have not only the opportunity to
partake of the benefits but also to share in making such possible.

All the proposals to date are characterized by a timidity that will not generate a spontaneous appeal to the public as a whole. I am convinced a bolder
approach having universal appeal is needed to stir the imagination and to
stimulate public action.

The outline that follows presents my beliefs as to what the program should
comprise and how it can be best and most equitably financed. While I am
not completely satisfied with some of the details, nonetheless, it comes closer
to meeting the public desires and consequently the public fancy than anything yet proposed. Certainly it is the most practical and economical way of
providing all, old and young, rich and poor, with that greatest of all needs of
an increasingly complex society, the opportunity for healthful and meaningful associations with the outdoors.

1. Composition of a Nationwide Recreation and Open Space Program

The system would comprise all segments of public land use devoted to the
social and recreational benefits of the public. Regardless of political jurisdiction, locale or managing authority, all of the following kinds of park and recreation lands would be part and parcel of the System. Only though such a
balanced and integrated system can we expect to achieve a maximization of
benefits with a minimization of land needs.

Urban (Towns, Cities, Counties)

Playgrounds, recreation centers, parks and parkways in cities and metropolitan areas, county parks and open space or greenbelts surrounding
metropolitan areas; choice open spaces for conservation and study areas.

State and Regional

The necessary land to complete the state park system and to provide the
desired recreational opportunities and facilities in state forests; land for
picnic and rest areas and protection of scenic qualities and views along
major highways, both state and inter-state; land for recreation areas at
reservoirs both publically and privately owned.

Federal

A Nationwide Recreation and Open Space Program for all levels of
government would not be worthy of the name if it did not include
the outstanding historic, scenic and scientific area comprising the
National Park System with such additional lands as are necessary to

make it fully representative. Nor would it be complete without the National Forests—America's Playgrounds as the U.S. Forest Service now refers to them—or without the other public lands managed by the Fish and Wildlife Service, Bureau of Land Management, Corps of Engineers, Bureau of Reclamation, or the Department of Defense, with additional land as is necessary to develop their recreational potential.

If there could be acceptance of such a glorious concept of public service, with all agencies of government and all political jurisdictions participating to the extent of their capabilities, in a common cause, with each retaining their individual identities and responsibilities that what benefits one benefits all. Then, too, there would come the realization that any financing of such a system of parks and recreation areas would include the needs of all as part and parcel of the over-all scheme. In unity there is strength. With all participating and sharing, the financing loses some of its formidable aspects as it is a common problem that can be solved in unison.

2. Financing the Nationwide Recreation and Open Space Program

Close cooperation and support of all agencies and political bodies will come into being when the aforementioned concept is understood. Once it is understood by the American public I am sure they too will want to participate and invest in a legacy of which they are the prime beneficiaries.

I would suggest that a meeting be arranged with representatives of the oil, automobile, and boating industries, and the automobile clubs. The purpose being to acquaint them with the following and to get their reaction:

A. The need for the social and cultural values of the program outline in part 1. I would also acquaint them with the subsidiary benefits as reflected in the personal consumption of expenditures induced by travel to parks and recreation areas and the contribution such makes to both the local and national economy.
B. The magnitude of the financing and the desire to have the public directly participate through the purchase of Conservation Stamps, using gasoline dealers as the retail outlet for the stamps. The authorization for such an undertaking would have to come from the Congress, so I would present to them the essence of a bill that would provide for the following:

1. The bill would be in effect for five years.
2. Each gasoline dealer would be required to distribute Conservation Stamp Books and to sell Conservation Stamps. Each book would have space for 700 stamps.
3. Each purchaser of gasoline, whether for use in an automobile or in a boat, would be required to purchase the same number of stamps as

gallons of gasoline purchased as his contribution to the green legacy. (For example, 10 gallons of gasoline, 10 stamps at 1 cent each or 10 cents for the 10 gallons.)

4. Purchasers of the stamps would place them in the stamp book. When the book was filled (700 stamps), the owner would exchange it at a post office for a conservation sticker which would be registered in his name. The owner of the sticker would place it on the designated spot on his car. The sticker would be good for one year.

5. When a sticker is placed on a car that indicates to the gasoline dealer the driver of the car is under no obligation to buy stamps for the balance of the year in which the stamp was issued.

6. As an extra inducement, any individual who so desires may purchase a conservation sticker as a reduced rate of $6.00, thus eliminating the need to buy stamps at the filling station unless he wishes to further contribute.

7. Receipts from the sale of stamps would be deposited with the U.S. Treasury to be used only for acquiring needed land.

8. The receipts for each year would be distributed in the following manner:

   a) Twenty-five percent of the total retained by the federal government for the projects it sponsors and with administer.

   b) One million dollars to each of the states, the District of Columbia and the Territories, for a total of $52 million.

   c) The balance of the receipts to be distributed to the recipients in (b) above, pro-rated on the basis of their population and area, and to the respective national total. Of the total balance, 80 percent would be distributed on the basis of population and 20 percent on the basis of area. Thus each state would share in proportion to their population and area. (For example, a state whose population is 10 percent of the national total and whose area is 10 percent of the national total would receive 10 percent of the earmarked 80 percent and 10 percent of the 20 percent making 10 percent of the total balance.)

   d) Each state would apportion its share within the state for non-federal projects of the type outlined in 1 as being components of the National Park and Recreation System.

9. As an added incentive, the federal government would match the individual contributions with appropriations from such funds as are available. For Federal projects the matching would be on a dollar-for-dollar basis. For the states it would be the same, but only to the extent that the states provided matching funds from state revenues.

C. Distribution of the funds is best illustrated by a hypothetical example. Last year there were 60 million passenger cars on the road. Assume the total number of stamps sold averaged out as a sticker for 40 million cars, the total receipts deposited with the U.S. Treasury would be about $280 million. The distribution would be as follows:

$70 million for Federal projects.

$210 million for state projects, of which $52 million would be an across the board distribution of $1 million each. The balance of $158 million would be distributed on a pro-rate basis as outlined.

By matching funds on a dollar-for-dollar basis, the total for Federal projects would be $140 million. If each state participated to the extent outlined, the $210 million from stamp purchases would be matched by $210 million of Federal funds and $210 million dollars of state funds, making a total of $630 million for state proposed projects per year.

3. Matching Funds

Instead of making a direct appropriation from general revenue funds, I would suggest the matching funds be derived from oil leased lands on the outer shelf, which is now being held pending court decisions. In addition, other conservation funds obtained from land uses and entry fees could also be used. The reason I suggest such funds is that it would be a reinvesting of the profits of the business of natural resource conservation in the business of human resource conservation. The reinvesting would be on a one-for-one on Federal projects and a one-for-two on state projects.

4. Public Acceptance

I believe the program as outlined should be developed so all the details are worked out and all the answers available before there is any public announcement. Being somewhat of a voluntary program with a yearly limit on individual contribution and of short duration, only five years, I am sure we could get such a proposal off the ground and get the full support of the people, the business interests, and the governments. The proposal is in effect a joint undertaking of the aforementioned in which all contribute and all benefit.

The conservation sticker not only marks the car owner as an individual who is personally interested in the objectives and values of the overall National Park and Recreation programs, but also one who has invested in the future well-being of his country and his offspring. There would also be tangible benefits that go with the sticker. Entrance fees at National and State Parks would be waived for cars displaying the sticker.

As an aid to park visitors, both National and State Park entrance stations would be furnished conservation stickers. Thus a visitor could redeem a partially filled stamp book for a sticker by paying the balance due on his stamp book. If the visitor had no stamp book, he could purchase a sticker at the reduced rate of $6.00.

The proposal appeals to me and I believe it has a lot of merit. If it appeals to you, I would like to spend more time perfecting the proposal and talking with certain individuals who should be consulted on such a proposition.

Conrad L. Wirth
Director

Source: NARA RG79, Administrative Files, 1949–1971, Box 333

Appendix 5.2
Bureau of Outdoor Recreation Land Classification System, 1965

Class I: High Density Recreational Areas

Class Examples: Intensively developed portions of Palisades Interstate Park, N.J. and N.Y.; Jones Beach, N.Y.; intensively developed parts of Cook Co. Forest Preserve, Ill.; Huntington Beach State Park, Calif.; Patapsco State Park, Md.; beach and boardwalk area in Atlantic City, N.J.; Colter Bay recreation center in Grand Teton National Park, Wyo.

Physical Characteristics: Physiographic features such as topography, soil type, drainage, etc., should be adaptable to special types of intensive recreation use and development. An attractive natural setting is desirable; however, manmade settings are acceptable. There are no specific size criteria and there is great variation in size from one area to another.

Location: Usually within or near major centers of urban population but may occur within such units as national parks and forests remote from population concentrations.

Activities: Intensive day or weekend type, such as picnicking, water sports, group field games, winter sports, and other activities for many people. Although high density areas are subject to heavy peak load pressure at certain times, they often sustain moderate use throughout the year.

Developments: High degree of facility development which often requires heavy investment. They are usually managed exclusively for recreation purposes. Development may include a road network, parking areas, bathing beaches and marinas, bath houses, artificial lakes, playfields, and sanitary and eating facilities.

Responsibility: Commonly held under municipal, county, regional, or State ownership. Many commercial resorts have similar characteristics and collectively provide a significant portion of recreation opportunities for urban population centers.

Class II: General Outdoor Recreation Areas

Class Examples: Rock Creek Park, Washington, D. C.; Kensington Park, Huron Clinton Authority, Mich.; and Golden Gate Park, San Francisco, Calif.

Physical Characteristics: May have varied topography, interesting flora and fauna within a generally attractive natural or manmade setting adaptable to providing a wide range of opportunities. These areas range in size from several acres to large tracts of land.

Location: Usually more remote than Class I areas, however, relatively accessible to centers of urban population and accommodate a major share of all outdoor recreation. Included are portions of public parks and forests, public and commercial camping sites, picnic grounds, trail parks, ski areas, resorts, streams, lakes, coastal areas, and hunting preserves.

Activities: Extensive day, weekend, and vacation use types such as camping, picnicking, fishing, hunting, water sports, winter sports, nature walks, and outdoor games.

Developments: Generally less intensive than Class I areas. Includes, but not limited to, access roads, parking areas, picnic areas, campgrounds, bathing beaches, marinas, streams, natural and/or artificial lakes. Areas are equipped with some manmade facilities, which may vary from simple to elaborate. Thus, campgrounds may have only the barest necessities for sanitation and fire control or they may have ample and carefully planned facilities such as cabins, hot and cold running water, laundry equipment, stores, museums, small libraries, entertainment, juvenile and adult playfields. Other features may include permanent tows for ski areas, fully equipped marinas, lodges, dude ranches and luxury hotels.

Responsibility: Federal, State or local governments, including regional park and recreation authorities, and private clubs and other forms of private ownership assisted by public agencies on problems of access and development of basic facilities.

Class III: Natural Environment Areas

Class Examples: Portions of the Allagash country of northern Maine and cutover areas in northern Lake States. Public lands of this category often adjoin outstanding natural Class IV, and primitive Class V areas in national and state parks and forests as in the case in the Grand Teton National Park and the Superior National Forest.

Physical Characteristics: Varied and interesting land forms, lakes, streams, flora and fauna within attractive natural settings.

Location: Usually more remote from population centers than Class I and II areas and occur throughout the country and on an acreage basis are the largest class in both public and private ownership.

Activities: Extensive weekend and vacation types dependent on quality of the natural environment, such as sightseeing, hiking, nature study, picnicking, camping, swimming, boating, canoeing, fishing, hunting, and mountaineering. The primary objective is to provide for traditional recreation experience in the out-of-doors, commonly in conjunction with other resource uses. Users are encouraged to enjoy the resource "as is," in natural environment.

Developments: Access roads, trails, picnic and campsite facilities and minimum sanitary facilities. There may be other compatible uses of the area such as watershed protection, water supply, grazing, lumbering, and mining provided such activities are managed so as to retain the attractiveness of the natural setting.

Responsibility Federal, State, or local governments, including regional park and recreation authorities and private ownerships.

Class IV: Outstanding Natural Areas

Class Examples: The scenic sites and features in this class are limited in number and are irreplaceable. They range from large areas within Yosemite Valley and the Grand Canyon to smaller sites such as Old Faithful in Yellowstone National Park; Old Man of the Mountain, N.H.; and the Bristle Cone Pine Area in the Inyo National Forest, Calif.

Physical Characteristics: Outstanding natural feature associated with an outdoor environment that merit special attention and care in management to insure their preservation in their natural condition. Includes individual areas of remarkable natural wonder, high scenic splendor, or features of scientific importance. One or more such areas may be part of a larger administrative unit, such as a national park or forest.

Location: Any place where such features are found.

Activities: Sightseeing, enjoyment, and study of the natural features. Kinds and intensity of use limited to the enjoyment and study of the natural attractions so as to preserve the quality of the natural features and maintain an appropriate setting. May be visited on a day, weekend, or vacation trip.

Developments: Limited to minimum development required for public enjoyment, health, safety and protection of the features. Wherever possible, access roads and facilities other than trails and sanitary facilities should be kept outside the immediate vicinity of the natural features. Visitors encouraged to walk to the feature or into the area when feasible. Improvements should harmonize with and not detract from the natural setting.

Responsibility: Public agencies, (Federal, State, and local), and private landowners, with assistance from public agencies, who may identify, set aside, and manage natural features. Generally, the Federal Government assumes responsibility for the protection and management of natural areas of national significance; the States for areas of regional or State significance; and local government and private owners for areas of primarily local significance.

Class V: Primitive Areas

Class Examples: This class will be composed of two types of areas: V-A includes only those areas designated under the provisions of P.L. 88–577, the Wilderness Act (78 Stat. 890; 16 U.S.C. 1131). Examples: Bob Marshall Wilderness, Flathead and Lewis & Clark National Forests, Montana;

Great Gulf Wilderness, White Mountain National Forest, N.H. V-B includes all other areas having the characteristics of this class. Examples: Sawtooth Primitive Area, Boise, Sawtooth and Challis National Forests, Idaho; the undeveloped portion of Anza Borrego Desert State Park, Calif. Note: Some Federal lands may change from V-B to V-A under the provisions of the Wilderness Act.

Physical Characteristics (V-A and V-B)

Extensive natural, wild and undeveloped area and setting essentially removed from the effects of civilization. Essential characteristics are that the natural environment has not been disturbed by commercial utilization and that the areas are without mechanized transportation. The area must be large enough and so located as to give the user the feeling that he is enjoying a "wilderness experience." The site may vary with different physical and biological conditions and may be determined in part by the characteristics of adjacent land. Size may vary in different parts of the country. These areas are inspirational, esthetic, scientific, and cultural assets of the highest value.

Location: V-A: Wherever established by law. V-B; usually remote from population centers.

Activities (V-A and V-B): Those activities that are usually done without or with a minimum of mechanized transportation or permanent shelter or other conveniences.

Developments: V-A As prescribed in Wilderness Act. V-B-Usually no development of public roads, permanent habitations or recreation facilities except trails. No mechanized equipment allowed except that needed to control fire, insects and disease. Commercial use of the area that may exist at time of establishment should be discontinued as soon as practical.

Responsibility: V-A • Federal. V·B • Usually Federal but may also be by State agencies or private landowners (such as the high mountain country held by large timber and mining companies,)

Class VI: Historic and Cultural Sites

Class Examples: The Hermitage; Mount Vernon; the Civil War battlefields; and historic Indian dwellings, Mesa Verde National Park.

Physical Characteristics: These are sites associated with the history, tradition or cultural heritage of National, State or local interest and are of enough significance to merit preservation or restoration.

Location: The location of the feature establishes the site.

Activities: Sightseeing, enjoyment, and study of the historic or cultural features. Kinds and intensity of use limited to this type of study and enjoyment.

Developments: Management should be limited to activities that would effect such preservation and restoration as may be necessary to protect the features from deterioration and to interpret their significance to the public. Access to the area should be adequate but on-site development limited to prevent overuse, Development should not detract from the historic or cultural values of' the site.

Responsibility: Public agencies (Federal, State, and local), and private land-owners who identify, set aside, and manage historic and cultural areas.

Source: "Outdoor Recreation Grants-in-Aid Manual," Bureau of Outdoor Recreation, 1965.

Appendix 5.3
National Natural Landmarks
Program, 1965

Objectives

The objectives of the Natural Landmarks program are to encourage the preservation of sites importantly illustrating the geologic and ecologic character of America; to enhance the educational and scientific value of sites so preserved; to strengthen the cultural appreciation of the natural history of America among people; and to foster a greater concern and involvement in the conservation of America's natural heritage among Federal, state, and local governments, citizens organizations, and individuals.

Standards

Sites will qualify for Natural Landmark status when found to satisfy the following criteria:

I.   The site contains an object, feature, or assemblage of biological or geological features that importantly illustrates a principle, process, or condition of nature.
     These include, but are not limited to:

     •   Outstanding geological formations or features illustrating geological processes.
     •   Significant fossil evidence of the development of life on earth.
     •   An ecological community which significantly illustrates characteristics of a physiographic province or biome.
     •   A biota of relative stability maintaining itself under prevailing natural conditions, such as a climatic climax community.
     •   An ecological community illustrating the process of succession and restoration to natural condition following disruptive change.
     •   A habitat supporting a vanishing, rare, or restricted species.
     •   A relict flora or fauna persisting from an earlier period, or as a remnant of a population formerly more widespread.

- A seasonal haven for concentrations of native animals, or a vantage point for observing concentrated populations, such as restricted migration route.
- A site containing evidence which illustrates important scientific discoveries.

II. The site possesses a quality distinctly above the average of its kind.

III. The natural object, feature, or assemblage of features, identified as the basis for landmark consideration, presents a true, accurate, undistorted natural example of the same.

- The object, feature, or features will have been created, and will be found to exist, for the most part, under the influence of natural forces.
- Manipulation of the environment is acceptable to the degree necessary to neutralize unnatural influences, to perpetuate a rare or particular species, or to better expose a geologic feature for study or interpretation.

IV. The site is of such size and location as to give reasonable assurance that the feature, its quality, and its naturalness can be preserved.

- In this respect, the site will be large enough to maintain the essential quality of its geological or ecological character, and to adequately illustrate the process or feature. It will be so located as to be reasonably invulnerable to deterioration by developments outside its boundaries.

V. The site is in responsible ownership, sympathetic with landmark objectives and agreeable to preservation of the values for which it is designated.

Source: NPS Advisory Board Minutes, 52nd Meeting, April 12–15, 1965.

Appendix 7.1

Conservation by Preservation of
Our Heritage, 1964

If my topic is less than crystal clear to you, be not faint of heart. Even for me, it doesn't sparkle with lucidity, notwithstanding the fact that it was my adaptation of an original—and more understandable—suggestion by your program chairman. Thus, you must not hold her responsible—for what I said I would say to you today, nor for that matter, what I will say.

Perhaps we can communicate more easily if you will accept my semantics. Preservation is the keeping of man-made structures or objects from decay, injury, or destruction; conservation, the safe-keeping of God-given natural bounties, such as forests, rivers and park areas. But there is, I suggest, a further subtle distinction: conservation is not only a broader and more comprehensive term, but even has an official connation and is perhaps more authoritative. That may explain the name of one of the committees of this joint meeting. Some would argue that conservation subsumes preservation. If it does not, then I submit that some re-thinking is in order, for conservation in its broadest and most patriotic sense cannot ignore historic preservation. I am not necessarily promoting the organization of a new committee, but I am asserting that what we have in mind and in common is the safeguarding of thing important, meaningful and beautiful in our past and present, for the future, whether God-given or man-made.

I should perhaps really begin by quoting from one of our great naturalists and lovers of the outdoors, such as Thoreau or Frost. Let me instead set the keynote for my speech by repeating what a dynamic man in another field, that of music, has said about tradition.

Stravinsky, in his Musical Poetics, says:

> A real tradition is not a relic of the past that is irretrievably gone; it is a living force that animates and informs the present.

I give you this quotation in order to stress the fact that conservation and preservation are living things—and not dust-covered anachronisms. I hope we shall see the day when the leading conservationists and preservationists of this country number many of our younger Americans—vigorous guardians of the dimensional evidence of this country's past achievements for future generations.

To an extent greater perhaps than we are aware of, the United States has been a country of very rapid growth and development—perhaps unparalleled in the history of the world. In the pioneering era of discovery and the old frontier, there was both time and space in which to develop. The coming of the industrial revolution reshaped the nature of our communities, and the advent of the machine changed the face of our country.

Triumphs of American engineering and ingenuity, such as our superhighways, often destroy the very natural sites to which they give access, and create such scenic disasters as the parking lot and the automobile graveyard. If we are not watchful, the improvements in our standard of living will themselves destroy the natural beauty of our land and all traces of our cultural heritage.

If public apathy is perhaps the worst enemy of our heritage, unity may well prove the answer. When the tiny Continental Army faced a superb British force across the Delaware there may have been some who thought the odds too great, the effort not worthwhile. But they did not give up then, and we should not give up now.

It is incumbent upon the leaders of our society, no matter what their walk of life, to unite in common concern, and ensure that the heritage of the past is preserved for the benefit and enlightenment of the future.

It is vital that conservationists and preservationists should present a public image of leadership and unity, or professional competence, and aggressiveness in a righteous cause. It is only thus that we may touch public awareness and enjoy its favorable opinion and support—the most powerful force in the land. It is only thus that we may put an end to the isolation that the preservation movement has suffered all too long.

Concerned as you are with the gardens, parks, and horticulture of this great nation, I do not have to tell you of the fine work of our National Park Service and our local city and state park boards. Suffice it to say here that the vital conservation of our natural bounty of parks, forests, water, shore, and wilderness must go hand in hand with the preservation of our historic sites and buildings. Together they weave the tapestry of this country's historical and cultural development.

From the calm of Walden Pond to the majesty of Bryce and Zion, conservationists are fighting to preserve this tapestry. From support for creation of potential national parks, to pressures on local governmental units to preserve adequate open spaces for the graceful growth of our cities, citizens everywhere must be on the alert to preserve what Thomas Jefferson called "the face and character" of this nation.

Though the soil can be conserved and forests replanted, our historical sites and structures, once destroyed by the wrecker's ball, are forever lost—they are the tangible and irreplaceable testimonials of our past. Reconstruction or copies can be made, but not in situ and they are always nothing more than full scale models, in an alien setting, of original documents since destroyed.

Although the National Park Service has the threefold responsibility of conserving our scenic assets, our scientific treasures and our historic sites, this task far exceeds the available or anticipated resources of that agency, or any governmental agency. This is the reason why the National Trust for Historic Preservation, a private organization, came into being.

. . . .

The National Trust opposes the destruction, or mutilation, of significant historic sites and structures. It serves as a clearing house for information on preservation needs, projects, techniques and problems, and is a source of technical advice and counsel for all preservationists wherever they may be.

It constantly encourages higher standards of restoration and preservation through its publications, re-prints, consultation services, conferences and seminars, and other educational programs. It is empowered to accept property to be maintained for the public use and enjoyment. Finally and perhaps its most important task of all it seeks to promote an awareness in the broad mass of the American people of the need for the preservation and conservation of their cultural, natural, and historic heritage. In this task, we have only begun to scratch the surface.

. . . .

Let me assert here that no matter what legislation is passed, be it at a federal, state, or local level, the ultimate responsibility for and success in the preservation of our nation's heritage lie within its citizens.

In the face of our rapid urban growth the citizen must be vigilant. Will our country be "Heritage or Honky Tonk?" Let us unite to ensure that the natural beauty of this country may be enjoyed without hindrance of billboard, unsightly commercial development, trash, or junkyard. Let us attack disorder, visual monotony, and, above all, public indifference. Prevention of blight calls for enlightened leadership and unselfish citizens in the cause of both conservation and preservation.

. . . .

Let us therefore educate through three dimensional historical documents. Let the past illuminate the present. Let us teach people to perceive—and as they perceive, be re-vitalized. Let the architecture of yesterday be a source of inspiration for the architects of the future. Let our historic sites inspire our young leaders, and the wilderness refresh them for their daily tasks.

As the late President Kennedy said at Amherst College in 1963: "I will look forward to an America which will not be afraid of grace and beauty, which will protect the beauty of our natural environment, which will preserve the great old American houses and squares and park of our national past, and which will build handsome and balanced cities for our future."

Sections from: "Remarks of Gordon Gray at the Garden Club of America, New York, Marcy 11, 1964" RG 421 NTHP Gray.

Index